MADE SIMPLE

Leigh E. Zeitz, Ph.D.
University of Northern Iowa
Associate Professor

Illustrations by Scott Nurkin

Made
Simple

BOOKS

A Made Simple Book
Broadway Books
New York

Produced by The Philip Lief Group, Inc.

PRINTED IN THE UNITED STATES OF AMERICA

Produced by The Philip Lief Group, Inc.
Managing Editors: Judy Linden, Jill Korot, Albry Montalbano.
Design: Annie Jeon.

First Broadway Books trade paperback edition published 2005

Library of Congress Cataloging-in-Publication Data

Zeitz, Leigh.
  Keyboarding made simple / Leigh Zeitz; illustrated by Scott Nurkin
        p. cm.—(Made simple series)
  "Originally published in a different form as Touch typing
  made simple by Doubleday in 1985 and subsequently reprinted
  by Broadway Books in 2001"—T.p. verso.
  Includes index.
  ISBN 0-7679-1705-7
  1. Keyboarding. I. Title.
  Z49.Z45 2005

652.3—dc22   2004062885

10 9 8 7 6 5 4 3 2 1

CONTENTS

INTRODUCTION

"I am trying to get the hang of this new fangled writing machine, but I am not making a shining success of it. However this is the first attempt I ever have made, & yet I perceive that I shall soon & easily acquire a fine facility in its use... One chiefly needs swiftness in banging the keys..."

Mark Twain's first typewritten letter:
December 9, 1874

Congratulations! You have decided to make a big move in improving your *communication* skills. That's right, I said communication skills. This book isn't about making your fingers move faster across the keyboard. It's about improving your ability to communicate in today's world of word processing, on-line chatting, and searching the World Wide Web (also called the Web).

Since you are reading this, I assume that you are tired of hunting and pecking around your keyboard and want to learn how to type quickly. This will involve more than just learning the location of the keys on the keyboard. You have taught yourself how to keyboard while writing e-mail or papers or chatting and probably developed some bad habits such as looking at the keyboard or watching the screen. You have reached a point at which you can't keyboard any faster, so you need to break some bad habits that are slowing you down. Remember that this process is one that takes time and needs to be nurtured. Following these lessons for as little as 20 minutes per day can lead to a dramatic increase in keyboarding speed and accuracy over a period of 6 weeks.

TYPING VERSUS KEYBOARDING

One question that arose repeatedly during the creation of this book was "What is the difference between typing and keyboarding?" The answer is, "Nothing"—nothing, that is, except for the machine on which the work is done and the contemporary decade. *Typing* was the term used to describe the process of producing documents by striking the keys of a typewriter (circa 1900–1985), whereas *keyboarding* is the term used to describe the process of entering data into a computer via a keyboard (1975–present). These dates are only approximations, because there were people still using typewriters after 1985, and there were computer users before 1975, but these dates show the evolution of the term. We shall use the more prevalent term *keyboarding* for consistency.

ELEMENTS OF LEARNING TO KEYBOARD?

So what does it take to learn how to keyboard? It takes technique, familiarity, and practice.

Technique involves:

- how you sit,
- how you hold your hands above the keyboard,
- how you tap the keys, and
- the strategies you use to optimize your keyboarding sessions.

You will develop familiarity with the location of the keys and the basic functioning of a word processor as you progress through the lessons in this book. These lessons begin by introducing the home row keys (ASDFJKL;) where your fingers rest. The remaining keys will be introduced through a progression that has been selected to facilitate memorization and muscle development. The sequence of letter introduction was also selected to provide letters to create words for your practice sessions. Learning to type *words* instead of just *letters* is the ultimate goal of keyboarding.

Practice involves repeating an activity until it becomes automatic. Recall the saying "Practice makes perfect." It is true but misleading. Repeated practice will improve your ability to do what you are doing. If you are practicing a technique that is incorrect, then you will perfect it incorrectly. That is not why you are using this book. You want to keyboard correctly, so that means that you must practice it correctly because "perfect practice make perfect." This book will lead you through a process that will help you practice keyboarding perfectly.

TECHNIQUE

As already mentioned, proper posture is an important part of keyboarding. The detached keyboard and laptop computers have made improper sitting even easier than when people used typewriters. I spent many hundreds of hours with my feet on the desk and the keyboard in my lap as I wrote letters, papers, and books. Unfortunately, for this reason I now suffer from serious lower back problems. I don't sit like that any longer. You *need* to take care of yourself as you work so you don't suffer the consequences of improper posture later.

Ergonomics is a term that has become quite important in homes, classrooms, and offices around the world. *Ergonomics* is the study of design factors in the workplace that maximize productivity by matching the conditions at the workstation with the mechanics of a person's body. These conditions include properly designed furniture that positions keyboards and monitors at the proper height, chairs that provide appropriate back support and allow adjustments to fit different body sizes, and even work schedules that incorporate periodic breaks to guard against injuries caused by repetitive actions. Proper positioning for keyboarding will be discussed in Lesson 1, but it is necessary to review here the important aspects of properly sitting at a keyboard.

The Occupational Safety and Health Administration (OSHA) is quite interested in ergonomics. It sponsors a wonderful Web site that describes proper sitting and keyboarding positioning (www.osha.gov/SLTC/etools/computerworkstations). Visit the Web site to review the in-depth discussion about workstation safety. Here are some of its highlights:

- Top of monitor at or just below eye level
- Head and neck balanced and in-line with torso
- Shoulders relaxed
- Elbows close to body and supported
- Lower back supported
- Wrists and hands in-line with forearms
- Feet flat on the floor

BUILDING KEYBOARD FAMILIARITY

Keyboarding is more of a sport than an academic skill. Academic skills typically involve learning new information and then using that information to make decisions or to do new things. A sport, like racquetball, involves making decisions as well, but it is more about automatic responses than thoughtfully applying new knowledge. Learning to keyboard involves developing such automatic responses. It involves building connections among the eye, the brain, and the fingers. These connections, often called *memory traces* in physiology, produce a response system that enables touch keyboarding. The eye sees a letter (or group of letters); the brain decides which finger addresses this letter and sends the appropriate signals to the proper finger. With enough practice, the conscious decision of which finger to use becomes an automatic response. When the eye sees a letter the finger almost twitches in anticipation of typing. This automaticity is the goal of any keyboarding program.

BREAKING BAD HABITS

Breaking bad habits is probably the toughest part of building efficient keyboarding. Because the census of 2000 found that more than 50 percent of homes in the United States have computers, and 40 percent of homes have Internet connections, chances are pretty good that you have been using a computer for a few years. You have been surfing the Web, sending e-mail, writing papers, or meeting in your favorite chat room, where you have been frantically tapping the keys. If you haven't memorized the location of the keys and developed an efficient way to press those keys in a rapid manner, you are probably engaging in bad habits that are requiring you to work much harder than you need to do. Bad habits in keyboarding typically involve two areas: looking at the keys (fondly known as the "hunt and peck" method of keyboarding) and using the wrong fingers to tap the keys.

LOOKING AT THE KEYS

Needing to look at the keys is obviously caused by not knowing the location of the keys on the keyboard. The problem with looking at the keys is that this process gets the job done (inefficiently) but promotes very little learning. The process usually involves the following:

- Look at the paper.

- Recognize the needed letter.

- Find the letter on the keyboard.

- Press the letter on the keyboard.

- Look at the monitor screen to see that you got the letter right.

This process does not involve anything that will make keyboarding more efficient. As noted earlier, practicing this method of keyboarding is helping the learner perfect an imperfect form of keyboarding. No connection is being made between the letter to be keyed and the finger that needs to be used to tap it.

USING THE CORRECT FINGERS

Learning occurs when you consistently make a connection between a letter to be keyed and the finger that will be used to tap it. This consistency involves having a specific point of reference where you always place your fingers (the home row) and then moving the appropriate finger in the correct direction to tap the desired key.

But looking at the keyboard is so tempting! What can you do to keep your eyes from wandering down there? The options are plentiful.

1. Get a neck brace that will prevent you from looking down. (Only joking: this is a bit drastic!)

2. Purchase or create a keyboard cover out of cardboard, wood, or plastic. This is like an upside-down three-sided box that doesn't affect the keyboard but keeps roaming eyes from looking at the keyboard. (This is done in classes across the nation.)

3. Purchase a keyboard overlay/skin. This is a custom-fit rubberized overlay that prevents you from seeing the letters on the keys. It costs about 10 dollars and is becoming a popular option. Alternatively, just place 1/4" stickers over the keys. It is less expensive but much less appealing.

4. "NoPeekee" towel. This is actually just a dishtowel that is laid over the hands. The trick is to use your right hand to place the towel on your left hand, sneak your right hand underneath it, and begin keyboarding.

But how can you know where the keys are if you don't look at the keyboard? You can begin by going through the lessons in this book. They are designed to provide you with an orderly and consistent introduction to the letters. But sometimes you might forget which letter goes where. You need some sort

of reference device, something that will tell you where to find the keys so you can use the correct finger without looking at the keyboard. Enter the NoPeekee Keyboard!

NOPEEKEE KEYBOARD

This is a small paper keyboard diagram that shows the location of the keys as well as the fingers that are responsible for pressing each of the keys. Remember that the thumb is always used for the space bar. You probably don't want to cut the keyboard out of the page here, but you can make a copy of it or go to http://www.keyboardingresearch.org, where you can download a color version, print it out, and use it.

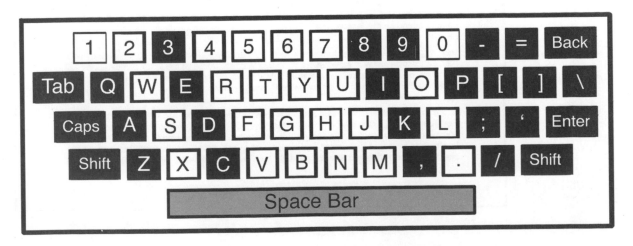

You can place this small keyboard at about the same height as the top of the monitor (preferably not *on* your monitor, because that will cause you to repeatedly look at your monitor). If you are transcribing from hand-written copy, you can place the paper keyboard at the top of the paper. If you are just composing at the keyboard, then you can place it on the document holder (if you have one) to refer to as necessary.

x://us.f112.mail.yahoo.com/ym/ShowLetter?box=Inbox&Msgid=...

Look at the monitor screen to see that you got the letter right. (This will happen less as you become more confident in your keyboarding.)

This will be slower at the beginning, but you are actually going through a muscular learning process when you consciously tell your fingers which key to press. Unlike the hunt and peck method where you have to visually find the key and press it, you are developing the muscular memory that connects the letters with the fingers with the keyboard. THAT is the key (pun intended) to rapid keyboarding!

Practice

Your success in developing your keyboarding speed is based completely upon how much time you spend practicing. You are developing a skill that can only be improved through practice – perfect practice. This means that you must develop a learning and practice regimen. This book has been designed to assist you in progressing through the learning curve of keyboarding. Here is how it works:

SCOTT: This section needs to be updated. I will do it tomorrow.

The first 10 lessons introduce the letters. The next 10 lessons introduce letter combinations and numbers. The last 4 lessons describe the process of writing various letters and using formatting processes.

Each lesson begins with a Warm-up section. This is VERY important because it provides a review of the letters (and words) you have already learned. You are only going to improve if you spend time practicing these keys. You might even find it helpful to practice this section a couple of times before progressing through the lesson. It's all a matter of how much time you have to spend on the lesson.

Next, you will be introduced to the new keys. These keys will be introduced individually and then in combination with other letters you have learned. Some of the letter combinations will be nonsense words but real words and sentences will be used as you progress through the book and the selection of letters available to you increases.

At the end of each lesson will be additional keyboarding practice in a section entitled Self-Testing Work. This is where you perfect your newly-learned keystrokes. Once again, you might want to practice this section a few times before progressing to the next lesson. Learning to keyboard is a great deal like learning to play the piano. You can learn how to play the correct notes in a musical passage but you usually need to practice the passage a

10/20/04 12:17 PM

So, now you have a way to prevent you from looking at the keyboard *and* a reference (NoPeekee Keyboard) to use to learn the location of keys. Instead of "hunting and pecking" described earlier above, you will use the following process to find and tap keys.

- Place your fingers on the home row.
- Look at the paper.
- Recognize the needed letter.
- Find the letter on the NoPeekee Keyboard.
- Identify the finger that needs to be used to press that letter.
- Press the letter on the keyboard.

Look at the monitor screen to see that you got the letter right. (This will happen less as you become more confident in your keyboarding.)

This will be a slow process at the beginning, but you are actually training your muscles when you consciously tell your fingers which key to press. Unlike visually hunting for the key and pressing it, you are developing the muscular memory that connects the letters with the fingers with the keyboard. *That* is the key to rapid keyboarding!

PRACTICING KEYBOARDING

Your success in developing your keyboarding speed is based completely on how much time you spend practicing, so you must develop a learning and practice regimen. This book has been designed to assist you in progressing through the learning curve of keyboarding.

- The first nine lessons introduce the letters.

- The next eleven lessons introduce characters and numbers. (You will notice that some symbols, including ^, [,], {, }, |, and \ are not taught. These symbols are rarely used.)

- Throughout the book, lessons are dedicated to developing your ability to key letter combinations as easily as you can key individual letters. These letter combinations include short words (AutoWords) and letter combinations (AutoBlends). These will be introduced in Lessons 6, 10, 12, and 16.

- Lesson 21 introduces the numeric keypad.

- Lessons 22 and 23 explore formats used to write personal and business letters.

- Lesson 24 surveys the many aspects of electronic communication.

- In the last chapter you will create a two-column newsletter with graphics.

Each lesson begins with a warm-up section. This is *very* important because it provides a review of the letters (and words) you have already learned. You are going to improve only if you spend time practicing these keys. You may even find it helpful to practice this section a few times before progressing through the lesson, depending on how much time you have to spend on the lesson.

Next, you will be introduced to the new keys. These keys will be introduced individually and then in combination with other letters you have learned. Some of the letter combinations will be nonsense words, but real words and sentences will be used as you progress through the book and the selection of letters available to you increases.

At the end of each lesson will be additional keyboarding practice in a self-test where you perfect your newly learned keystrokes. Once again, you may want to practice this section a few times before progressing to the next lesson. Learning to keyboard is a great deal like learning to play the piano. You can learn how to play the correct notes in a musical passage, but you usually need to practice the passage a number of times to feel comfortable with it.

You may have heard of (or even used) the phrase, "The quick brown fox jumps over the lazy dog." You may not know that this type of phrase is called a pangram. A *pangram* is a sentence that contains all the letters in the alphabet. Keyboarding pangrams is good practice for a keyboarder. Beginning in Lesson 11, you will discover at least one pangram in each lesson. Enjoy them.

Beginning with Lesson 3, timed tests will be incorporated into every other lesson. These tests will begin with 1-minute timings. This is where you can finally test yourself for speed. You can use an egg timer or download a timer to your computer that will allow you to focus on your timing instead of on watching the clock. Keyboarding speed in words per minute (WPM) is calculated by counting the number of letters typed and dividing by 5 (the average word is considered to be five letters long). This won't require any fancy mathematical computation, because numbers in the text will assist you in computing your WPM. You will see that the text has been arranged in a way that will make calculating your WPM almost automatic. In Lesson 11, your timings will extend to 3 minutes. Lesson 17 introduces 5-minute tests to measure how fast you can key in a prolonged session. Don't worry too much about mistakes now. Some systems subtract 1 WPM for every error, but you need to build your confidence and speed before you start penalizing yourself for inaccuracy.

Keeping track of your progress is an important part of developing your skill level and self-confidence. You will find a progress chart in the appendixes where you can keep track of your work either in the book or by copying this page and posting it in an easily accessible and visible place for yourself. This is where you can watch yourself progress through the program. It is also where you hold yourself accountable by recognizing when you haven't been applying yourself to building your keyboarding skills. Remember that your success depends on your desire and motivation.

The appendixes are filled with helpful lists and activities. There are a couple of self-support pages, home row hints, and sitting hints that you can copy (or tear out) from the book to hang on your wall by your computer. Practice lists of AutoBlends, AutoWords, pangrams, and the five hundred most frequently used English words are included to provide you with additional activities. Additional keyboarding timings are also included if you want to practice your keyboarding.

Good luck on building your communication skills, and *Happy Keyboarding*!

J F K D SPACE ENTER

OUTCOMES

- Open a word processor
- Create a new file
- Become acquainted with the parts of a word processor
- Save your file
- Sit properly in front of the keyboard
- Set font type for word processing
- Keys: J F K D Space and Enter

PREPARING TO KEYBOARD

Begin by placing this book to the right of your computer keyboard. If you are left-handed, you may want to place it at the left of your keyboard. You may be able just to prop it against something on your desk, but you will probably have more success if you use an acrylic or wooden book holder that is sold to hold open cookbooks, for example. You may have one of these in the kitchen (see Figure 1.1).

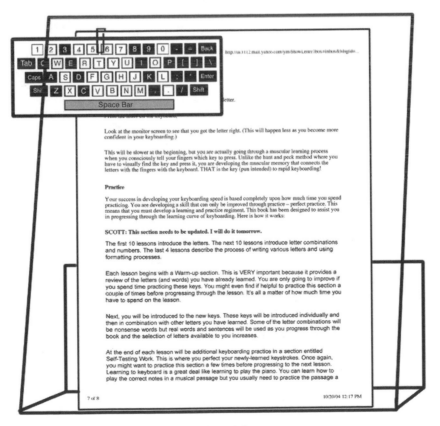

Figure 1.1

Now, turn on your computer. Find the word processor you will use. Currently, the most popular word processor is Microsoft Word, which is part of the Microsoft Office package, but you can use any word processor you choose. Word processors are quite similar, especially when it comes to the activities you will use to learn keyboarding; however, for the sake of continuity, this book will refer to Microsoft Word installed on a Windows-based computer.

Once you have started your word processor you need to create a new file for your keyboarding. A *file* is an electronic collection of information that has a unique name; it may be stored on the hard drive of the computer or on a CD, DVD, or other external memory device. You can create a file by clicking on the **File** menu at the top of the screen and selecting **New**. A blank document will appear on your screen. It is named **Document1**.

Let's set up the file management system you will be using by creating a folder that is dedicated to the files you will create as you learn the keyboard.

Click on **File** in the menu bar at the top of the screen and select the **Save** command from the drop-down menu that appears. A *drop-down menu* is a group of selections in a box that appears ("drops down") when a selection on a menu is clicked.

Double-click on the **My Documents** folder in the left column, then click **File**. A drop-down menu will appear. Click on **New**, then **Folder**. Name the folder **Keyboarding**. This is where you will keep all your files you create throughout the book.

Now it is time to set your fonts to match what is used in this book:

1. Click on the **Format** command in the menu bar at the top of the screen.

2. Drag the cursor to the **Font** command; that is, press the left mouse button and move the arrow to the **Font** command.

3. Release the button to select the **Font** command. The **Font** dialog box should appear. A *dialog box* is a box that appears on the screen where settings and selections are made.

4. Select the following settings:
   a. Font: **Times Roman Bold**
   b. Font style: **Regular**
   c. Size: **12**

5. Click on the **OK** button.

These settings will work with all the upcoming practice exercises, but you will be instructed to change the font when you get to your timings. Now that you have your book, computer, and word processor ready, let's see where you and your hands fit into this combination.

LEARNING TO KEYBOARD

The proper sitting and keyboard positioning was mentioned in the introduction, but let's review it now.

Follow these **Sitting Hints** (see Figure 1.2):
- Sit at the center of the keyboard. Align the center of your body with the line that divides the G and H keys.
- Sit up straight in your chair in front of your keyboard.
- Make certain your lower spine is at the back of your chair.
- Keep about 9 inches between you and the keyboard.
- Position both feet flat on the floor with one foot slightly ahead of the other.

Figure 1.2—Sitting Hints

NAMING YOUR FINGERS

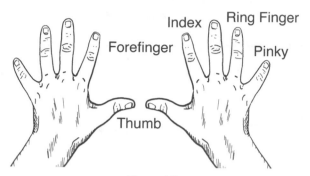

Figure 1.3

Learning how to tap the proper key with the most efficient finger involves naming the fingers. As you can see in Figure 1.3, we name the fingers Thumb, Forefinger, Index, Ring Finger, and Pinky. Hold your hands out and name your fingers beginning with the left pinky.

HOME ROW

Home row is located in the middle of your keyboard and is where your hands automatically go to rest.

Place your left fingers on the A S D F keys, with the forefinger on the F key. Do you feel the bump on the F key? (Some keyboards may have these bumps on the K and D keys, but either way, identify their locations and learn to use them to find your position on the home row without looking.)

Place your right fingers on the J K L ; keys, with the forefinger on the J (see Figure 1.4). Do you feel the bump on the J key?

Figure 1.4—Home Row

POSITION OF HANDS

You have to develop a natural position for keyboarding. This is how your fingers will always return to the home row in preparation for rapid touch keyboarding.

Follow these **Home Row Hints**:

- Curve your fingers naturally. (Think of how you would bend your fingers if you were scratching someone's back.)

- Find the bumps on the F and J keys. Lay your forefingers on the bumps. These bumps are on these keys to allow you to return to them without looking.

- Having landed your forefingers on F and J, lightly lay the rest of your fingers on the home row keys.

- Keep your wrists low but *not* touching the keyboard or table.

- Keep your elbows close to your body.

- If you are right-handed, let your right thumb drop to the space bar below and let your left thumb curl under.

- If you are left handed, use your left thumb for the space bar.

USING THE SPACE BAR

Sit at your keyboard. Place your fingers over the home row. Use the side of your chosen thumb to sharply tap the space bar (see Figure 1.5). Notice that the *cursor* (the vertical line that indicates where the letters will appear on the screen when you press a key on the keyboard) is moving to the right. Keep hitting it until you get to the end of the line. You will notice that the cursor jumps to the next line. That is called word wrap. *Word wrap* is a feature that causes text to move automatically to the next line after it has filled the current line.

Figure 1.5

USING THE ENTER KEY

Sometimes you want to force the cursor to move to the next line even when you haven't gotten to the end of the line. This can be done by tapping the Enter key with your right pinky finger (see Figure 1.6).

Sit at the keyboard. Place your fingers over the home row. Without moving your forefingers from the J or F keys, reach over with your right pinky finger and tap the Enter key. Notice that the cursor jumps to the next line.

Tap the Enter key repeatedly until you get to the bottom of the screen. Keep tapping the Enter key and watch the screen scroll.

You have just begun keyboarding by filling the screen with nothing. Sure, this is not too rewarding, but at least you didn't make any mistakes. Let's move on to learning the keys in the home row. Use the up arrow to move the cursor back to the beginning of the document.

Figure 1.6

STRIKING THE KEYS

This may seem like a "no brainer" but it is useful to discuss how you will strike the keys. You won't be "pressing" the keys. Think of it more as quickly tapping the keys. Tapping the home row keys isn't too difficult, but when you get to the other keys on the keyboard, you will tap the key with the appropriate finger and then return that finger to its home key on the home row.

STRATEGY FOR INTRODUCING KEYS

As with most keyboarding books, we are starting with the home row; however, most keyboarding books begin with the A and S keys. The only reason I can surmise for doing this is that these keys are the first ones you see when you read the home row keys from left to right. This is not a very substantial reason. Although this approach has been used for many years, it doesn't make much sense to begin your introduction to keyboarding technique using your two weakest fingers—your pinky and your ring finger.

Considering a psychomotor approach to learning how to keyboard, it makes more sense to introduce keyboarding using your strongest fingers—your forefinger and index fingers. Therefore, you will notice that the forefinger and index fingers are emphasized in the first few lessons. You will learn more than the typical home row keys at the beginning, but you will feel better about the process if you are tapping with your stronger fingers than if you are fumbling with your less dominant digits.

Figure 1.7

NEW KEYS J AND F

Sit at your keyboard. Place your fingers over the home row. Feel the raised buttons on the J and F keys (see Figure 1.7). Feel the J key with your right forefinger. Tap the J key three times with your right forefinger and then strike the space bar.

Tap the J key three more times followed by the space bar. Continue doing this until you have filled a line on your screen like this:

jjj jjj jjj jjj jjj jjj jjj jjj jjj jjj jjj jjj jjj jjj jjj jjj jjj jjj jjj jjj jjj jjj jjj jjj jjj jjj jjj jjj jjj jjj jjj

Good job! You are now a keyboarder. Let's add the letter F. Feel the F key under the forefinger on your left hand. Using the J and F keys, type these two lines. Say the letters as you type them.

jjj fff jjj fff jjj fff jjj fff jjj fff jjj fff jjj fff jjj fff jjj fff jjj fff jjj fff fff jjj fff jjj fff jjj fff jjj fff

jf jf jf jf jf jf jf jf fj fj fj fj fj fj fj fj jfj jfj jfj jfj jfj jfj fjf fjf fjf fjf jfj jfj jfj jfj jfj jfj fjf fjf fjf

NEW KEYS TRYOUT J AND F

Now it's time to try out the J, F, and the space bar. This means that you will read the letters to be typed from the book and then type them without looking.

Without looking is the key phrase here. You may have keyboarded while looking at the keys in the past, but you will become a *fast* keyboarder only if you can do it without looking at the keys. But what if you forget the location of the keys? How can you select the correct key if you don't remember where it is?

You need a reference chart. You have already seen a couple of illustrations that show the location of the keys; however, if you are work-ing on page 12 and the illustration is on a different page, then it isn't much use to you. As we described earlier, there *is* an answer.

Turn to the Introduction and look at the keyboard figure on page xvii of the Introduction that is specifically designed for you to use— your NoPeekee Keyboard. Photocopy the figure and cut it out for a small, 1.5" × 4" reference keyboard that you can clip to the page where you are working. Placing the reference keyboard where you can see it instead of looking at your fingers will help build the memory traces that were described in the introduction.

Copy these three lines exactly. Tap the keys sharply. Say the letters as you type them.

jf jf jf jf jf jf jf jf jf jf jf jf jf jf jf jf fj fj fj fj fj fj fj fj fj fj fj fj fj fj fj fj fj fj fj fj fj fj fj fj fj fj

jjff jjff jjff jjff jjff ffjj ffjj ffjj ffjj ffjj jjff jjff jjff jjff ffjj ffjj ffjj ffjj jjff jjff jjff jjff ffjj ffjj

j jf jfj jfjj f fj fjf fjff j jf jfj jfjj f fj fjf fjff j jf jfj jfjj f fj fjf fjff jf j jf jfj jfjj f fj fjf fjff jf j jf

Congratulations! You are beginning to develop your keyboarding skills. Keyboarding with two fingers may not seem like a great

conquest, but it is just the beginning. Soon you will be able to keyboard the preamble to the U.S. Constitution.

Save your work.

SAVE YOUR WORK

It's time to save your work. It may not seem important saving three lines of gibberish, but is a necessary habit to acquire. You must remember to save, and save often.

1. Click on the **File** command in the menu bar at the top of the screen.

2. Click on the **Save** command in the drop-down menu that appears.

3. Alternatively, press the (left) mouse button and drag the cursor to the **Save** command, and release the button to select. The **Save**

window should appear and you should be in the **My Documents** folder.

4. In the **Save As** box that appears, enter **Lesson1.doc** in the **File name** box.

5. Click on the **Save** button in the window. (You can also select this button by simply pressing the Enter key.)

Now, stop keyboarding for a moment or two and relax. Shake your hands loosely at the wrists. Stretch your arms above your head. Turn your head slowly from side to side. It is important to do this every fifteen minutes or so to help prevent undue repetitive stress on muscles.

Figure 1.8

NEW KEYS K AND D

Sit at your keyboard again. Place your fingers over the home row. Feel the raised buttons on the J and F (or K and D) keys (see Figure 1.8). Feel the K key with the right index finger.

Tap the K key three times with your right index finger and then strike the space bar. Tap the K key three more times followed by the space bar. Continue doing this until you have filled a line on your screen like this:

kkk kkk kkk kkk kkk kkk kkk kkk kkk kkk kkk kkk kkk kkk kkk kkk kkk kkk kkk

Now let's add the letter D. Feel the D key with the left index finger. Tap the D key three times and then strike the space bar. Continue until you have filled the screen with Ds.

ddd ddd ddd ddd ddd ddd ddd ddd ddd ddd ddd ddd ddd ddd ddd ddd ddd ddd ddd

Let's mix it up a little.

kd kd kd kd kd kd kd kd kd kd kd kd dk dk dk dk dk dk dk dk dk dk dk dk dk dk dk dk

kkdd kkdd kkdd ddkk ddkk ddkk kkdd kkdd kkdd kkdd ddkk ddkk kkdd kkdd kkdd

k kd kdk kdkk d dk dkd dkdd k kd kdk kdkk d dk dkd dkdd dkdk k kd kdk kdkk d dk

Save your work.

Saving is a simple process, since you have already named the file and told your computer where to save it.

Click on the **File** command in the toolbar menu at the top of the screen.

1. Press the left mouse button and drag the arrow cursor to the **Save** command.

2. Release the button to select the **Save** command. Your updated file will replace your original file.

NEW KEYS TRYOUT K AND D

Now practice using what you learned. Type these letters as they appear.

kkk ddd kkk ddd kkk ddd kkk ddd kk dd kkk ddd kkk ddd kk dd kkk ddd kkk ddd
kkk ddd kkk ddd kkk ddd kkk ddd kk dd kkk ddd kkk ddd kk dd kkk ddd kkk ddd

kkkk dd kkkk dd kkk ddd kkkk dddd kk dd kkk ddd kkkk dddd kk dd kkk ddd kkkk
kkkk dd kkkk dd kkk ddd kkkk dddd kk dd kkk ddd kkkk dddd kk dd kkk ddd kkkk

SELF-TEST

You are now the master of four letters: J, F, K, and D. These are the letters that you can access using your strong forefingers and index fingers. Not only that, but you are also an experienced user of the Space (thumb) and Enter keys (right pinky).

Let's finish this lesson practicing these letters. Here are a few hints for doing your self-test:

• Keep your eyes on the book.

• Don't look at your fingers.

• If you forget the location of the letter, look at your NoPeekee Keyboard reference chart.

• Don't look at the screen until you have finished keyboarding.

• Don't worry if you make a mistake. Just go ahead. Don't stop to correct.

• Don't worry about going fast. Seek accuracy, and the speed will come later.

• Say the letters as you use them. This provides an auditory input to accompany the visual input.

You will notice that you will be typing jumbles of letters. You will learn some vowels in the next lesson so you can type words as well as letters. Notice that there is a *single space* between most of the letters in the first two lines.

j f k d j f k d j f k d   j f k d j f k d j f k   f j d k f j d k f j d k   f j d k f j d k f j d k

d k f j d k f j d k f j   d k f j d k f j d k f   k d j f k d j f k d j f   k d j f k d j f k d j f

jjj fff kkk ddd jjj fff kkk ddd fff jjj ddd kkk fff jjj ddd kkk jfkd fff jjj ddd kkk fff jjj

kkk ddd jjj fff kkk ddd jjj fff ddd kkk fff jjj ddd kkk fff jjj dkfj ddd kkk fff jjj ddd kkk

(Take a 10-second break.)

ddkkffjj ddkkffjj ddkkffjj jjffkkdd jjffkkdd jjffkkdd jjffkkdd jjffkkdd jjffkkdd jjffkkdd

ffjjddkk ffjjddkk ffjjddkk kkddjjff kkddjjff kkddjjff kkddjjff kkddjjff kkddjjff kkddjjff

jdfk jdfk jdfk jdfk fkjd fkjd fkjd fkjd jdfk jdfk jdfk fkjd fkjd jdfk jdfk jdfk fkjd fkjd

jkdfjd jkdfjd fdkjfk fdkjfk dkfjjd dkfjjd kdjfjf kdjfjf kkdjfd dkfjjd dkfjjd kdjfjf kdjfjf

IMPROVEMENT WORK

Perfect practice makes perfect!

Did you like the digital gymnastics? How did you do? Did you find a rhythm?

Now it's time to return to the Self-Test and practice the lines again. See if you can key them more smoothly and more accurately. Remember to say the letters as you go.

Hold it! Don't skip to the next section. You will become a better keyboarder *only* if you practice! Go back and give it a try. You will do well.

REVIEW

Good job! You are now a keyboarder.

In this lesson you learned to use your fore-fingers and index fingers to key J, F, K, and D. You used your thumb to tap the Space Bar and your right pinky to press the Enter key. This is just the beginning, but as long as you keep your eyes on the paper while you work, you are on your way to becoming a rapid keyboarder.

The key to success is to build those memory traces that cause you to twitch the appropriate finger when you see/think of a specific letter. You can improve your keyboarding skills if you practice even when you are away from your keyboard.

As you walk down the street or wait in a doctor's office or sit on a bus, think of the keys and then press the appropriate finger. You may have heard of playing "air guitar"— that is, someone pretends to play the guitar while listening to music. Here is your opportunity to type on an "air keyboard." You don't even have to worry about hitting the correct key. Just move the correct finger.

Happy practicing and good luck.

H G I E

OUTCOMES

- Open a word processor
- Create a new file
- Save your file
- Sit properly in front of the keyboard
- Print a document
- Proofread your work
- Keys: H G I and E

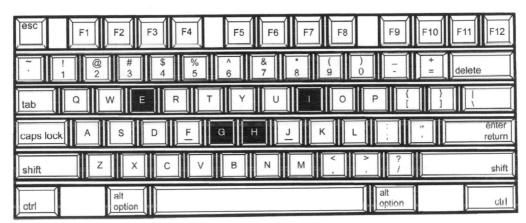

Figure 2.1

WARM-UP (5 MINUTES)

Just as a pianist needs to warm up before a concert, it is important for you to warm up your fingers before you keyboard. This will help you achieve maximum performance. Each lesson will begin with a warm-up section of exercises involving the keys you have already learned. These will be limited to 5 minutes. If you complete the exercises before the time, then start again at the beginning and continue until your timer rings.

Now, turn on your computer. Open your word processor. Create a **New** file.

Save your file to your **Keyboarding** folder and name it **Lesson2.doc**.

Set up your workspace.

- Clip your NoPeekee Keyboard to the top of your page for reference if you need it. You may not need it now, but you may as you learn more keys.

- Place your book into your book holder.

- Place your book holder to the right of your keyboard.

Pay attention to how you are sitting at your keyboard.

- Sit at the center of the keyboard. Align the center of your body with the line that divides the G and H keys.

- Sit up straight in your chair in front of your keyboard.

- Make certain your lower spine is at the back of your chair.

- Keep about 9 inches between you and the keyboard.

- Position both feet flat on the floor with one foot slightly ahead of the other.

Place your fingers on the home row.

- Curve your fingers naturally. (Think of how you would bend your fingers if you were scratching someone's back.)

- Find the bumps on the F and J keys. Lay your index fingers on the bumps.

- Having landed your index fingers on F and J, lightly lay the rest of your fingers on the home row keys.

- Keep your wrists low but *not* touching the keyboard or table.

- Keep your elbows close to your body.

Now you are ready to begin.

- Set your timer to 5 minutes.

- Key the following four lines exactly.

- DON'T look at the keys. Refer to your NoPeekee Keyboard if you need to know the location of a key.

- Say the letters to yourself as you work.

jjj fff kkk ddd jjj fff kkk ddd jjj fff kkk ddd jjj fff kkk ddd jjj fff fff kkk ddd jjj fff kkk ddd
jjff kkdd jjff kkdd jjff kkdd jjff kkdd jjff kkdd jjff kkdd jjff kkdd jjff kkdd jjff kkdd jjff

jfkd jfkd jfkd jfkd jfkd jfkd fjdk fjdk fjdk fjdk fjdk fjdk fjdk fjdk jfkd jfkd jfkd fjdk fjdk
jdkf fkdj jdkf fkdj kdjf dkfj kdjf dkfj kfdj djkf kfdj djkf fjdk fjdk kfj kfdj djkf kfdj djkf

Save your file by selecting **Save** from the **File** command in the toolbar menu at the top of the screen.

NEW KEYS H AND G

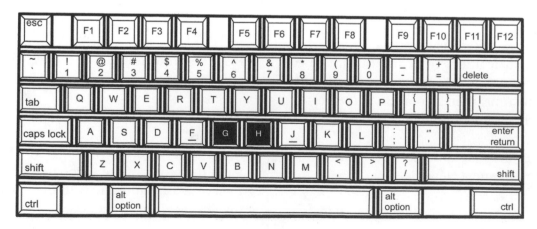

Figure 2.2

How did you do with the warm-up? How many times did you make it through the exercise? Did you notice the patterns in the letter combinations? Words are patterns as well. You will learn some vowels in this lesson so you can begin working with words.

Your new keys are H and G. These are located directly to the inside of your index fingers on the home row (see Figure 2.2).

Now it's time to practice these keys. Remember that your index fingers consider the J and F keys their home. After you tap the H key, you must return your right index finger to the J key. You must also return your left index finger to the F key after your tap the G key.

Try it out. Say the letters as you work.

jjj hhh jjj hhh jjj hhh jj hh jj hh jj hh jj hh jj hh jj hh jj hh jj hh jj hh jj hh jj hh jj hh jj hh

Did you feel how satisfied your right index finger felt when it returned to its home on the I key? Try it with the F and G keys.

fff ggg fff ggg fff ggg ff gg ff gg ff gg ff gg ff gg ff gg ff gg ff gg ff gg ff gg ff gg ff gg ff

That felt good, didn't it? F to G and back to F. It works every time and leaves you ready for the next letter.

NEW KEYS TRYOUT H AND G

You've keyed H and G in isolation. Now try them with the other four letters you have learned.

jjj hhh fff ggg jjj hhh fff ggg jjj hhh fff ggg jjj hhh fff ggg jjj hhh fff ggg jjj hhh fff ddd
jjj fff hhh ggg kkk ddd jjj fff hhh ggg kkk ddd jjj fff kkk ddd jjj fff hhh ggg kkk

kk dd jj ff hh gg kk dd jj ff hh gg kk dd jj ff hh gg kk dd jj ff hh gg kk dd jj ff hh gg kk
kk jj hh gg ff dd ff gg hh jj kk jj hh gg ff dd ff gg hh jj kk jj hh gg hh jj kk jj hh gg hh jj

k d j f h g j f k d d k f j g h f j d k k d j f h g j f k d d k f j g h f j d d k f j g h f j d d k f
hhh ggg hhh ggg hhh ggg hhh ggg hh gg hh gg hh gg h g h g h g hhh ggg hhh ggg hh

kjhgfd dfghkj kjhgfd dfghkj dkfjghfjdk dkfjghfjdk gjfkdh gjfkdh dkfjghfjdk dkfjghfjdk
dkfjghfjdk dkfjghfjdk gjfkdh gjfkdh kjhgfd dfghkj kjhgfd dfghkj gjfkdh kjhgfd dfghkf

Save your file by selecting **Save** from the **File** command in the menu bar at the top of the screen.

NEW KEYS I AND E

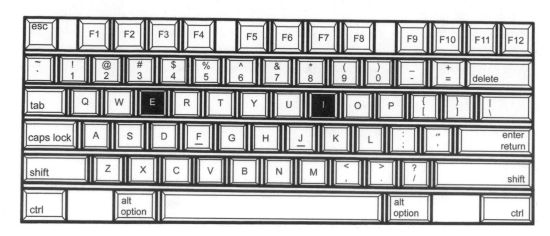

Figure 2.3

Now it is time to move away from the home row. You will use your middle fingers to find the vowels I and E in the upper row (see Figure 2.3).

Remember that the home row is where your fingers are most comfortable. Your right middle finger will move from the K key to tap the I key. Your left middle finger will move from the D key to tap the E key. Don't allow your fingers to wander around the keyboard.

Always bring them back to the home row.

kkk iii kkk iii kkk iii kkk iii kkk iii kkk iii kkk iii kkk iii kkk iii kkk iii kkk iii kkk iii

Now try keying with your left hand.

ddd eee ddd eee ddd eee ddd eee ddd eee ddd eee ddd eee ddd eee ddd eee ddd eee

Welcome to the world of vowels.

NEW KEYS TRYOUT I AND E

kkk iii ddd eee kkk iii ddd eee kkk iii ddd eee kkk iii ddd eee kkk iii ddd eee kkk iii

eee iii eee kkk ddd fff jjj ggg hhh iii eee kkk ddd fff jjj ggg hhh iii eee kkk ddd fff jjj

di di di fi fi fi gi gi gi hi hi hi ji ji ji ki ki ki ig ig ig ih ih ih ij ij ij ki ki ki ig ig ig ih ih

de de de de he he he he hi hi hi hi id id id id if if if if fi fi fi fi ik ik ik de he hi id if fi def def def fej fej fej geg geg geg hej hej hej jid jid jid ijg ijg ijg def fej geg hej jid ijg

dig dig dig fig fig fig ide ide ide egg egg egg hid hid hid jig jig jig kif dif ikj jff his jif

kige kige kige jike jike jike dihi hidi hidi hidi gegi gegi gegi kige jike dihi hidi gegi

fiji fiji fiji hike hike hike geek geek geek fide fide fide kidd kidd kidd fiji hike geek

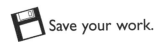 Save your work.

SELF-TEST

Test your mastery of the eight letters you have learned so far. Key the following twelve lines.

Keep your eyes on the book (and use the NoPeekee Keyboard) as you work. Don't look at the keyboard. Don't rush. Emphasize accuracy, not speed. Try to build a rhythm.

ded ded ded kik kik kik def def def jik jik jik ged ged hik hik dej dej ded kik def jik

ked ked ked dek dek dek hed hed hed gik gik gik hig hig geh geh ked dek hed gik hig

did did did kid kid kid fed fed fed keg keg keg gig gig gig dig dig did kid fed keg gig

dei dei dei egg egg egg jig jig jig die die die hid hid hid fid fid fid dei egg jig die hid

deed deed deed dike dike dike feed feed feed heed heed heed eddie eddie eddie heed

hide hide hide hike hike hike hifi hifi hifi hedge hedge hedge eddie hide hike hifi

def deg di feg fid fej geg gej gid heg hif hig jej hig jeg jej jid kik def deg di feg geg gej

deek deeg dife fide ffej geed gide heik jeke jigg keed kige dije egde deek deeg dife fide

de dei die did dig ed egg fig fed gig he hi hid jig keg kid eek de dei die did dig ed egg

deed feed heed dike hide hifi hike jeff kidd geek hedge edge deed feed heed dike hide

hi jill he did dig jeff fed fig egg feed fig jig ed hid a keg egg fell eddie did feed

dig egg hide hedge kid did hike dike eddie feed fig   heed jig jill did dig jigged egg

The "sentences" weren't too exciting, but they will get more interesting as you add letters and capitalization to your repertoire.

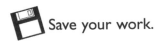 Save your work.

CORRECTIVE WORK

It is always important to proofread your work. Some keyboardists like to do their proofreading on the screen, but often it is useful to print your work to paper and edit it there.

1. To print your document:

   • Click on the **File** command in the menu bar at the top of the screen.

   • Press the left mouse button and drag the pointer to the **Print** command.

   • Release the button to select the **Print** command. The **Print** dialog box should appear on your screen.

   • Click on the **OK** button to print your document. (If you have printing problems, it is beyond the scope of this book to troubleshoot them. Contact a computer expert or technician to help you with this problem.)

2. Proofread your work by comparing your printout with the text in this book, word for word.

3. Circle the words or letter clusters that are incorrect: typographical error, wrong word, additional word, or omitted word.

4. Write a list of the corrected words on a separate sheet of paper.

5. Create a new document and save your practice file as **L2Practice.doc** in your **Keyboarding** folder.

6. Key each of these words five times correctly and save your file to the **Keyboarding** folder.

IMPROVEMENT WORK

How did you do on the self-test? Did you have to retype many words? If you are unsatisfied with your accuracy on that task, you should go back and do it again. You will get only as much out of these lessons as you put into them.

REVIEW

In this lesson you expanded the reach of your index and middle fingers. You extended to the middle of the keyboard with the H and G keys. You reached into the upper row and added vowels to your repertoire with the I and E keys. You typed actual words and collections of words that resembled sentences.

You continued your work on building the memory traces connecting letters with your fingers. You completed the activities without looking at the keyboard (didn't you?). You continued on your journey toward developing the skills necessary to become a proficient keyboarder.

Keep practicing and play your air keyboard whenever you can.

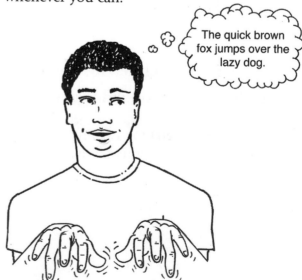

The quick brown fox jumps over the lazy dog.

L S A ; (SEMICOLON)

OUTCOMES

- Open a word processor
- Create a new file

- Save your file
- Sit properly in front of the keyboard
- Keys: L S A and ; (semicolon)
- One-minute timed test

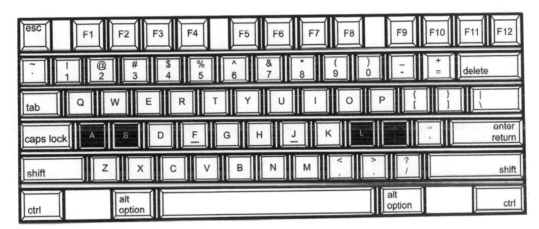

Figure 3.1

WARM-UP (5 MINUTES)

It's time to limber up your dexterous digits. Begin by creating a **New** file and saving it in the **Keyboarding** folder. Name it **Lesson3.doc.**

Remember to:

- Clip your NoPeekee Keyboard to the top of the page.

- Place your book in the holder and set it to the right of your keyboard.
- Sit at to your computer following the **Sitting Hints**.
- Set your timer to 5 minutes.
- Place your fingers lightly on the home row considering the **Home Row Hints**.

 Now you are ready to begin. Start your 5-minute timer. Go!

fff jjj ddd kkk ggg hhh eee iii jjj fff kkk ddd hhh ggg iii eee fff kkk ddd ddd hhh ggg iii eee
ffjj ddkk gghh eeii jjff kkdd gghh iiee ffjj ddkk gghh eeii jjff ffjj ddkk gghh eeii jjff kkdd
kdjjfhgie dkfjghei kjhgfdie dfghjkei kdjjfhgie dkfjghei kjhgfdie kdjjfhgie dkfjghei kjhgfdie

jjff kkdd jjff kkdd jjff kkdd jjff kkdd jjff kkdd jjff kkdd iiee jjff kkdd jjff kkdd jjff kkdd

de dei die did dig ed egg fig fed gig he hi hid jig keg kid id de dei die did dig ed egg fig

deed feed heed eddie dike hide hifi hike jeff kidd geek hedge deed feed heed eddie dike

 Save your work.

NEW KEYS L AND S

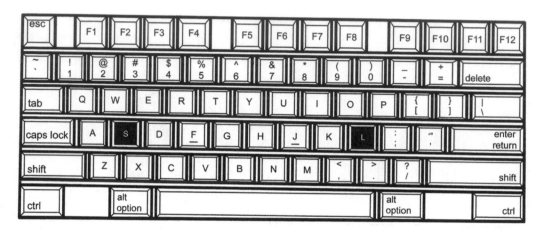

Figure 3.2

In this lesson you will learn the rest of the keys in the home rows. The L and S keys are each pressed with your ring fingers (see Figure 3.2). Your ring finger is the most difficult of all your fingers to control. You will notice that when you move your ring finger your other fingers will move involuntarily as well. This is something that will become less of a problem as you perfect your keyboarding skills.

lll lll lll lll lll lll lll lll lll lll sss sss sss sss sss sss sss sss sss sss lll lll lll lll lll lll ll sss sss sss

Good job! You are now a keyboarder, but your skills are not too useful yet. Using the L and S keys, type these two lines. Say the letters as you key them.

lll sss lll sss lll sss lll sss lll sss lll sss lll sss lll sss lll sss lll sss lll sss lll sss lll sss lll sss lll

ls ls ls ls ls ls ls ls sl sl sl sl sl sl sl sl lsl lsl lsl lsl lsl sls sls sls sls sls lsl lsl lsl lsl lsl sls sls

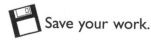 Save your work.

NEW KEYS TRYOUT L AND S

Let's put it all together now. Key these lines. Remember to say the letters as you work. Try to build a rhythm as you go.

lll sss lll sss ll ss ll ss ls ls ls ls ssll ssll ssll slsl slsl slsl s sl sls slss lll sss lll sss ll ss ll ss ls

jjll ffss kkll ddss hhll ggss iill eess jjll ffss kkll ddss hhll ggss iill jjll ffss kkll ddss hhll

ll ss kk dd jj ff hh gg ii ee hh gg jj ff kk dd ll ss ii ee sdfg hjkl ie gg ii ee hh gg jj ff kk dd ll

ss ii s h d j f k g l e i l g k f j d h s i e s h d j f k g l e i l g k f j d h s i e s h d j f k g l e i l g k f j

lid lid fig fig dig dig fed fed gel gel hid hid kid kid she she he he lid fig dig fed gel hid kid she he sell sell fish fish said said hide hide shed shed gill gill liss liss sell fish dish hide shed

leigh likes life les hides leeks leif slid ledges leslie did jigs jill hid gills egg gel kids sid jigs she sells shells she hid hedge seeds she sells hifi gigs kel did dig figs

 Save your work.

Do you notice that the words and sentences are making more sense? You still have a way to go, but as your repertoire expands, so will your keyboarding sophistication.

Take a break. Shake your hands loosely at the wrists. Stretch your arms above your head. Slowly turn your head from side to side. Stand up and walk around a little to relax your body.

NEW KEYS A AND ; (SEMICOLON)

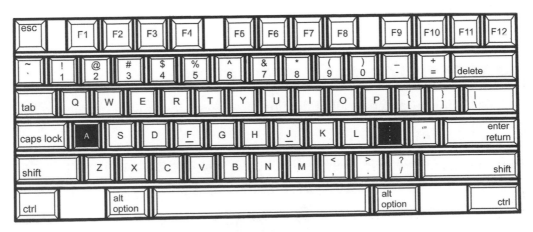

Figure 3.3

Now, you are going to add punctuation. You may be wondering why the semicolon is on the home row. Tradition has it that the typewriter inventor, C. L. Sholes, arranged the keys on the original typewriter keyboards to reduce the jamming of the mechanical keys.

Did you notice the pattern of letters in the home row? They are *almost* in alphabetical order. Ignoring the letters B, C, E, I, and S, the alphabet from A through L is in the home row (see Figure 3.4).

A b c D e F G H i J K L

Figure 3.4

Now, it's time to begin with your weakest finger, your pinky. Look at the keyboard and you will see that, aside from the A key, the more seldom-used letters are going to be pressed by the pinky, Q, Z, P, /, ', along with an assortment of brackets. The right pinky is responsible for pressing as many as ten keys, but most of them are used seldomly.

Sit at your computer and practice your pinky keys:

;;; ;;; ;;; ;;; ;;; ;;; ;;; ;;; ;;; **aaa aaa aaa aaa aaa aaa aaa aaa aaa aaa** ;;; ;;; ;;; ;;; ;;; ;;; ;;; **aaa aaa**

Good job! Remember to say the letters as you key them. You may want to say "semi" instead of "semicolon" for simplicity.

;;; aaa ;;; aaa ;;; aaa ;;; aaa ;;; aaa ;;; aaa ;;; aaa ;;; aaa ;;; aaa ;;; aaa ;;; aaa ;;; aaa ;;; aaa ;;;

;a ;a ;a ;a ;a ;a ;a ;a a; a; a; a; a; a; a; a; ;a; ;a; ;a; ;a; ;a a;a a;a a;a a;a a;a a; a; ;a ;a ;a; ;a; a;a

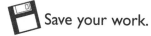Save your work.

NEW KEYS TRYOUT A AND ; (SEMICOLON)

You have now been introduced to all of the home row keys. It's time to practice your whole repertoire.

;;; aaa ;;; aaa ;; aa ;; aa ;a ;a ;a ;a aa;; aa;; aa;; a;a; a;a; a;a; a a; a;a a;aa ;;; aaa ;;; aaa ;; aa ;;

jj;; ffaa ll;; ssaa hh;; ggaa ii;; eeaa ll;; ssaa jj;; ffaa ll;; ssaa hh;; ggaa ii;; jj;; ffaa ll;; ssaa hh;;

;; aa ll ss kk dd jj ff hh gg ii ee hh gg jj ff kk dd ll ss ;; aa ;lkjh asdfg ;; aa ll ss kk dd jj ff hh

a h s j d k f l g ; e i ; g l f k d j s h a a h s j d k f l g ; e i ; g l f k d j s h a h s j d k f l g ; e i ; g l f ag ag; if if; all all; ads ada; his his; fad fad; lad lad; had had; dad dad; add add; glee glee; aids aids; lass lass; said said; added added; aided aided; asked asked; addled addled; egad

ada aids ali; aiko added all ag ads; adele alleges that al aided all his allies; adie adds as she alda asked adia; adli asked if a fad lad had gadflea ideas; lass said dad had disliked glass

 Save your work.

You just keyed an eight-word sentence. I hope you remembered to keep your eyes on the book instead of peeking at the keyboard. This is how you will build your skills as a keyboarder. If you peeked a couple of times as you were doing the previous exercises, you may want to go back and do them again. Remember that you are trying to build the memory traces from your brain to your fingers, so refer to your NoPeekee Keyboard instead of looking at your computer keyboard.

Break time! Stretch your arms. Shake your hands. Slowly turn your head from side to side. Walk around a bit and relax for a couple of minutes before continuing.

SELF-TEST

dad dad dad; aid aid aid; age age age; had had had; fad fad fad; add add add ; sea sea sea; lid lid lid; jig jig jig; jag jag jag; leg leg leg; sag sag sag; gas gas gas; ilk ilk ilk; see see see

age age age; fig fig fig; gel; gel gel; hag hag hag; his his his; led led led; lad lad lad; she she has has has; sad sad sad; sea sea sea; sis sis sis; eel eel eel; add add add; dig dig dig; eel

aide aide; deal deal; dell dell; heal heal; fade fade; gall gall; gash gash; dish dish; safe safe; head head; fell fell; held held; keel keel; lake lake; lash lash; idea idea; glad glad; said said;

less less; heals heals; hedge hedge; seals seals; heads heads; lease lease; shields shields; shall shall; shield shield; glass glass; shade shade; shake shake; likes likes; gails gails; dis

dee has a salad; jeff hiked hills; he held his head high; lad adds flags as he hides his shades dad has a hifi head; ed did dig a fig; iggi is eldest; i feel safe here; shasha sees high shields

al has a glass heel; dale heeds his less selfish ideas; he likes his digs; he shall sail sea sis shakes figs as she fells a shade hedge; she has had a glad saga; fiji fish feel less dike

a seahag has shellfish; gigi likes less shellfish; a desk easel is safe; les has a lead leg; he likes a fish flashed as she dashed; eels feel keels ahead; jig jag flasks leak; sasha feels feed classes

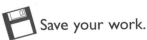 Save your work.

CORRECTIVE WORK

Proofread your work.

- Print the file, **Lesson3.doc**.

- Identify the words that were keyed incorrectly.

- Create a new file and save it as **L3Practice.doc**.

- Key each of these words five times correctly and save your file.

IMPROVEMENT WORK

Return to the Self-Test. Open the file **Lesson3.doc** and key these lines again. You should be able to complete the task more quickly and more accurately.

WORDS PER MINUTE (WPM)

You have learned twelve keys so far. Knowing the keys is important, but you are using this book to build your keyboarding speed. The only way you will know how successful you are at building speed is to take a timed test. Here is your opportunity to measure your speed. It will identify a starting point on your road to improvement.

If you haven't ever taken a keyboarding test before, let's go over the rules. You are trying to find how many words per minute (WPM) you can key. The term *words per minute* can be a little misleading. As you know words come in various sizes. Should the short word *it* be considered the same as the longer word *inspiration*? The answer is no. A "word" is generally considered five characters long. This means that if you key fifty letters (spaces included) it will count as ten words. That's easy to compute if you key a number of letters

that can be evenly divided by 5. Unfortunately, you have a greater chance of keying a number of letters that cannot be divided evenly by 5. What do you do?

Partial Words. What do you do if you key fifty-four letters? What about fifty-two letters? Here's the rule:

- If you key the first or second letter of a word, *round down*. Thus, if you key fifty-two letters, it counts as fifty letters (10 words).

- If you key three or four letters of a word, *round up*. Thus, if you key fifty-three or fifty-four letters, it counts as fifty-five letters (11 words).

What about errors? Don't worry about errors now. You want to do your best, and your accuracy will build as you gain experience. You will count errors in the future.

THE ONE-MINUTE TEST

On page 25, you will find three lines of text to key for a 1-minute test. You must set your timer (or ask a friend or family member to time you) for 1 minute and then try to key as much of the text as possible. Don't worry about errors or try to go back and correct mistakes. Just keep a steady pace and *always* move forward. For simplicity, tap the Enter key at the end of each line. This is not what you usually do when keyboarding, but it will keep the format the same as on the printed page.

Tips on Setting Your Timer

You have been using a timer for the 5-minute warm-ups throughout the book.

Using a timer for a 1-minute exercise needs to be a bit more precise. Whether you use an egg timer or the timer on your watch, a certain amount of time elapses between when you tap the start button and when you can begin keyboarding.

Here's a suggestion. Instead of hurting yourself trying to make the quick transition, try setting your timer for 10 seconds extra. If you are timing a one-minute test, set your timer for 1 minute and 10 seconds. This will give you 10 seconds to press the start button and then get set in front of your keyboard. Good luck!

If you complete all three lines, you will have keyed at 36 WPM, which is very good. If you run out of words, just start at the first line again and continue until your timer goes off.

Setting the Font

You will notice that the font used in the timing test is different from the font used elsewhere in the practice activities. This font is called Courier. It is used because each of the letters is the same width. This makes it easier to use the index at the top of the selection to help you calculate how many words you completed. In contrast, you will notice that in the font used for this sentence the letters are proportionally spaced. This means that an *i* uses less space than an *m*.

You can change your font using the same process you used in Lesson 1 for your practice work. Set your font to **Courier, Regular, 12 point**.

Preparing Properly

Ready to begin? Use the sitting hints to prepare for your test. Use the home row hints to ensure that your fingers are set and ready to go. Don't look at the keyboard. You are trying to break bad habits and/or build new habits as you work. If you forget the key location, refer to your NoPeekee Keyboard.

The text for this timing has been laid out with 12 words (60 characters) per line. It also requires a 6"-wide page, so set your left and right margins to 1.25".

 Set your timer…and…go!

```
         3              6              9             12
al is glad he is a dad; he hid eggs; del said he did dishes;
        15             18             21             24
dee had ideas; she likes jig jag ideas; jeff dislikes eels;
        27             30             33             36
seals eat shellfish; sis hikes hills; gigi fishes his lakes;
```

How did you do? It is OK if you completed only 3 WPM. That means that you were tapping a key every 4 seconds. The most important part of the timed test is that you didn't look at the keyboard. If you did look at your fingers during the timed test, go back and do it again. Find out how many keys you can tap in one minute without looking at your fingers. Even if you are referring to your NoPeekee Keyboard, you are building good habits instead of resorting to being a hunt-and-peck keyboarder.

This is your starting point. Turn to the Self-Progress Chart at the back of the book and write the total number of words you keyed in 1 minute. Notice that you compute the WPM by dividing the total words by the number of minutes. This isn't much of a mathematical challenge when you are dividing by 1 minute. The mathematical calculations will require a few more steps when you get to the 5-minute tests.

U R Y T

OUTCOMES

• Keys: U R Y and T

Figure 4.1

WARM-UP (5 MINUTES)

Are your fingers ready for some more challenges? This lesson will expand your repertoire to eighteen keys.

Begin by creating a **New** file and saving it in the **Keyboarding** folder. Name it **Lesson4.doc**. You are building quite a collection of files in your Keyboarding folder, aren't you?

Remember to:

• Clip your NoPeekee Keyboard to the top of the page.

• Place your book in the holder and set it to the right of your keyboard.

• Sit at your computer following the **Sitting Hints**.

• Set your timer to 5 minutes.

• Place your fingers lightly on the home row considering the **Home Row Hints**.

 Now you are ready to begin. Start your 5-minute timer. Go!

kkk ddd jjj fff uuu rrr ;;; aaa iii eee hhh ggg ;;; aaa uuu rrr kkk ddd kkk ddd jjj fff uuu rrr ;;;
kkdd jjff llss ;;aa iiee hhgg kkdd jjff llss ;;aa iiee hhgg ;;aa llss jjff kkdd jjff llss ;;aa iiee

a he is an dad has sid jif she eggs leg eel hid shed fake lake lass ugly jade alas sage self sill
fish kiss deed said seeks sells feeds jade desk salad ahead seals seeds feels skill shade

sid sells jade; eddie feeds fish; she is ahead; he hid fake eggs; dad said he seals deed
dale has a salad; he seeks a safe jade desk; a shed shields hags; fae has skilled fish
a lad has a fake leg; alas a lass sells a kiss; a fish seeks a shade lake; hal feels he has

 Save your work.

NEW KEYS U AND R

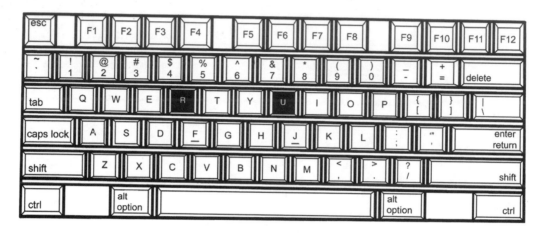

Figure 4.2

In this lesson you will learn the rest of the top row keys that you reach with your forefingers. The U and R keys are both directly above the J and F keys (see Figure 4.2). Remember to bring your forefinger immediately back to the home row after you have tapped the top row keys. Give it a try while tapping the U key. Say the letters as you tap the keys.

jjj uuu jjj uuu jjj uuu jjj uuu jjj uuu jjj uuu jjj uuu jjj uuu jjj uuu jjj uuu jjj uuu jjj uuu jjj

Way to go! Now try it with the R key. Remember to obey the "rubber band" that will bring your left forefinger directly back to the F key after tapping the R key.

fff rrr fff rrr fff rrr fff rrr fff rrr fff rrr fff rrr fff rrr fff rrr fff rrr fff rrr fff rrr fff rrr fff rrr

 Save your work.

NEW KEYS TRYOUT U AND R

Your skills are expanding and your knowledge is skyrocketing. Your selection of letters is becoming even more varied. U R going to know how to key words with U and R now. Remember to clip your NoPeekee Keyboard to the book and try these exercises. Say the letters as you work. Build a rhythm as you proceed.

jjj uuu fff rrr jjj uuu fff rrr jjj uuu fff rrr jjj uuu fff rrr jjj uuu fff rrr jjj uuu fff rrr jjj uuu

jjuu ffrr jjuu ffrr jjuu ffrr kkii ddee ;e;aa ssll ddkk ffjj jkl fds ujk rfd ujk rfd lkju sdfr rufj

uu rr ii ee jj ff gg hh dd kk ss ll aa ;; ss ll dd kk ff jj gg hh uu rr ii ee kk dd ll ss ;; aa jj

a ; s l d k f j g h r u e i h g j f k d l s ; a i e u r h g j f k d l s ; a s l d k j f h g u r i e s l d

red red; rug rug; rush rush; real real; rigs rigs; rash rash; read read; used used; usher read read; sails sails; rails rails; radar radar; raked raked; rigger rigger; real real; rural

uri used a ukulele; usher is useful; a real red rudder sails radar rigs; a ruffled rug rash rafe reared a red radar; rhad hugs red rigs; rural rails are ragged; rugged rural rulers

Let's put it all together now. Key these lines. Remember to say the letters as you work. Try to build a rhythm as you go.

jjj uuu fff rrr jjj uuu fff rrr jjj uuu fff rrr jjj uuu fff rrr jjj uuu fff rrr jjj uuu fff rrr jjj uuu fff

ffrr jjuu kkii ddee jjhh ffgg aa;; ffrr jjuu kkii ddee jjhh ffgg aa;; ffrr jjuu kkii ddee jjhh

uu rr ii ee hh gg jj ff kk dd ll ss ;; aa uu rr ii ee hh gg jj ff kk dd ll uu rr ii ee hh gg jj ff kk

u r i e h g j f k d l s ; a u r i e h g j f k d l s ; a u r i e h g j f k d l s ; a u r i e h g j f k d

jug jug; full full; surf surf; sure sure; rule rule; huge huge; rude rude; deer deer; fur fur; fuses fuses; furies furies; rake rake; gushed gushed; refuse refuse; sushi sushi; rulers

fake fuses issue furies; a jug full of ideas gushed ahead; her hushed heels hugged rare surf sure urges surges; rulers rule huge rude sushi; red deer refresh real refuse

Save your work.

Take a break. Loosen up your arms, wrists, and head. Stand up and stretch.

NEW KEYS Y AND T

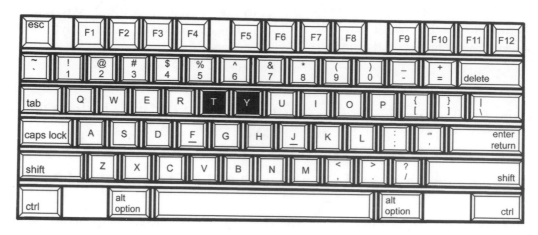

Figure 4.3

You have limbered up your forefingers, so it's time to reach toward the middle on the top row (see Figure 4.3). Introducing Y and T will expand your keyboarding vocabulary greatly. You will now be able to use adverbs like "easily" and "daily." You will be able to write numbers like "thirty" and "fifty." The opportunities are endless. Try keying the Y key. Remember to bring your forefinger back to the home row after you make the long stretch to these keys. Say the letters as you tap.

jjj yyy jjj yyy jjj yyy jjj yyy jjj yyy jjj yyy jjj yyy jjj yyy jjj yyy jjj yyy jjj yyy jjj yyy jjj yyy jjj

Now it's time to work on the left hand. Tap that T and return to the F key to rest.

fff ttt fff ttt fff ttt fff ttt fff ttt fff ttt fff ttt fff ttt fff ttt fff ttt fff ttt fff ttt fff ttt fff ttt fff

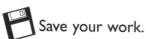Save your work.

NEW KEYS TRYOUT Y AND T

You are becoming a keyboarding expert, so it's time to practice your newly learned skills. Say the letters as you tap them and try to build a rhythm.

Remember your NoPeekee Keyboard!

jjj yyy fff ttt jjj yyy fff ttt jjj yyy fff ttt jjj yyy fff ttt jjj yyy fff ttt jjj yyy ttt fff
jjyy fftt jjuu ffrr kkii ddee llss ;;aa fftt jjyy ffrr jjuu ddee kkii ssll jjyy ffrr ddd

yy tt uu rr ii ee hh gg jj ff kk dd ll ss ;; aa yy tt uu rr ii ee ll ss ;; aa hh dd kk ttt uuu

y t u r i e h g j f k d l s ; a y t u r i e h g j f k d l s ; a y t u r i e l s ; a d y j k r y a t u l s g

yak yak; yes yes; yay yay; the the; say say; yard yard; tied tied; died died; tigers tigers; tree tree; sure sure; takes takes; three three; true true; truth truth; ready ready; fast; fast;

yis yak has a yaw; yigi yelled yes; the yard yak read true; three ukeleles yelled loudly tara takes three till tikes; ted tied the dead tree; tasha tried trials;

 Save your work.

Break time! Stretch your arms. Shake your hands. Slowly, turn your head from side to side. Walk around a bit and relax for a couple of minutes before continuing.

SELF-TEST

the the; dry dry; see see; try try; rat rat; his his; fat fat; jar jar; his his, rut rut; tar tar; fill fill; yard yard; eyes eyes; huge huge; get get; salty salty; hair hair; dusk dusk;

tried tried; salad salad; treat treat; yells yells; tight tight; drudge drudge; truth truth; heard heard; giggle giggle; lilies lilies; eight eight; frugal frugal; died died; yelled

share share; rarely rarely; really really; easily easily; trash trash; illustrates illustrates; guest guest; surely surely; retire retire; greatest greatest; shirt shirt; yak yak; tiger;

the yard grass is really dry; fill the basket; try the lilies; sheila heard high giggles; dad easily sees the dirt; see the dark shirt; it is right there; get it; she likes the shirt

that fat rat has huge eyes; she has really large feet; she likes her treats; ted gets her sal tells us that eight eggs is the greatest way to start the day; he likes to eat real eggs

kathy guesses his age easily; he is rarely at his desk at dusk; ted tries tofu eggs darla has taught us; she is a great ally; her hair is real dark; the truth is huge they had heard the firefighter; he is the greatest firefighter; kids like Ted; he is funny that kid is rude; he yells angrily; he illustrates cat hats; his hat is tight; tigers yell

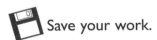 Save your work.

CORRECTIVE WORK

Proofread your work.

- Print the file, **Lesson4.doc**.

- Identify the words that were keyed incorrectly.

- Create a new file and save it as **L4Practice.doc**.

- Key each of these words five times correctly and save your file.

IMPROVEMENT WORK

Return to the preceding fourteen lines. Open the file **Lesson4.doc**, and key these lines again. You should be able to complete the task more quickly and more accurately.

How much are you practicing a day? Haven't you been able to get to the keyboard enough? Have the days been too beautiful to practice? Remember your air keyboard! It will go with you anywhere.

N V B M C

OUTCOMES

- Keys: N V B M and C
- One-minute timed test

Figure 5.1

WARM-UP (5 MINUTES)

One, two, three, four. One, two, three, four. Loosen up those hands and wrists and arms and get ready to learn five letters this time. You will use your forefingers again, but this time you will venture to the center of the bottom row (see Figure 5.1). At the end of this lesson, you will have learned twenty-one of the twenty-six letters in the alphabet. You will also have the opportunity to time yourself again to see how your keyboarding fluency is progressing. You are well on your way to writing a letter using proper fingering on your computer.

Create a **New** file and save it in the **Keyboarding** folder. Name it **Lesson5.doc**.

Remember to:

- Clip your NoPeekee Keyboard to the top of the page.
- Place your book in the holder and set it to the right of your keyboard.
- Sit at your computer following the **Sitting Hints**.
- Set your timer to 5 minutes.
- Place your fingers lightly on the home row considering the **Home Row Hints**.

 Now you are ready to begin. Start your 5-minute timer. Go!

yyy ttt nnn vvv hhh ggg jjj fff iii eee kkk ddd lll sss ;;; aaa jjj fff ;;; aaa yyy ttt nnn vvv hhh

ggg lll sss kkk ddd iii eee hhh ggg jjj fff nnn vvv yyy ttt aaa ;;; asdfg ;lkjh lll sss kkk ddd iii as he it is to the eat try all she egg ever deal that good easy tried salad treat great feels ready fuels truth heals radar liked salty daily treats stated dessert furies ushers liked eating basket greater

has he tried the egg salad; it is his treat; try it as a dessert treat; he ate it in the desert she stated that she sleeps a great deal; her fraud feud fuels less selfish dislikes; she shakes good treats are easy eating; she tastes treats; truth heals greater furies; fifty ushers ate

 Save your work.

How many times did you make it through the warm-up exercises? Are you getting faster? Do you feel more comfortable using the home row–based keyboarding method?	Are you referring to the NoPeekee Keyboard instead of looking at the computer keyboard? Keep at it and you will become a proficient keyboarder.

NEW KEYS N AND V

Figure 5.2

You have been extending your fingers into the upper row for letters like T, Y, E and I. Now it is time to move to the lower row to the N and V keys (see Figure 5.2). You will notice that all five of the keys in this lesson will be tapped with forefingers. Your forefingers are the busiest keyboarding fingers. This is good because they are your strongest and most agile fingers.

Place your fingers on the home row and feel the J and F keys. Move your J finger (right forefinger) down and to the left and you will find the N key. Go ahead and look at the keyboard and see how natural it is to move your right forefinger from the J to the N key. Remember to move your finger back to the J key. Always return to the home row. Do this a couple of times to get the feel of it. Key the row on the next page. Say the letters as you key them.

jjj nnn jjj nnn jjj nnn jjj nnn jjj nnn jjj nnn jjj nnn jjj nnn jjj nnn jjj jjj nnn jjj nnn jjj nnn jjj

Nicely done! Now, try it with the V key. Move your left forefinger from the F key to the V key. Notice how natural it feels.

fff vvv fff vvv fff vvv fff vvv fff vvv fff vvv fff vvv fff vvv fff vvv fff fff vvv fff vvv fff vvv fff

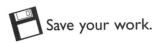 Save your work.

NEW KEYS TRYOUT N AND V

Now it's time to give your Ns and Vs some practice. Say these letters as you key them.

jjj nnn fff vvv jjj nnn fff vvv jjj nnn fff vvv jjj nnn fff vvv jjj nnn fff vvv jjj nnn fff vvv jjj ffvv jjnn ffgg jjhh fftt jjnn ffrr jjuu ddee kkii ssll aa;; jjnn ffvv jjuu fftt ffvv jjnn ffgg

ff vv jj nn ff gg jj hh ff tt jj nn ff rr jj uu dd ee kk ii ss ll aa ;; jj nn ff vv ff vv jj nn ff n v h g y t u r j f i e k d l s ; a n v h g y t u r j f i e k d l s ; a n j v f n v h g y t u r j f i e

nine nine; knee knee; shine shine; sang sang; very very; vase vase; tunes tunes; saved; valet valet; never never; vines vines; value value; veiled veiled; vanilla vanilla; varying

the nine nursery nannies sing little tunes; laura sang the tunes very fast; tiny tunes varying vanilla fudge varieties taste fine; val had funny valentines; vinnie veiled jan the valet never valued the vase; it is very dear; van vines saved vera; she never gave

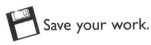 Save your work.

Break time. Spend a minute shaking your arms and stretching your back. Stand up.

NEW KEY B

Figure 5.3

The letter B is introduced by itself because it is stuck in the center of the lower row (see Figure 5.3). It is an equal stretch for the right or left forefinger to get to the B. This book recommends that you use your right forefinger to reach for the B, but if you are left-handed or it just feels better to reach for the B with your left forefinger, go for it! (If you decide to use your left forefinger for the B key, replace the Js in the following practice line with Fs.)

jjj bbb jjj bbb jjj bbb jjj bbb jjj bbb jjj bbb jjj bbb jjj bbb jjj bbb jjj bbb jjj bbb jjj bbb

Save your work.

NEW KEY TRYOUT B

Let's put it all together now. Key these lines. Remember to say the letters as you work. Try to build a rhythm as you go.

jjj bbb fff bbb nnn vvv hhh ggg uuu rrr nnn aaa iii eee kkk ddd lll sss ;;; jjj bbb fff bbb
jjbb ffbb jjhh ffgg jjll fftt jjuu ffrr kkii ddee ll;; ssaa jjbb ffbb jjhh ffgg jjbb ffbb jjhh

jj bb ff bb ;; aa ll ss kk dd ii ee jj ff uu rr bb tt hh gg nn vv bb nn vv jj ff jj bb ff bb ;; aa
b n j b v f j g h d k s l a ; t y r u e i b n j b v f j g h d k s l a ; t y r u e I b n j b v f j g h d

by by; big big; bugs bugs; buys buys; bags bags; bins bins; blast blast; burst burst
being being; brings brings; better better; burger burger; bakery bakery; baseballs base

billy brings big bugs at breakfast; betty bags brian by being better; barney bugles badly brett has a burger business by the barn; he buys big bakery bags; baseballs blast by betty

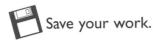 Save your work.

Take a break. Loosen up your arms, wrists, and head. Stand up and stretch.

NEW KEYS M AND C

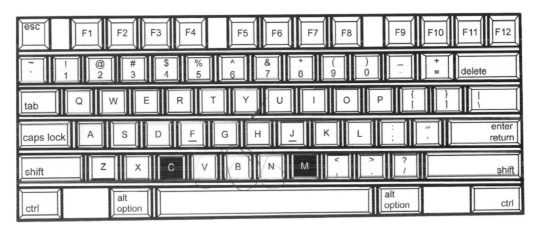

Figure 5.4

Now, it is time to reach for the Ms and the Cs (see Figure 5.4). Once again, you will use your forefingers to tap these keys. This time, you will move your fingers backward toward the palm of your hand to reach the M and C keys.

Place your fingers on the home row and try touching the M and C keys.

Begin keying M with your right forefinger using the following practice activity.

jjj mmm jjj mmm jjj mmm jjj mmm jjj mmm jjj mmm jjj mmm jjj mmm jjj mmm jjj

OK, lefty, your turn. Return your forefinger to F after you tap the C.

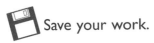 Save your work.

NEW KEYS TRYOUT M AND C

Let's mix up the Ms and Cs with the other letters you have learned so far. Build a rhythm as you work and remember to refer to your NoPeekee Keyboard as necessary.

jjj mmm fff ccc jjj mmm fff ccc jjj mmm fff ccc jjj mmm fff ccc mmm ccc jjj mmm fff jjmm ffcc jjnn ffvv bbbb jjuu ffrr jjyy fftt jjhh ffgg kkii ddee llss ;;aa mm cc jjmm ffcc

mm cc nn bb jj ff hh gg tt yy uu rr kk dd ii ee ll ss ;; aa cc mm vv nn bb mm cc nn bb jj m c n v b j f h g y t u r i e k d l s ; a m c n v b j f h g y t u r i e k d l s ; a m c n v b j f h

me me; men men; can can; many many; make make; chit chit; chat chat; made made; cats cats; chess chess; casual casual; create create; emails emails; cradles cradles; mighty

mighty mary emails me many messages; many men make measurements; martin married chris checkmates chuck in chess; charlie can create casual chit chat; carl cradles cats

Save your work.

You deserve a break. You don't have to take a long one: just give yourself an opportunity to stretch and to loosen up your muscles. You know how to do it by now. Take a 60-second break before you start the following self-test.

SELF-TEST

fun fun; has has; his his; eat eat; try try; are are; and and; had had; tab tab; near near; this this; they they; very very; this this; girl girl; year year; made made; many many; suit;

treats treats; vivid vivid; river river; tarts tarts; never never; small small; falls falls; laugh; scary scary; there there; ideas ideas; these these; three three; cedar cedar; tried tried; shiny;

dance dance; light light; tasty tasty; river river; leaves leaves; future future; sailed sailed island island; heading heading; family family; friends friends; teacher teacher; dessert

alice has never navigated the cedar river; she sailed many rivers in maine; the rivers run he sailed by a small island near the falls; heading for the falls was scary; he fell by me

chris is graduating thursday; his family and friends will be there; he can be a fine teacher
he has many future ideas; these ideas include taking a trip by nebraska; he leaves tuesday

ana has tried the egg salad; it is very tasty; it takes three eggs; try it as a nice dessert treat
she makes great blueberry tarts; they are light, fluffy and very tasty; the great taste is vivid

the dancing girl likes the shiny suit; she made the children laugh; she is talentedly funny
it was clear that she had taken classes in ballet dancing; her river dance started well

 Save your work.

CORRECTIVE WORK

Proofread your work.

- Print the file **Lesson5.doc**.
- Identify the words that were keyed incorrectly.
- Create a new file and save it as
  L5Practice.doc.
- Key each of these words five times correctly
  and save your file.

IMPROVEMENT WORK

Return to the Self-Test. Open the file
Lesson5.doc, and key these lines again.
You should be able to complete the task
more quickly and more accurately.

ONE-MINUTE TIMING

You have now learned twenty-one keys. You
just learned five keys in this lesson alone. It's
time to check your speed again. You may have
to think a little harder to remember the placement of the more recently introduced keys,
but you should be comfortable with the home
row keys and those that were introduced in the
earlier lessons.

Remember that this timing measures your
speed while you keyboard without looking
at the keyboard! You may be getting tired of
hearing this, but disciplining yourself to look
only at the book and your NoPeekee Keyboard
is building the positive habits that will lead to
successful keyboarding.

Remember to:

- Use the **Sitting Hints** to address your
  keyboard.
- Use the **Home Row Hints** to position
  your fingers.
- Use the NoPeekee Keyboard for reference.
- Tap the Enter key at the end of each line.

The text for this timing has been laid out with
12 words (60 characters) per line. This timing
should be done using 12-point New Courier
font. It also requires a 6"-wide page so set your
left and right margins to 1.25".

Start your timer. Go!

```
             3                6                9               12
tammy likes starfruit after her lunch; her guru taught her
            15               18               21               24
sheila studies art a great deal; she likes attending fairs
            27               30               33               36
jack carries his flute by the market tuesday and thursday
            39               42               45               47
abe giggled at silly games yesterday; his father laughed
```

How did you do this time? Did you improve? You are now responsible for almost twice as many keys as in Lesson 3, so it's OK if you did the same speed. Chances are good, however, that you are feeling more comfortable at the keyboard and that you were able to recall and respond to more keys more quickly this time.

Turn to the Self-Progress Chart at the back of the book and enter the total number of words per minute (remember to round up) and calculate your total WPM.

AUTOWORDS

OUTCOMES

• Keying AutoWords
  if, is, me, am, an, it, he, be, by, in, my

You have spent the past five lessons learning one key after another. You have had the opportunity to test your proficiency at key-boarding. You should be feeling pretty good about yourself by now.

There is a trick for learning to key faster. That trick is to key *words* rather than *letters*. You will learn more about that method in this lesson.

WARM-UP (5 MINUTES)

Try this warm-up to get your communicative juices flowing.

Create a **New** file and save it in the **Keyboarding** folder. Name it **Lesson6.doc**.

Remember to:

• Clip your NoPeekee Keyboard to the top of the page.

• Place your book in the holder and set it to the right of your keyboard.

• Sit up to your computer following the **Sitting Hints**.

• Set your timer to 5 minutes.

• Place your fingers lightly on the home row considering the **Home Row Hints**.

 Now you are ready to begin. Start your 5-minute timer. Go!

mmm ccc nnn vvv bbb hhh ggg jjj fff kkk ddd lll sss ;;; aaa yyy ttt uuu rrr iii eee ggg hhh aaa ;;; sss lll ddd kkk ccc mmm vvv nnn bbb iii aaa ;;; sss lll ddd kkk ccc mmm vvv nnn

us is at the men cut all can any try give that here many best like rate save cash make feel human treat makes keying feeling illustrate buying successful mar line taste thanks biggest letters advance ability available markets individual fast run tiger balance

give us the biggest ice cream treat that is available here; mmmmmm; i like vanilla best many men like buying merchandise at cut rate markets; they save cash and time buying it keying these letters at a fast rate can make any human feel talented; rate is desired here feeling skilled can advance human ability; it makes any individual try much harder;

Save your work.

The warm-up activities are getting longer, but you are becoming more capable. Notice that with the extended number of keys/letters that you can key, the sentences are becoming longer and much more interesting. The few important letters that you still need to learn, like O, P, and W, will be covered in the next couple of lessons.

KEYING WORDS

Until now, you have been keying a lot of letters. Remember when you were sitting on the bus or in front of the television playing your "air keyboard"? You were just thinking about the letters. You thought of an *I* and you moved your right index finger. You thought of an *F* and you moved your left forefinger. You spelled the word *if* but did you ever think of that?

Remember when you were first learning to read? No? I don't either. Think of how children first learn to read. First, they learn the alphabet and then learn the sounds that go with each of the letters. Reading is the process of seeing the letters presented in a word and then making the sounds in sequence to say that word.

If the word *if* is presented, the reader first says the sound for *i* and then the sound for *f*. Combining these sounds makes the word *if*. This process works for reading short single words, but it becomes quite clumsy and time-consuming when the early reader is trying to read whole sentences and paragraphs. The efficient reader learns to recognize whole words and connect to their meaning with the meaning of the other words in the sentence to create understanding.

Keyboarding works in a similar but reverse manner. The keyboarder produces the word *if* by first keying the letter *i* and then keying the letter *f*. This means that the keyboarder first sees the letter *i* on the paper that he/she is copying. As a result of extensive keyboarding practice (*without looking at the keyboard while keying*) the keyboarder's right index finger moves (almost automatically) and taps the *I* key and returns to the *K* key in the home row. The keyboarder next sees the *f* on the paper, and the left forefinger quickly taps the *F* key. These two processes are the automated result of practice. Since they are done by "feel," they are quick and efficient. But they are still two processes. What if they could be consolidated into a single process?

Imagine considering *if* as a two-finger movement instead of two single-finger movements: Thus, whenever you saw the word *if* you would immediately start twitching your right forefinger and left forefinger (preferably in the correct order). This would definitely increase your response time and speed up your keyboarding, wouldn't it?

You may be asking yourself, how, since I am just beginning to learn the fingering for single letters, will I be able to key whole words? Don't worry. If you don't feel ready for this move toward more efficient keyboarding, then just go through the exercises using the single-key method. But watch—you may find yourself thinking of these little words in a different way by the end of the lesson.

AUTOWORDS

if, is, me, am, an, it, he, be, by, in, my

Have you never heard of an AutoWord? An *AutoWord* is a word that you automatically key when you see it. When you read the word *it*, you don't have to sound it out. You automatically recognize it and integrate it into the meaning of the sentence. AutoWords are words that you consider as multiple-finger movements instead of as multiple single-finger movements.

Let's begin by keying some two-letter words that involve both hands. Say the word *if* instead of the letters *i* and *f* individually as you key. Start slowly and increase speed until you are keying rapidly.

if if if if if if if if if if if if if if if if if if if if if if if if if if if if if if if

Now look away from the book and key *if* five times.

Did you feel the movement? You didn't have to think about the letters. You just thought about the word.

Obviously you haven't turned *so* into an AutoWord yet, but keying the word as a whole without looking at your keyboard (or even the NoPeekee keyboard) is the process for developing your ability to use AutoWords.

Let's try some more. Say each word as you key it. Start each line slowly and increase speed until you are keying each AutoWord rapidly:

is is is is is is is is is is is is is is is is is is is is is is is is is is is is is is is is is is is is is is is

me me me me me me me me me me me me me me me me me me me me me me me

am am am am am am am am am am am am am am am am am am am am am am am

an an an an an an an an an an an an an an an an an an an an an an an an an

it it it it it it it it it it it it it it it it it it it it it it it it it it it it it it it it it it it it it it it

he he he he he he he he he he he he he he he he he he he he he he he he he he he he he he

be be be be be be be be be be be be be be be be be be be be be be be be be be be be be be

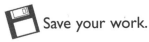 Save your work.

Let's mix it up a bit.

if if if is is is me me me am am am an an an it it it he he he be be it it if if if is is me me an an he he it it an an am am me me is is if if he he be be it it an an am am an an he he it it if it is me; me is it; if me is an it; he is me; it is he; me is he is it; it is me if it is me;

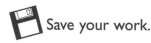 Save your work.

Do that last row again. Notice that you are keying words, not letters. If you don't think you have mastered this yet, that's OK. This is just the beginning. The more words that you turn into AutoWords, the more efficient a keyboarder you will become.

There are one-handed AutoWords too. This means that your other hand has an opportunity to rest while you key these words.

LEFT-HAND AUTOWORDS

at at at at at at at at at at at at at at at at at at at at at at at at at at at at at at at at at at at at

The next one is difficult because it uses your two weakest fingers.

as as as as as as as as as as as as as as as as as as as as as as as as as as as as as as as as as as as

RIGHT-HAND AUTOWORDS

by by by by by by by by by by by by by by by by by by by by by by by by by by by in in in in in in in in in in in in in in in in in in in in in in in in in in in in in in in in in my my my my my my my my my my my my my my my my my my my my my my my my my

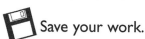 Save your work.

Mix it up a bit.

at at at as as as by by by in in in my my my at at as as by by in in my my at as by in my as by in at as by my in my in by as at as at by my in my at at at as as as by by by in in in my my at he is by me; he is in it; as at it; he if me; he as me; my as he; in my by; by me my; my me

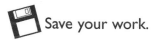 Save your work.

Although they don't make much sense, you are keying words instead of letters here. Good job!

COMPOSING AT THE KEYBOARD

The most important reason to learn to key AutoWords is that you will be composing at the keyboard. The world of keyboarding/typing has changed. In the 1970s, every business had rooms full of secretaries whose job it was to type letters that had been handwritten by their bosses or to read from the shorthand notes they took as their bosses dictated letters. None of the bosses had typewriters. Secretaries would sit at their typewriters and look at handwritten papers and transcribe them. They were copying the writing into a more readable format.

In the early 1980s, the personal computer became a common office machine. This machine was used for more than to type letters. It was used to create spreadsheets for business planning. It held databases of information for managers to search. It was used to communicate via e-mail. Interestingly, since these machines also had word processors on them, many of the managers decided to write their own letters, so they didn't need to have their secretaries type them.

Today, in the twenty-first century, the World Wide Web has created a keyboard-based world. Whether you are answering e-mail or composing a story, doing it directly through the keyboard is the most efficient way to do it. The ultimate way to compose is to be able to keyboard as fast as you can think. This is not easy to do, but your goal should be at least to develop the ability to think of the word "my" and have the appropriate fingers tap the appropriate keys without interrupting the thinking process so your thoughts can flow onto the screen.

If you are going to be keying your correspondence at your computer, it is faster just to key it directly at the computer instead of first writing it out and then copying it into the computer. However, some people still write their letters first because they are poor keyboarders. The process of finding the keys is so difficult that they can't concentrate on what they are writing, so they just write their thoughts on paper and key them later. You will not have to do this because you are becoming a proficient keyboarder.

SELF-TEST

if if if is is is me me me am am am an an an it it it he he he be be be at at at as as as by by in in my my my if is me am an it he be at as if is me if if if is is is me me me am am am an

it is my he by in me as him can all the can try fun idea that fall date much tell make will head thin real stir rest call begin learn needs start tries successful teacher string

dance using music keeps happy harder skills better essay change classes several address finding cabinet sentences greatness revealed listening catch mitt baseball net hard run

it is my idea that he begin classes; he can learn all the skills he needs; he is as ready as can be
she believes that she starts classes by the fall; her start date is in several days; she is my daughter

if he can change certain sentences in the essay it will be much better; it is my belief
if he tries harder he can achieve greatness; tell me if he makes it; i believe he can get it

he can see me as my head is revealed by the thin sheet; it reveals the illustration little by little
i can dance like the rest; using dancing as activity is fun; my flat feet have a great rhythm

it is music that makes me glad; i believe in listening carefully; try it; it is fine by me
he can be here; if he needs aid in finding my address call me; he has my cell number

 Save your work.

CORRECTIVE WORK

Proofread your work.

- Print the file **Lesson6.doc**.

- Identify the words that were keyed incorrectly.

- Create a new file and save it as **L6Practice.doc**.

- Key each of these words five times correctly and save your file.

IMPROVEMENT WORK

Return to the Self-Test. Open the file **Lesson6.doc**, and key these lines again. You should be able to complete the task more quickly and more accurately.

O W P Q

OUTCOMES

- O W P and Q
- One-minute timed test

Figure 7.1

You are almost there. You have learned to key most of the alphabet letters, but you have been limping along keying words that don't contain Os or Ps (see Figure 7.1). Count how many words have those letters in this paragraph alone.

WARM-UP (5 MINUTES)

Your keyboarding charisma is about to elevate with these warm-up activities.

Create a **New** file and save it in the **Keyboarding** folder. Name it **Lesson7.doc**.

Remember to:

- Clip your NoPeekee Keyboard to the top of the page.
- Place your book in the holder and set it to the right of your keyboard.
- Sit at your computer following the **Sitting Hints**.
- Set your timer to 5 minutes.
- Place your fingers lightly on the home row considering the **Home Row Hints**.

 Start your 5-minute timer. Go!

ccc vvv bbb nnn mmm aaa ;;; sss lll ddd kkk fff jjj ggg hhh ttt yyy rrr uuu eee iii iii eee

fff jjj aaa ;;; sss lll ddd kkk ccc mmm vvv nnn bbb ccc vvv bbb nnn mmm aaa ;;; sss lll

it is he be if an at by has his red can the him her has fun huge shag fine feet blue like

feels green needs likes rural merits tables chairs running iguana ferret terrific residence believe mel has a huge shag rug in his rural residence; it feels fine with his feet; it is green

he likes mushing in it; he can be at the residence if his sis needs him; his sis is terrific;

she likes her animals; she has an iguana and a ferret; her cats are cute; they can have fun

they like running by the tables and chairs in the residence; they rarely cause large snags

 Save your work.

How did you do on that warm-up? Were you using your AutoWords? Did you find yourself keying the letters as a two-motion word instead of as a two single-motions word? If you did, you are becoming a more efficient keyboarder. If you are still at the single-motion/letter level, don't worry. You will learn to use AutoWords as you consciously try to integrate them into your keyboarding behavior.

NEW KEYS O AND W

Figure 7.2

Now, it's time to address more of the upper-row letters (see Figure 7.2). This time you will be using your ring fingers to do this. The ring finger can be a difficult finger to use because of the way your hands are constructed. Hold your hands up in front of you. Move your thumb and watch to see if any of your other fingers move. They don't, do they? That's because the thumb was designed as an opposable digit that can be used for picking up and holding things. Now, move your forefinger. None of the other fingers move either. Move your index (middle) finger. Some of your other fingers (most likely your ring finger) will move a little. Move your ring finger and your middle finger will most likely move. This is because of the way the tendons are connected in your fingers. This can be a small problem when you are first learning to keyboard, but you will learn to move your ring finger rather independently with practice. Place your fingers on the home row and feel the J and F keys. The row is starting to feel like home, isn't it? Move your right ring finger forward to tap the O key. See how natural it is to move the ring finger to the O key. Move the ring finger back home to the L key. Always return to the home row. Give it a try. Repeat tapping O and returning to the L key a few times.

lll ooo lll ooo lll ooo lll ooo lll ooo lll ooo llll ooo lll ooo lll ooo lll ooo lll lll ooo lll ooo

Well done. Now let's move to the left hand and work on the W key. Reach your left ring finger into the upper row to tap the W key. Move it back home to the S key. Do that again a few times until it feels natural.

sss www sss www sss www sss www sss www sss www sss www sss www sss www sss

 Save your work.

NEW KEYS TRYOUT O AND W

Practice your work with Os and Ws. Remember to say the letters as you key them.

lll ooo sss www lll ooo sss www lll ooo sss www lll ooo sss www ooo lll ooo sss www
lloo ssww lloo ssww llww ssoo llww ssoo ooww llss ooww llss wwoo lll ooo sss www

gg hh ff jj dd kk ss ll aa ;; oo ww ii ee uu rr yy tt bb vv nn cc mm oo ww tt bb vv nn cc mm oo
b v n c m ; a l s k d j f h g t y r u e i w o g h s l e o w i e u t y r ; a m c n b i w o g h s l e o w i

who who; owns owns; was was; will will; often often; with with; orders orders; warm warm; objects objects; wanted wanted; older older; wished who who; owns owns; was;

ollie often orders oriental; oliver owns ocean objects of original origin; orson oscillates will was working with william who wanted warm woolens; wan wished woody won outside officers often warn wild workers wonderfully; will oki offer woodrow wings

 Save your work.

Take a rest. Shake those muscles. Taking periodic breaks is important for good health.

NEW KEYS P AND Q

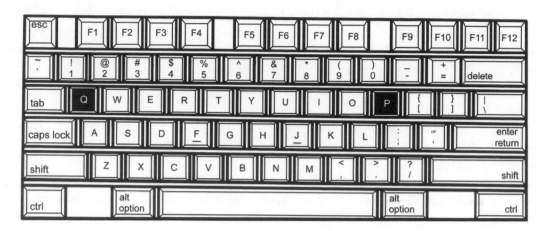

Figure 7.3

Wonderful! At last you can key words like *keyboard* and *monitor* and *winner* in your self-testing work. You still have a few more letters to learn, but adding all four letters in this lesson will enable you to key at least 95 percent of the words in the English language.

The P and Q keys are pinky keys (see Figure 7.3). They require you to extend your pinky to the upper row. At first, you may see your whole hand moving, but your pinky will become more independent as you continue to practice.

Place your hands on the home row. Wiggle your pinky fingers. Reach for the P key using the right pinky finger. Bring it back home to the ; key. Do that enough times so that you feel comfortable.

;;; PPP ;;; PPP ;;; PPP ;;; PPP ;;; PPP ;;; PPP ;;; PPP ;;; PPP ;;; PPP ;;; PPP ;;; PPP ;;; PPP ;;;

Now it's time to get that left hand moving. Reach for the Q key with your left pinky. Return your pinky to its home on the A key. Do it again…and again…and again….

aaa qqq aaa qqq aaa qqq aaa qqq aaa qqq aaa qqq aaa qqq aaa qqq aaa qqq aaa qqq aaa

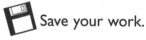Save your work.

NEW KEYS TRYOUT P AND Q

Practice your Ps and Qs. Remember to say the letters as you key them.

;;; ppp aaa qqq ;;; ppp aaa qqq ;;; aaa ppp qqq ;;; qqq aaa ppp aaa qqq ;;; ppp qqq ;;; qqq ;;pp aaqq jjuu ffrr lloo ssww kkii ddee jjmm ffvv jjbb ;;pp aaqq lloo ssww ffvv jjbb ;;pp

pp qq ll ss ;; aa ii ee kk dd oo ww jj ff uu rr yy tt hh gg nn vv bb cc mm pp qq ll ss ;; aa ii
m c n v b a ; s l d k f j g h q p w o e i r u t y h g a ; p q l s k d j f i e w o m c n v b a ; s l d

patti proposes potentially playful possibilities; peter paid paul presently; pretty portia quinn quickly quelled quaint quarrels; quentin quaffed quadrupled quinine quarts perry quaintly practiced quantum physics questioningly; qwin passes quagmires

 Save your work.

SELF-TEST

was was; for for; way way; one one; when when; older older; object object; olive olive; today today; room room; write write; would would; was was; for for; way way; one one;

winter winter; waders waders; people people; prefer prefer; requires requires; ornate ornate; thoughts thoughts; keyboard keyboard; windows windows; wallow wallow; wish;

quilting quilting; quality quality; promises promises; workers workers; professional; wonders wonders; programs programs; pilot pilot; quick quick; pummel pummel;

ona would prefer quilting or weaving pure quality; oscar promises one quality quilt quality is one promise given by professional workers; paula wonders; why today

learning to keyboard properly is an important skill for everyone today; people use email to communicate; they use instant messaging programs; quietly winning friends

success in chat rooms requires users key their thoughts easily and quickly; schools require students to research the web and write original essays; good writing wins

trying to find keys on the keyboard gets in the way of communication; it is key to build keyboarding skills through practice and autowords; suggest some practice

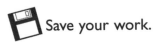 Save your work.

CORRECTIVE WORK

Proofread your work.

- Print the file **Lesson7.doc**.

- Identify the words that were keyed incorrectly.

- Create a new file and save it as **L7Practice.doc**.

- Key each of these words five times correctly and save your file.

IMPROVEMENT WORK

Return to the Self-Test. Open the file **Lesson7.doc**, and key those lines again. You should be able to complete the task more quickly and more accurately.

ONE-MINUTE TIMING

Here's your opportunity to see how you have improved. You have had two more lessons of practice and learned about using AutoWords The rules for this timed test are the same as in Lesson 5.

- Don't look at the keyboard!

- Use the NoPeekee Keyboard for reference.

- Use the **Sitting Hints** to address your keyboard.

- Use the **Home Row Hints** to position your fingers.

- Tap the Enter key at the end of each line.

 It's time to start your trial run. Set your timer for 1 minute (and 10 seconds). Go!

```
            3              6              9             12
the rain is coming down hard; the hail is a mass of marbles;
          15             18             21             24
i hope that hail does not seriously damage trucks or windows;
          27             30             33             36
it is enjoyable to watch some big lightning strikes in storms;
          39             42             45             48
the lightning forks and the whole sky sparks as they strike;
```

Did you do better this time? Even if you improved by one word, you should be proud.

Turn to Appendix K and enter the total number of words per minute in the first column and compute your total WPM.

Keep at it. You are getting better.

SHIFT KEY : (COLON)

OUTCOMES

- Shift keys for capital letters
- Key : (colon)

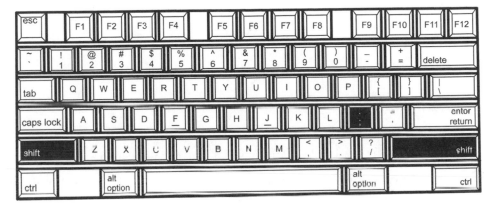

Figure 8.1

You have been keying strings of words so far. Some of them have even been sentences, but they didn't have capital letters at the beginning or periods at the end. Using the Shift keys can be a little tricky, but it adds clarity to your writing when your readers can tell where sentences begin and end (see Figure 8.1).

WARM-UP (5 MINUTES)

Rev up your power and punch up your potential with these warm-up exercises.

Create a **New** file and save it in the **Keyboarding** folder. Name it **Lesson8.doc**.

Remember to:

- Clip your NoPeekee Keyboard to the top of the page.
- Place your book in the holder and set it to the right of your keyboard.
- Sit at your computer following the **Sitting Hints**.
- Set your timer to 5 minutes.
- Place your fingers lightly on the home row considering the **Home Row Hints**.

Set your 5-minute timer. Go!

lll ooo sss www ;;; ppp aaa qqq jjj uuu fff rrr kkk iii ddd eee lll ooo sss www jjj nnn fff ggg jjj mmm fff ccc uuu rrr yyy ttt bbb nnn mmm ooo lll ooo sss www ;;; ppp aaa qqq jjj

the sit you one body your body with line that keys back nine both feel vary feet flat foot front align chair helps avoid lower spine arrow elbow floor ahead strain other center should inches divides correct forearm between imagine keyboard slightly straight distance

proper body positioning in front of the keyboard center is important; it avoids strain; align the center of your body with the line that divides the g and h keys; sit properly now sit straight up in your chair with your lower spine at the back of your chair the distance between you and your computer keyboard should be about nine inches; both feet should be flat on the floor with one foot slightly ahead of the other one;

 Save your work.

Did you recognize the text? Yes, it included the Sitting Hints you have been following so far in the book. It's nice to be able to produce as well as read the hints, isn't it? Remembering and using those hints is as important as remembering to use your AutoWords when you key. They are the basis for efficient keyboarding.

USING THE SHIFT KEYS

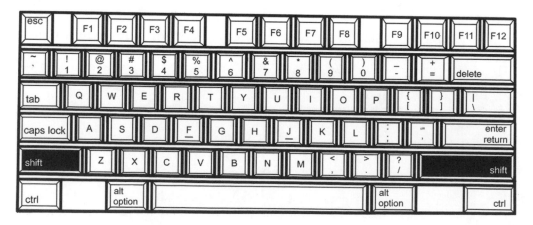

Figure 8.2

Find the Shift keys on both sides of your keyboard (see Figure 8.2). One is to the left of the Z key and the other is to the right of the / key. If you press these keys, you won't see anything appear on the screen. These are called *complementary keys* because they are used with other keys on the keyboard. If you hold down a Shift key and press one of the letter keys, you will see a capital letter appear on the screen. Try it with the initials in your name.

The trick is knowing which Shift key to hold down when tapping another key. The rule is: **To key a capital letter, use the Shift key on the opposite side of the keyboard**. In practice, this means that since you use a finger on your right hand to tap a key such as the J key,

you will use your left pinky finger to hold down the left Shift key. If you use fingers on your left hand to tap a key such as the F key, you will use your right pinky finger to hold down the right Shift key. It's just a matter of building the habit of using the Shift key opposite the finger keying a key.

Let's try it for a while. You will use the left Shift key with your right hand first and then the right Shift key with your left hand. Then you will get the challenge of using both.

Be slow. Be deliberate. Say the letters as you key them. You will need to build coordination to make this work.

J J J K K K L L L : : : H H H Jj Kk Ll Uu Yy Ii Oo Pp Bb Nn Mm Jj Kk J J J K K K L L L

Now try the left hand.

F F F D D D S S S A A A G G G Ff Dd Ss Aa Tt Rr Ee Ww Qq Vv Cc F F F D D D S S S A

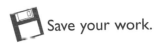 Save your work.

NEW KEY TRYOUT (SHIFT)

Let's mix it up a bit.

Jj Jj Kk Kk Ll Ll Yy Yy Uu Uu Hh Hh Gg Gg Ff Ff Dd Dd Ss Ss Aa Aa Jj Jj Kk Kk Ll Ll Yy Vv Vv Cc Cc Tt Tt Rr Rr Ee Ee Ww Ww Bb Bb Nn Nn Mm Mm Yy Yy Vv Vv Cc Cc Tt Tt Rr

Uu Uu Ii Ii Oo Oo Rr Rr Ee Ee Ww Ww Pp Pp Jj Jj Ll Ll Qq Qq Ff Ff Uu Uu Ii Ii Oo Oo Aa Aa Ss Ss Dd Dd Ll Ll Kk Kk Jj JJ Vv Vv Cc Cc Ee Ee Bb Bb Nn Nn Aa Aa Ss Ss Dd Dd

Jj Jj Ff Ff Kk Kk Dd Dd Ll Ll Ss Ss Aa Aa Yy Yy Tt Tt Uu Uu Rr Rr Jj Jj Ff Ff Kk Kk Dd Dd Ii Ii Ee Ee Oo Oo Ww Ww Pp Pp Qq Qq Hh Hh Gg Gg J F K D L S A Ii Ii Ee Ee Oo Oo

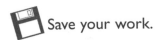 Save your work.

Did you begin to get the hang of it? It takes a little while to build the coordination required for changing from one pinky to the other, but with practice it will become a habit.

SELF-TEST

Take your time with these. Work on building the habit of using the Shift key on the side opposite the key that you are tapping.

AA AA CC CC IA IA NE NE US USKLA KLA LPN LPN LVN LVN ASAP ASAP HDTV AAA
Sharon Australia Joe Robin New Guinea Malaysia Thailand Indonesia Bali Dan Licensed

Sharon flew KLA airlines to Australia; She met Joe and Robin there; She got there ASAP
She later flew to New Guinea; Malaysia; Thailand; Indonesia and Bali; The trip was AOK

Rae Ann enjoys being an LPN; LPN means Licensed Professional Nurse; It is LVN in CA
Dan is studying to be an LPN; He is earning his AA from Hawkeye CC; This CC is in NE IA

Save your work.

Are you worn out from all the pinky pushups you have been doing in this lesson? Take a break. Stand up. Shake it out. Get back to work and learn about the colon.

NEW KEY : (COLON)

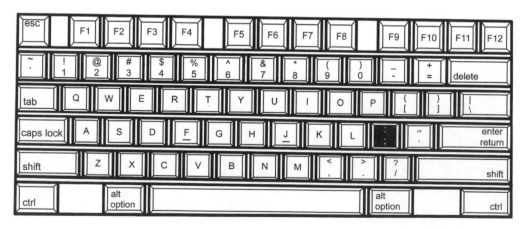

Figure 8.3

You have started to master the Shift keys to produce capital letters. Every time you used a Shift key with a letter key, you produced an uppercase version of that letter. Have you noticed that there are more than twenty keys on your keyboard that produce completely different characters when you use a Shift key?

The first one you will explore is the relative of the semicolon (;), the colon (:) (see Figure 8.3).

Hold down the left Shift key and tap the semicolon (;). You have produced a colon (:). Now, let's move between the semicolon and the colon for a while.

; ::: ; ::: ; ::: ; ::: ; ::: ; ::: ; ::: ; ::: ; ::: ; ::: ; ::: ; ::: ;:;: ;:;: ;:;: ;:;: ;:;: ;::: ;:::

Save your work.

NEW KEY TRYOUT : (COLON)

;;; ::: ;;; ::: ppp PPP qqq QQQ ccc CCC uuu UUU ggg GGG kkk KKK ;;; ::: ;;; ::: ppp PPP ikIK esES inIN egEG qtQT noNO pgPG rmRM ydYD gmGM hrHR ikIK esES inIN egEG

aa PP ww LL kk TT II :: qq OO ee JJ ss HH gg UU rr VV bb CC nn mm aa PP ww LL kk G f H j D s K l A ; Q p O w E i U r T y B v C n M : F d L a P e Y t V c G f H j D s K l A ;

Types of Flowers: Bird of Paradise; Venus Flytrap; Belles of Ireland; Dusty Miller; Types of Lilies: Yellow Ribbons; Casa Blanca; Black Beauty; Kiss Me Kate; Scarlet Dear John; Dear Dr McDonald: UNI and U of O have all replied to you: Sincerely:

Save your work.

SELF-TEST

IA IA; MA MA; BA BA; her her; MIT MIT; did did; BYU BYU has has; and and; the the; CPA CPA; from from; pass pass; exam exam who who; CPA CPA; ROI ROI; BMOC BMOC

pass pass; from from; earn earn; game game; hard hard; lunch lunch; which which; spoke earned earned; worked worked; offers offers; number number; decided decided; resided

college college; helping helping; Baseball Baseball; hurried hurried; officer officer; official returned returned; statistics statistics; Remembering Remembering; dedication dedication

Jay earned his BA from UCLA; He worked to pass his CPA test ASAP; He liked his ROI
Moira earned her MBA from Pepperdine University in LA; She did well on her ROI also

Pedro has had scholarship offers from UNI; MIT; BYU; Harvard and USC; He was BMOC
He hasn't decided which college to attend to earn his BA and MFA; He is quite talented

Baseball is a game of statistics like: AB; R; H; HR; RBI; BB; SO; ERA; E; it can be so EZ
Remembering the numbers is not hard; Remembering who earned them is; It is all MLB

Shelly PFC hurried PDQ to the HQ; She had just returned from PT; She spoke with an EMT
She had an MRE for lunch; The MP was helping the GIs get to the APO; They got there

Save your work.

CORRECTIVE WORK

Proofread your work.

- Print the file **Lesson8.doc**.

- Identify the words that were keyed incorrectly.

- Create a new file and save it as **L8Practice.doc**.

- Key each of these words five times correctly and save your file.

IMPROVEMENT WORK

Return to the Self-Test. Open the file **Lesson8.doc**, and key these lines again. You should be able to complete the task more quickly and more accurately.

LESSON 9

X Z , . CAPS LOCK

OUTCOMES

- X Z , . and Caps Lock
- One-minute timing

Figure 9.1

You are at the end of the alphabet. This lesson will introduce you to X and Z as well as the period and the comma. You will be able to write any sentences you want and punctuate most of them. You will also learn about the Caps Lock key (see Figure 9.1). This is a tool you can use to key large groups of capital letters more quickly.

WARM-UP (5 MINUTES)

Quick key clicking requires limber limbs and flexible fingers. Warm-up for this final lesson on the alphabetic keys.

Create a **New** file and save it in the **Keyboarding** folder. Name it **Lesson9.doc**.

Remember to:

- Clip your NoPeekee Keyboard to the top of the page.
- Place your book in the holder and set it to the right of your keyboard.
- Sit at your computer following the **Sitting Hints**.
- Set your timer for 5 minutes.
- Place your fingers lightly on the home row considering the **Home Row Hints**.

Set your 5-minute timer. Go!

qqq ppp aaa ;;; www ooo sss lll eee iii kkk ddd ::: ccc uuu rrr jjj fff mmm vvv yyy ttt hhh ggg nnn bbb sss lll ddd kkk ccc mmm vvv nnn bbb www qqq ppp aaa ;;; www ooo sss the row lay low but not feel your love home find keys rest keep body place hints curve bumps contents wrists table close quite having landed faster elbows lightly forearms quickly fingers keyboard naturally touching separately terrific wonderful happiness

Place your fingers on the home row; Curve your fingers naturally; This is their new home; Find the bumps on the F and J keys; Lay your index fingers on the bumps; Feel the bump; Having landed your index fingers on F and J; lightly lay the rest of your fingers on the home row keys; Keep your elbows close to your body; Not too close however; It can be uncomfortable; Keep your wrists low but NOT touching the keyboard or table;

 Save your work.

Did you recognize these lines? Yes, they are the home row hints. You may have found yourself checking your positioning as you keyed these hints. That's good. It shows you are conscious of your positioning.

NEW KEYS X AND Z

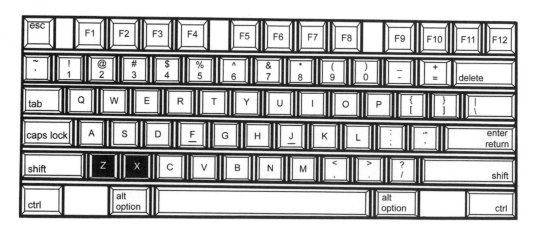

Figure 9.2

Look for the X and Z keys in the lower left row (see Figure 9.2). Identify which fingers are used to tap these keys.

Notice that you use your left ring finger to tap the X, and you use your left pinky to tap the Z key.

Place your fingers on the home row. Move your left ring finger from the S key to the X key and then return to the home row. Do this a few times. Here's a practice row for you to get the feel of it. Remember to say the letters as you key them.

sss xxx sss xxx sss xxx sss xxx sss xxx sss xxx sss xxx sss xxx sss xxx sss sss xxx sss xxx sss

Good job! Now it's time to add the final letter to your repertoire. Place your fingers on the home row. Lift your left pinky, and reach down into the lower row and tap the Z key. Tap it a couple of times to get familiar with it and then practice with the following exercises. Say the letters as you key them.

aaa zzz aaa zzz aaa zzz aaa zzz aaa zzz aaa zzz aaa zzz aaa zzz aaa aaa zzz aaa zzz aaa

 Save your work.

NEW KEYS TRYOUT X AND Z

aaa zzz sss xxx jjj mmm fff ccc kkk iii ddd eee lll ooo sss www ;;; ppp aaa zzz sss xxx jjj
aaa qqq jjj yyy fff ttt hhh ggg ccc nnn vvv bbb ,,, ... rrr uuu ausj dkel aaa qqq jjj yyy fff ttt

zz xx jj ff hh gg kk dd ll ss ;; aa cc ,, vv nn bb pp qq ww oo ee ii rr uu tt yy zz xx jj ff hh gg
a b c d e f g h i j k l m n o p q r s t u v w x y z y x w v u t s r q p o n m l k j a b c d e f g h i

Zen Zen; xrays xrays; zones zones; Zeon Zeon; zilched zilched; exalts exalts; zenith; zigged zigged; expected expected; exercise exercise; oxygen oxygen; extended extended;

Xavier examined xrays excitingly; Xi expected exercise extended oxygen; Xantara; Zestful Zachary zagged Zen ziggles; Zealot Zeon zigged zenith zones; Zan zilched zulu

SELF-TEST

zoo zoo; zero zero; zoic zoic; zaps zaps; zips zips; zeal zeal; zinc zinc; axes axes; xrays; exits exits; zings zings; zones zones; axles axles; exist exist; ozone ozone; exited exited;

oxygen oxygen; zapped zapped; zipped zipped; zagged zagged; zigged zigged; zenith; zigzag zigzag; exhaled exhaled; zilched zilched; extolled extolled; zoonomy zoonomy

azimuths azimuths; explores explores; exercise exercise; extended extended; excluded examples examples; zillions zillions; existing existing; exactness exactness; extinction

Xena exhaled excellent exhaust; Xander explored existing external exits; Xiu extolled Xalvadora expects exorbitant expectations; Xandy exhibited examples; Xerxes exited

Zelda zapped zero zoo zebras; Zoey zestfully zipped zooming zeppelins; Zaltana zips Zabrina zinged zinc zarfs; Zahina zoned zoic zoos; Zubird zaps zucchini; Zamir zings

Xia zoomed exhibited zeppelins excellently; Zi excluded zealot expressions; Xuxa Zsa Zsa expelled zestful exercise zeal; Xiang zilched excluded zinc axles; Zaci zones

Zaire exports zillions of existing zigzag axes; Xarles explores old Ozark zoos; Zamora Extended ozone exhibits of Aztec examples exist; Azure oxygen in Izmir; Extraordinary

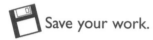 Save your work.

NEW KEYS , AND .

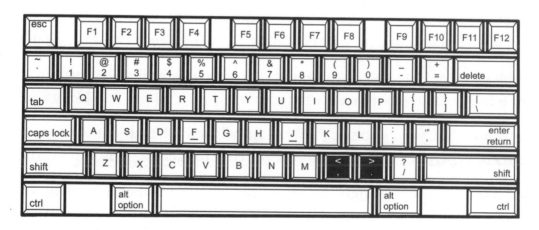

Figure 9.3

Now let's add some punctuation to your repertoire. With the comma and the period, you will be able to correctly punctuate a list of your friends and end your sentence with a period (see Figure 9.3).

Find the home row. Tap the K key a couple of times and then move your index finger toward the lower row to tap the comma (,) key. Do this again and again until you feel comfortable. Key the following practice lines while saying the letters as you key them.

kkk ,,, kkk ,,, kkk ,,, kkk ,,, kkk ,,, kkk ,,, kkk ,,, kkk ,,, kkk ,,, kkk ,,, kkk kkk ,,, kkk ,,, kkk ,,, kkk

That's it! Now move one key to the right on the home row and work with your right ring finger. Move your right ring finger down from the L key to the period (.) key

lll … lll … lll … lll … lll … lll … lll … lll … lll … lll … lll … lll … lll … lll lll … lll … lll

 Save your work.

NEW KEYS TRYOUT , AND .

kkk ,,, lll … kkk ,,, lll … kkk ,,, lll … kkk ,,, lll … kkk ,,, lll … kkk ,,, lll … kkk ,,, lll …
kk,, ll.. ssxx aazz ddcc kk,, ffvv jjmm hhnn ggbb jjyy fftt jjuu ffrr kkii ssxx aazz ddcc kk,,

kk ,, ll .. ss xx aa zz kk ii dd ee ll oo ss ww ;; pp aa qq jj mm ff vv hh gg . kk ,, ll .. ss xx aa
, z x m n c v b a ; s l d k f j g h q p w o e i r u t y . , z x m n c v b a ; s l d , z x m n c v b a ;

U.S.A. N.A.S.A J.P.L N.S.S.D.C. O.O.S.A. U.N. U.S.P.S. A.S.A.P. E.G.B.D.F F.I.N.E.
the, pump, space, prizes, helmet, shades, include, agencies, bicycle, finishers, exhaust,

Space agencies of the U.S.A. include: N.A.S.A, J.P.L., and N.S.S.D.C. O.O.S.A is in the U.N.
The prizes include: . . . er . . . a bicycle, a helmet, . . . er . . . a bicycle pump and tires.
The finishers are Lance, Gilberto, Emanuele, Marzio, Mica, and Elmo. Lance rode best.

 Save your work.

USING THE CAPS LOCK KEY

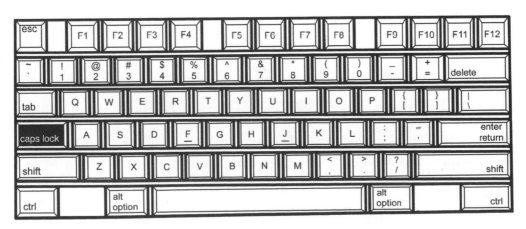

Figure 9.4

You have done a good job of learning all the letters and how to key capital letters. The Shift key is useful for capital letters at the beginning of sentences or names, but it can be a bit clumsy to use if you are capitalizing full words, titles, or acronyms.

The Caps Lock key is a time-saver. This key locks the keyboard into a CAPITAL LETTER mode.

Use your left pinky to tap the Caps Lock key (a Caps Lock indicator will probably light up on the Caps Lock key or somewhere on the keyboard) and it will "turn on" capital letters for all the keys on your keyboard (see Figure 9.4).

Now, try the practice sentences. Use the Caps Lock key, *not* the Shift key.

CAPITAL letters ARE easy WHEN you USE the CAPS lock KEY. IT should be USED ONLY when KEYING multiple CAPITAL letters, NOT when CAPITALIZING single LETTERS.

 Save your work.

SELF-TEST

zinc zinc, city city, exit exit, chat chat, zero zero, plans plans, extra extra, agree agree, means means, north north, cities cities, PLZ PLZ, MYOB MYOB, FOMCL FOMCL

garden garden, played played, Zurich Zurich, zoning zoning, exports exports, Excited, postings postings, include include, exalted exalted, exhausting exhausting, ZYDECO

acronyms acronyms, excellent excellent, exhausting exhausting, exquisitely exquisitely, improvement improvement, population population, exuberantly, POPULATION

The zoning board exuberantly exalted the EXCELLENT plans for a zoological garden EXIT. Excited Zurich musicians played exhausting ZYDECO tunes EXQUISITELY all night.

Online chat acronyms include: LOL, TNX, MYOB, BTW, SWAK, PLZ, FOMCL, and TGIF TNX bcuz I LOL at Ur postings. PLZ MYOB I do not agree. WYSIWYG and YMMV.

ZIP means ZONE IMPROVEMENT PLAN. XO is an eXecutive Officer in the Navy. ZPG means ZERO POPULATION GROWTH. XL means EXTRA LARGE as in XL eggs.

ZAIRE exports zinc to external countries. ZACATECA is a silver mining city in Mexico. IXTAPA and ZIHUATANEJO are two cities on the Mexican Riviera north of ACAPULCO.

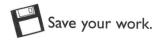 Save your work.

Take a break. Stand up and shake your arms for 30 seconds. Relax your body.

CORRECTIVE WORK

Proofread your work.

- Print the file **Lesson9.doc**.

- Identify the words that were keyed incorrectly.

- Create a new file and save it as **L9Practice.doc**.

- Key each of these words five times correctly and save your file.

IMPROVEMENT WORK

Return to the Self-Test. Open the file **Lesson9.doc**, and key these lines again. You should be able complete the task more quickly and more accurately.

ONE-MINUTE TIMING

Here's another opportunity to measure your improvement. You now know all the letters in the alphabet (including capital letters) *plus* some punctuation. Review the instructions for a one-minute timing on page 26. Remember the rules!

- Don't look at the keyboard!

- Use the NoPeekee Keyboard for reference.

- Use the **Sitting Hints** to address your keyboard.

- Use the **Home Row Hints** to position your fingers.

- Tap the Enter key at the end of each line.

 It's time to start your trial run. Set your timer for 1 minute. Go!

```
            3                 6                 9              12
Spring brings flowers and butterflies. It brings warm sun.
           15                18                21              24
I love to walk outside and explore the woods during spring.
           27                30                33              36
Monday I saw three deer stand on a riverbank in the forest.
           39                42                45              48
I tried to get close to them but I sneezed, and they ran.
```

How well did you do? Did you find that the capital letters slowed you down a little? Don't worry about it. You will become quite proficient as you practice.

CALCULATING ERRORS

Did you make any errors? Look back at what you keyed and you might see red lines under the words that are incorrect. Success in keyboarding requires accuracy. Yes, some word processors can catch your errors and even correct your mistakes as you work, but the key is not to make those errors in the first place.

We didn't worry about errors in the first three tests because it was important for you to learn the process of taking a timed test. *Now*, it's time to deal with accuracy. Now, it's time to count your errors.

What is an error? Errors come in many shapes and sizes—from keying the wrong letter to completely forgetting a word. Here are some types of errors you might make:

• Keying the wrong letter (e.g., keyboatd).

• Keying letters in the wrong order (e.g., keyborad).

• Leaving out a letter (e.g., kyboard).

• Leaving out a word (e.g., Learning to quickly improves your communications).

• Not including a space where needed (e.g., Learning tokeyboard quickly).

• Including too many spaces (e.g., Learning to   keyboard quickly).

If you are using the option "Check spelling as you type" included in Word and other word processors, you will probably find jagged lines under the errors you made while keying. This is not a foolproof way to find your errors because it won't show omitted words, but it is a good beginning indicator. Look for your errors and count them.

COUNT only one error per word. Sometimes you may make multiple errors in one word. Instead of keying "keyboard," you may key "keybotad." Notice that you keyed a wrong letter *and* you keyed the letters in the wrong order. This is too confusing to figure out, so just count it as one error.

Errors are going to cost you, the keyboarder, in WPM (remember, words per minute?). Each error will cost you one WPM. This means that you compute the number of words per minute and then subtract the number of errors.

Imagine that you keyed 23 WPM in a 1-minute test, and you made 4 errors.

Total words keyed 23
Subtract errors . . . .– 4
Correct words per minute 19

Consider your performance on this past test and enter the statistics in the "1-Minute Test #1" row of the following table.

	Total Words Keyed	Number of Errors Correct WPM	Total Words Keyed Minus Number of Errors
1-Minute Test #1			
1-Minute Test #2			
1-Minute Test #3			

Return to the 1-minute keyboarding test and take it two more times. Enter your statistics in the appropriate rows in the table.

Turn to the back of the book and enter the information about your *best* time on the Self-Progress Chart.

Keep at it! You are getting better!

AUTOBLENDS

OUTCOMES

- Keying letter combinations (AutoBlends) ay, at, as, ag, ap, ack, ank, ail, ot, ip, ell, ill, ick, ing, unk

You have now learned all twenty-six letters and four different forms of punctuation. In Lesson 6, you were introduced to AutoWords. These were short words that are used commonly enough that they should be considered single multistroke words instead of words composed of multiple single-stroke letters. This lesson introduces you to AutoBlends. *AutoBlends* are common letter combinations that can be combined with other letters to make up new words. AutoBlends are actually more useful than AutoWords because they are used in many words throughout the English language.

WARM-UP (5 MINUTES)

Quick key clicking requires fast flying fingers. Prepare to learn AutoBlends to speed your keying.

Create a **New** file and save it in the **Keyboarding** folder. Name it **Lesson 10.doc**.

Remember to:

- Clip your NoPeekee Keyboard to the top of the page.
- Place your book in the holder and set it to the right of your keyboard.
- Sit at your computer following the **Sitting Hints**.
- Place your fingers lightly on the home row considering the **Home Row Hints**.

 Set your 5-minute timer. Go!

hhh ggg jjj fff ;;; aaa ::: lll sss kkk ddd ppp qqq yyy ttt ooo www uuu rrr iii eee zzz …
xxx ,,, ccc mmm vvv nnn bbb ::: www mmm ccc hhh ggg zzz hhh ggg jjj fff ;;; aaa ::: lll

top you may not now but set: clip your page this will with need more keys book into; might learn place right timer, holder: provide; Keyboard NoPeekee reference workspace, action preparation anticipation operation.

Clip your NoPeekee Keyboard to the top of your page. This will provide you with a point of reference if you need it. You may not need it now, but you might as you learn more keys.

Place your book into your book holder. Place your book holder to the right of your keyboard. Set up your timer. This timer needs to be easily accessible so that you can start it and stop it easily. This means that you must place it within reach.

 Save your work.

These were more familiar sentences. They are the rules for setting up your workspace.

KEYING LETTER COMBINATIONS (AUTOBLENDS)

As explained earlier, keying efficiency is based on building memory traces between what you see and moving the appropriate fingers in the proper manner. You have already been introduced to the entire alphabet and a few AutoWords. The AutoWords are actual words that are commonly used. There are, however, letter combinations that are used in creating words. These letter combinations are called *blends*. Dr. Seuss based many of his beginning reader books (e.g., *Cat in the Hat* and *Hop on Pop*) on combining blends to create new words (e.g., at, cat, hat, fat, bat, mat, nat, pat, and sat). Learning the blend *at* and placing sounds before it is beneficial for reading. Consider doing the same thing for keying words. Learning to key the blend *at* as a multistroke single word and then placing single letters or other blends before or after *at* will make your keying more efficient and ultimately faster.

But which blends should you learn? Obviously, if you want your keying to be most efficient, you should perfect the blends that are used most often in the English language. Linguists have studied the use of blends (sometimes called *polygrams*) in English and have ranked them by occurrence. This book is not large enough to introduce all these blends, so only the top fifteen blends will be introduced during this lesson. The complete list of blends is listed in priority of occurrence in Appendix C. You may want to turn to that page and practice the blends that were not included in these lessons.

There are also a number of word beginnings (prefixes) and endings (suffixes) used in English. They will also be included as AutoBlends throughout the book.

LEARNING SOME AUTOBLENDS

ay, at, as, ag, ap, ack, ank, ail, ot, ip, ell, ill, ick, ing, unk

Let's begin by learning some of the blends beginning with the letter *a*. These are being introduced in an order that will help your learning. The first blend is *ay*. Remember to think of the blend as a single unit. As you did in Lesson 6 with AutoWords, think of it as *ay* instead of the letters *a* and *y* individually. Begin slowly and increase speed until you are keying rapidly. Say the blend *ay* as you work.

ay ay ay ay ay ay ay ay ay ay ay ay ay ay ay ay ay ay ay ay ay ay ay ay ay ay ay ay ay ay ay ay

Now, close your eyes and key *ay* five times.

Does it feel as if you are keying a single unit or two separate letters? The more you key this blend, the more automatic the movements will become. Remember that you want to build the memory traces with a two-finger movement.

Here are some more AutoBlends. Remember to say each AutoBlend as you key it. Begin slowly and increase your speed as it becomes more automatic.

at at at at at at at at at at at at at at at at at at at at at at at at at at at at at at at at at at at at at

as as as as as as as as as as as as as as as as as as as as as as as as as as as as as as as as as as as

ag ag ag ag ag ag ag ag ag ag ag ag ag ag ag ag ag ag ag ag ag ag ag ag ag ag ag ag ag ag ag ag ag

ap ap ap ap ap ap ap ap ap ap ap ap ap ap ap ap ap ap ap ap ap ap ap ap ap ap ap ap ap ap

ack ack ack ack ack ack ack ack ack ack ack ack ack ack ack ack ack ack ack ack ack ack ack

ank ank ank ank ank ank ank ank ank ank ank ank ank ank ank ank ank ank ank ank ank ank

ail ail ail ail ail ail ail ail ail ail ail ail ail ail ail ail ail ail ail ail ail ail ail ail ail ail ail ail ail

 Save your work.

NEW AUTOBLENDS TRYOUT

And now, let's mix up the blends a bit. Say the blends and words as you key them. Don't think of them as letters but as blends.

ay ay ay at at at as as as ag ag ag ap ap ap ack ack ack ank ank ank ail ail ail ay ay at at as ag ap ap ack ack ank ank ail ail ay at as ag ap ay ay ay at at at as as as ag ag ag ap ay ay ay

say hat has bag sap back tank bail sway that bass drag snap flack thank grail spray tray snag strap quack stank quail Sunday cravat canvas airbag mishap unpack shrank detail great extras dragged strap blank trail dank snail prank apple crank Braille

 Save your work.

Return to the previous five lines and key them again. Say the blends as you key them. You will notice that the blends in some of the words (e.g., scream) have different pronunciations but you can still consider each blend as

a single process. Practice will build the automaticity of keying these blends.

Let's expand your skills into keying full sentences with capital letters and punctuation.

The trail backpack had a gnat hat bag under the flap. You can yank the frayed bag from the back of the pack. Matt sprayed the pack's seams with wax. That way, they are less apt to leak.

That gray snail dragged its fat shell around the rail nail. Its trail was a glassy track. The trail gapped as it wrapped its way up the blank plank. He began to flail back.

The fat cat sat on a lap for a nap. It drank a tank of sappy tea. The cat wagged its sagging tail. Hank snagged a snack for the cat at the retail shack. The cat slapped a rail.

A stray quail delayed the relay today. The team repeated the race at the track. Their lead shrank with a clank but Frank stayed ahead of the pack. He lapped them at the tail end.

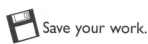Save your work.

THE REST OF THE AUTOBLENDS

If you have not mastered all the blends beginning with "a" yet, you will with time and practice. Key each of these blends. Remember to pronounce each blend as you key it. Begin slowly and increase your speed as you feel it become an automatic process.

ot ot ot ot ot ot ot ot ot ot ot ot ot ot ot ot ot ot ot ot ot ot ot ot ot ot ot ot ot ot ot ot ot ot ot

ip ip ip ip ip ip ip ip ip ip ip ip ip ip ip ip ip ip ip ip ip ip ip ip ip ip ip ip ip ip ip ip ip ip ip ip

ell ell ell ell ell ell ell ell ell ell ell ell ell ell ell ell ell ell ell ell ell ell ell ell ell ell ell ell ell ell

ill ill ill ill ill ill ill ill ill ill ill ill ill ill ill ill ill ill ill ill ill ill ill ill ill ill ill ill ill ill ill ill ill ill

ick ick ick ick ick ick ick ick ick ick ick ick ick ick ick ick ick ick ick ick ick ick ick ick ick ick

ing ing ing ing ing ing ing ing ing ing ing ing ing ing ing ing ing ing ing ing ing ing ing ing ing

unk unk unk unk unk unk unk unk unk unk unk unk unk unk unk unk unk unk unk unk unk unk

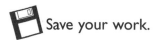Save your work.

AUTOBLENDS AS WORDS

You had an opportunity to try the AutoBlends by themselves. Now let's mix things up
a bit and see how they can be used in words.

ot ot ot ip ip ip ell ell ell ill ill ill ick ick ick ing ing ing unk unk unk ot ot ip ip ell ell ill ill
ing ing unk unk ot ip ell ill ick ing unk ot ip ell ill ot ot ot ip ip ip ell ell ell ill ill ill ick ick

sill mill fell well sick sell grip Hill fill junk sings picks areas tulip still skill quill shell
thick slick smells refill booted turnip skunk stunk quickly string sunken biking riding
tripped landing lifting uprooted training equipped barbells dumbbells unknown confusing

 Save your work.

It's time to hone your skills with these blends as well. Go back to the previous three lines and key them again. Remember to pronounce the blends as you key them. Here are some sentences to give you a chance to practice with real words.

Rick sings as he picks and smells a tulip. He used great skill to refill a quill from the
sill of a mill. The quill fell in a well when Rick's grip slipped as he tripped. A skunk
stunk of gunk junk.

Elliot booted a turnip beyond Shell Hill. By landing on a strip of mill fill, the
vegetable uprooted some sunken junk. The junk was swell but smelled. Elliot quickly
kicked the stick into the well.

Skip was training for biking up hills. His bike was equipped for riding races. He
was lifting dumbbells and barbells to build thick muscles for the ride. He would be
biking in unknown areas.

Phillip's airship was darting and dashing along an unknown path through the chilly
forest. He scooted the propelling shell to a slick landing. His trip plans were concise
but confusing.

 Save your work.

SELF-TEST

stay stay; away away; team team; back back; flag flag; grip grip; soap soap; flew flew; snags snags; thick thick; stick stick; snack snack; glass glass; mill mill; quill; quill; skunk skunk;

wings wings; stray stray; tails tails; cheap cheap; traps traps; tanks tanks; great great; wheat wheat; smell smell; sailed sailed; carrot carrot; spunky spunky; yummy yummy; tasty tasty;

skunks skunks; dunked dunked; treats treats; eating eating; cooing cooing; shilly shilly; muscles; quickly quickly; gripped gripped; slipped slipped; grabbed grabbed; splashed splashed; stream

Our swim team splashed upstream quickly. They tried to stay away from snags. They sailed back downstream in a glass sailboat with a flag. The flag flapped in the wind at the tail of the boat.

The parrot gripped the thick carrot. He slipped his grip and grabbed a stick. He snapped up a snack as he flapped his wings and flew away. Landing on an old tree trunk, he clanked a bell.

The stray skunks flicked their tails and repeatedly tripped cheap traps. Their smelly tails stunk. Frank skillfully treated the spunky skunks as he dunked them in tanks of soap. He has a real skill.

Jewell thanked Roswell for the great wheat treats. She was eating the alfalfa icing as she was cooing and crowing about its incredible taste and smell. She got another tray to share later.

Save your work.

Take a break. Stand up and shake your arms and hands to relax before you complete this lesson.

CORRECTIVE WORK

Proofread your work.

- Print the file **Lesson10.doc**.
- Identify the words that were keyed incorrectly.

- Create a new file and save it as **L10Practice.doc**.
- Key each of these words five times correctly and save your file.

IMPROVEMENT WORK

Return to the Self-Test. Open the file **Lesson10.doc**, and key these lines again. You should be able to complete the task more quickly and more accurately.

/ ? ' " AND AUTOBLENDS

OUTCOMES

- Keys: / ? ' and "

- AutoBlend Prefixes
  de, en, em, il, in, im,
  ir, dis, fore, anti

- Three-minute timing

Figure 11.1

Now, you will learn more punctuation for your repertoire. The four punctuation marks are on only two keys, but at the end of the lesson you will be able to list Web addresses (/); write questions (?); show possession ('); and convey what other people have said (") (see Figure 11.1).

WARM-UP (5 MINUTES)

Warm up and get ready to master more punctuation symbols.

Create a **New** file and save it in the **Keyboarding** folder. Name it **Lesson11.doc**.

Remember to:

- Clip your NoPeekee Keyboard to the top of the page.

- Place your book in the holder and set it to the right of your keyboard.

- Sit up to your computer following the **Sitting Hints**.

- Set your timer to 5 minutes.

- Place your fingers lightly on the home row considering the **Home Row Hints**.

Remember that we said that you would be able to key the Preamble to the Constitution of the United States of America? Here is your opportunity. You will notice that the capitalization seems to be a little strange. This copy of the preamble is capitalized *exactly* the way that Thomas Jefferson wrote it. He had wonderful handwriting and capitalized words that he considered important— not necessarily ones that grammatically *needed* capitalization.

Set your 5-minute timer. Go!

WWW ooo iii ttt ddd fff aaa mmm OOO UUU sss PPP ;;; SSS ::: ppp JJJ LLL AAA ,,, CCC …
TTT ggg eee ZZZ EEE III hhh qqq XXX BBB WWW ooo iii ttt ddd fff aaa mmm OOO UUU

do of in to We the for our and form more this Order Union secure People insure common United States ordain Justice defense promote Welfare Liberty America Liberty Blessings Constitution

We the People of the United States, in Order to form a more perfect Union, establish Justice, insure domestic Tranquility, provide for the common defense, promote the general Welfare, and secure the Blessings of Liberty to ourselves and our Posterity, do ordain and establish this Constitution for the United States of America.

 Save your work.

NEW CHARACTERS / AND ?

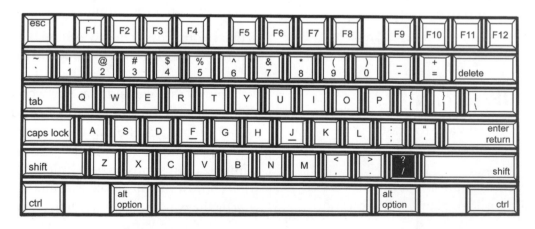

Figure 11.2

The / and ? reside on only one key (see Figure 11.2). You will find it on the bottom row below your pinky finger. The only difference is that you use the Shift key when you key the (?).

You can key the (/) with your right pinky. Keying the (?), however, requires you to first press the left Shift key with your left pinky and *then* press the /? key with your right pinky.

You will enjoy much pinky practice from this point forward.

Place your fingers on the home row. Move your right pinky from the (;) key to the (/)

key and return it to the (;) key in the home row. Do this a couple of times. Practice these movements by keying the following characters. Remember to say *semicolon* (or semi) and *slash* with each of the strokes.

;;; /// ;;; ///;;; /// ;;; ///;;; /// ;;; ///;;; /// ;;; ///;;; /// ;;; ///;;; /// ;;; ///;;; /// ;;; ///;;; /// ;;; /// ;;;

That wasn't too difficult, was it? Give that pinky a rest. Shake it and your whole right hand a bit to revive them. Let's get your left hand involved in the process. Now, hold down the left Shift

key with your left pinky and then repeat the same movement of using your right pinky to tap the /? key. This will produce a ?, since it is the Shift character for this key.

;;; ??? ;;; ??? ;;; ??? ;;; ??? ;;; ??? ;;; ??? ;;; ??? ;;; ??? ;;; ??? ;;; ??? ;;; ??? ;;; ??? ;;; ??? ;;; ???

Spend some time practicing these movements with this practice row of /s and ?s. Go through it a couple of times. Get the feel of it. Remember to say *slash* and *query* as you key them.

/// ??? /// ??? /// ??? /// ??? /// ??? /// ??? /// ??? /// ??? /// ??? /// ??? /// ??? /// ??? /// ??? ///

 Save your work.

NEW CHARACTERS TRYOUT / AND ?

Good job. Now, spend some time practicing your new characters.

;;; /// ??? ;;; /// ??? ;;; /// ??? ;;; /// ??? ;;; ??? /// ;;; ??? /// ;;; ??? /// ;;; ??? /// ;;; /// ??? ;;; /// ???

;;// ;;?? ;;// ;;?? ;;// ;;?? ?? ;; // ?? ;; // / ? ; ; ? / / ? ; ; ? / / ? ; / ? ; ; / ? ? / / ? ? ;;// ;;?? ;;// ;;?? ;;//

; : / ? , . URL, http://, website, many, www, org, exotic, Sixty, quickly, lazy, woven jute/bag/interesting/wizards/bag/picked/fox/brown/many/know/boxing/wildly/

Do you know the URL for a website on keyboarding? There are many. I want to find good one. The one I like is http://www.keyboardingresearch.org. It provides connections to good research.

The quick brown fox jumped over the lazy dogs. Sixty zippers were quickly picked from the woven jute bag. The five boxing wizards jump very quickly. Seventy exotic birds raced wildly.

 Save your work.

SELF-TEST

http:// http://; facts/ facts/; propaganda/ propaganda/; reviews/ reviews/ holy grail/ his/her his/her; He/she He/she; opinions opinions; website website; sentences

zinc zinc; find find; found found; spell spell; create create; chance chance; quart; oxide oxide; bright bright; paint paint; letters letters; unusual unusual; quickly

yesterday yesterday; operator operator; checker checker; corrected corrected; Pangrams Pangrams; apologized apologized; alphabet alphabet; containing containing; yesterday

Where did you find that fact? It is at http://www.interestingfactoids.com. I found it. I like that website because it has facts/propaganda/reviews/opinions there.

The operator tried to correct her/his error. Do you know how she/he did it? Yes. He/she found his/her error using the spell checker and then corrected it. He apologized.

Pangrams are sentences containing all the letters of the alphabet. The holy grail of pangrams contains only twenty-six letters. The following lessons have pangrams.

Want to see a pangram? Do you want a chance to key all the letters? A quart jar of oil mixed with zinc oxide makes a very bright paint. That is a fifty-three letter pangram.

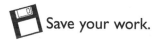Save your work.

Are you tired of doing keyboarding exercises? Do you know that "The quick brown fox jumps over the lazy dog" is a pangram. Keying it once is good exercise for your digits. It will provide lots of practice for keyboarding. Create a **New** file and enter the following:

=rand(200,99) (then tap the Enter key). Magically, more than 200 pages of the sentence will appear. This program is an "Easter egg" in Microsoft Word, hidden there by the Microsoft programmers who were tired of practicing their keyboarding.

NEW CHARACTERS ' AND "

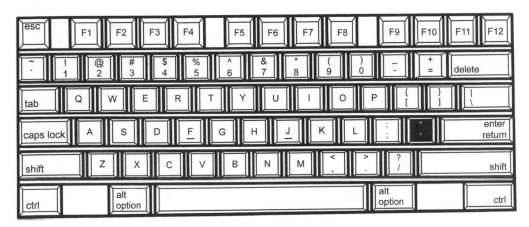

Figure 11.3

Being able to write using possessives and quotations is much more interesting than writing simple prose. You can do this when you use the key that is directly to the right of the (;) key (see Figure 11.3). That (;) key is getting a great deal of work in this lesson, isn't it?

Place your fingers on the home row. Tap the (;) key several times. Move your right pinky to the right to tap the (') key. Do it again.

Use the following practice lines to teach your pinky what to do and how to do it. Say *semicolon* and *apostrophe* as you key the characters. You may find that the first apostrophe is different from the rest of the apostrophes. This is because your word processor is designed to automatically place opening and closing apostrophes. Don't worry about this. It will be quite useful when you write.

;;; ''' ;;; ''' ;;; ''' ;;; ''' ;;; ''' ;;; ''' ;;; ''' ;;; ''' ;;; ''' ;;; ''' ;;; ''' ;;; ''' ;;; ''' ;;; '''

Now it's time to add quotation marks to your repertoire. This means that you can key what other people have said. Tap the (;) key and then move your left pinky to hold down the left Shift key. Once the Shift key is down, tap the (" ') key to yield a (") mark. Do this a couple of times. Practice the process using the following practice line. Say the characters at you key them.

;;; """ ;;; """ ;;; """ ;;; """ ;;; """ ;;; """ ;;; """ ;;; """ ;;; """ ;;; """ ;;; """ ;;; """ ;;; """ ;;; """

Practice both the ' and " using the following practice lines. Remember to say the names of the characters as you key them.

''' """ ''' """ ''' """ ''' """ ''' """ ''' """ ''' """"''' """ ''' """ ''' """"''' """ ''' """ ''' """ ''' """ ''' """ ''' """

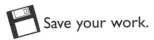
Save your work.

NEW CHARACTERS TRYOUT ' AND "

;;; ''' ;;; """ ;;; ''' ;;; """ ;;; ''' ;;; """;;; ''' ;;; """ ;;; ''' ;;; """ ;;; ''' ;;; """ ;; '' ;;; """ ;;; ''' ;;;
" ;; "" ;; " "" ;; // ?? ;; // ;; ?? ll .. kk ,, " "" ;; // ;; ?? ;; " ;; ""ll .. kk ,, " """ ;; "" ;; " "" ;; // ?? ;;

She's, "live", you're, "here", can't, "tell", I'm, "Please", we've, won't "move", shan't "tell",
"Thank you" she'll, "You're Welcome", doesn't, "Maybe", you've "Speak", don't "taste",

Sid said, "She's hoping you're aware she can't tell you I'm not here." He isn't "happy".
The words we've included are: "live", "here", "tell", "lead", and "peer". Are you "ready"?

I'm not sure she'll know he doesn't say "Please" or "Thank you." She says it's OK.
The public was amazed to view the quickness and dexterity of the juggler. She was sharp.

SELF-TEST

vex vex; name name; daft daft; mind mind; knew knew; Africa Africa; Zorro Zorro;
notice notice; Please Please; zebras zebras; piqued piqued; figure figure; correct correct;

pangram pangram; gymnasts gymnasts; believe believe; wondered wondered; instincts
psychics psychics; decided decided; quickly quickly; interested interested; historical

overall overall; success success; razorback razorback; opportunity opportunity;
observation; community community hero/swordsman/vigilante hero/swordsman;

I've always wondered why psychics ask, "What is your name?" They've had the
opportunity to read my mind. They should know. I don't tell them my name.

We've decided that you're correct. If you don't believe that she can't or won't do a good
job because she's not interested, "Please, go with your instincts!" Instincts are right.

While in Africa, Zorro noted, "How quickly daft jumping zebras vex." Notice the pangram?
It was an interesting observation by the hero/swordsman/vigilante. He was important.

Mr. Peabody watched the events come to pass and then queried, "How can razorback
jumping frogs level six piqued gymnasts in this quiet community?" This isn't logical.

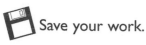 Save your work.

AUTOBLEND PREFIXES

de, en, em, il, in, im, ir, dis, fore, anti

Words have specific meanings, but they are often changed or redefined by the addition of a letter or a certain group of letters to the beginning of the words. This group of letters with a specific meaning is called a *prefix*. This part of the lesson will introduce you to some prefixes as AutoBlends. They may not be considered *blends* in the strictest sense of the word, but we will continue to use the label because prefixes are usually a group of letters instead of words. We note also that prefixes *imply* that there is a root word that can stand alone. From a keyboarding point of view, the importance is in the automation of keyboarding the letter sequence. This means that you will see some words such as *imply*, which includes the AutoBlend *im* but is not a true prefix in this case.

Remember that you are trying to learn to type these prefixes as single units. That is why only prefixes of three letters or fewer will be used. If you want to practice additional blends, you will find a list of the most commonly used ones in Appendix C.

Begin by slowly keying the following prefixes. Pronounce them as you work. Interestingly, prefixes such as *de* are pronounced *d* and *en* is pronounced *n*. Remember that the following or preceding vowels exist even though you don't pronounce them.

de de de de de de de de de de de de de de de de de de de de de de de de de de de de

en en en en en en en en en en en en en en en en en en en en en en en en en en en en

em em em em em em em em em em em em em em em em em em em em em em em

il il il il il il il il il il il il il il il il il il il il il il il il il il il il il il il il il il il il il il

im im im im im im im im im im im im im im im im im im im im im im im im

ir ir ir ir ir ir ir ir ir ir ir ir ir ir ir ir ir ir ir ir ir ir ir ir ir ir ir ir ir ir ir ir ir ir ir ir ir

ir ir ir ir ir ir ir dis dis dis dis dis dis dis dis dis dis dis dis dis dis dis dis dis dis

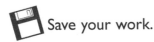 Save your work.

NEW AUTOBLEND PREFIXES TRYOUT

de, en, em, il, in, im, ir, dis, fore, anti

de de de en en en em em em il il il im im im ir ir ir dis dis dis de de en en em em il il

dis dis de en em il im ir dis dis ir im il em en de em de de de en en en em em em il il

debug debug, detail detail, entail entail, debate debate, encode encode, endear endear, delete delete, realize realize; illegal illegal, illicit illicit, timbers timbers; ground;

engaging; imploded imploded, defaulted defaulted; declined declined, opponent; exploded exploded, disappear disappear, important important, imitation imitation,

invitation invitation; irrelevant irrelevant; discussion discussion; impossible impossible; disinterested disinterested, irreversible irreversible, destruction destruction

His imitation shoes were illegal. His sorry excuse was irrelevant to the case.
I didn't realize the amount of detail this legal case would entail. It is an important case.

When the dynamite exploded, the building imploded. You might say the building was deconstructed. The owners watched their home disappear as the timbers fell.

The mayor was disinterested in the debate. She felt that engaging her opponent in discussion could endear her to the citizens. She declined this open invitation.

It was difficult to debug the irreversible problems and destruction caused by this computer virus. It seemed impossible to encode a solution to delete the troubles.

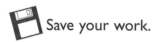Save your work.

SELF-TEST

crypt crypt, public public, empty empty, decay decay, image image, dismal dismal, amazed amazed, quickness quickness, dexterity dexterity, successful successful

youthful youthful, juggler juggler, remains remains, decades decades, slashes slashes, balance balance, writing writing, mummy mummy, illustrate illustrate, monitor monitor

recently recently, seemingly seemingly, disheveled disheveled, grammarians grammarians, questionnaire questionnaire, government government, discuss discuss,

The public was amazed to view the quickness and dexterity of the youthful juggler. She said, "I can balance two chairs on my nose but not my checkbook." Bad joke.

Many grammarians advise writers against using slashes in their writing. They say, "It makes writing look like a questionnaire/government/academic document."

My professor said, "It's amazing to see the many valuable resources that are available at http://www.broadwaybooks.com. Have you been there to see it all recently?"

After decades of decay, the image of the mummy was dismal. The seemingly empty crypt was filled with remains of days gone by. King Tut had been wrapped up.

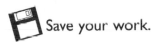 Save your work.

CORRECTIVE WORK

Proofread your work.

- Print the file **Lesson11.doc**.
- Identify the words that were keyed incorrectly.
- Create a new file and save it as **L11Practice.doc**.
- Key each of these words five times correctly and save your file.

IMPROVEMENT WORK

Return to the preceding fourteen lines. Open the file **Lesson11.doc**, and key these lines again. You should be able to complete the task more quickly and more accurately.

THREE-MINUTE TIMING

You have been able to test yourself to identify your WPM. The only problem is that you rarely key for only a minute. Often, you will find yourself getting into a flow after a few minutes. That is why you will begin to test your WPM using multiple-minute periods. You may find that on the same day with the same material you will key faster per minute over a 3-minute period than over only a 1-minute period.

Obviously, you will probably key at least three times the number of words in a 3-minute period than in a 1-minute period. This means that you will need to do some calculations to figure out your WPM as well as your errors. You may make three times as many errors in a 3-minute period, so you will need to calculate your EPM (errors per minute). We will cover how to do this after you take your next 3-minute timed test.

Now that you have learned and practiced more AutoBlends and AutoWords, you should be feeling pretty good about yourself. You are mastering the process of keyboarding. GOOD FOR YOU. Here is your opportunity to prove it. Remember the rules!

- Don't look at the keyboard!

- Use the NoPeekee Keyboard for reference.

- Use the **Sitting Hints** to address your keyboard.

- Use the **Home Row Hints** to position your fingers.

• Tap the Enter key at the end of each line.

The text for this timing has been laid out in a way to make computing your WPM simple. There are 12 words (60 characters) per line. This means that if you key all the characters in 1 minute, you will have completed 12 WPM. If you complete them all in 3 minutes, you will have keyed at 4 WPM. Notice that there are pairs of numbers throughout the text (e. g., 12/4). The first number (i.e., 12) indicates the number of words to that point. The second number (i.e., 4) indicates your WPM if you reach this point in 3 minutes.

 It's time to start your trial run. If you get to the end of the text, start at the top again. Set your timer for 3 minutes. Go!

```
              3/1            6/2            9/3           12/4
Learning to keyboard quickly will improve your communication.
             15/5           18/6           21/7           24/8
Faster keyboarding skills will improve your technology usage.
             27/9           30/10          33/11          36/12
You use your computer to write email, reports and letters.
             39/13          42/14          45/15          48/16
Your speed will not increase by simply writing all of these
             51/17          54/18          57/19          60/20
forms of communication. You must use them to develop memory
             63/21          66/22          69/23          72/24
traces for each letter so that you don't have to search the
             75/25          78/26          81/27          84/28
keyboard for letters. You will just see the letter and then
             87/29          90/30          93/31          96/32
use the correct finger to tap the proper key for the letter.
```

CALCULATING WPM

Look at all the words you keyed during this timing! It's almost three times as many as you did before, because you keyed for 3 minutes, not just one. That means that your WPM is only one-third of the number of words you keyed. Thus, to compute your WPM, divide the total number of words by 3. Do the same with the total number of errors.

Consider your performance on this test and enter the statistics in the "3-Minute Test #1" row of the following table. Complete the rest of your statistics by computing them as necessary.

	Total Words Keyed	Total Words Keyed in 1 Minute (Total Words/3)	Total Number of Errors	Total Errors in 1 Minute (Total Errors/3)	Correct WPM (Total Words Keyed in 1 Minute Minus Number of Errors in 1 Minute)
3-Minute Test #1					
3-Minute Test #2					
3-Minute Test #3					

Return to the 3-minute timing and take it two more times. Enter each of the results and do the necessary calculations.

Turn to the back of the book and enter the information about your *best* time in the Self-Progress Chart in Appendix K.

Keep at it. You are learning more and getting better.

MORE AUTOWORDS

OUTCOMES

• AutoWords
  do, go, in, no, on, of, or, to, up, the,
  for, all, and, end

The more AutoWords you know, the faster you
will go.

You have already been introduced to AutoWords
and AutoBlends. In this lesson, you will learn a
few more AutoWords. Remember that the goal
of learning AutoWords is to build your automaticity. You don't want to think of these
words as a collection of letters but as a single
group of keystrokes.

WARM-UP (5 MINUTES)

You are moving forth in your pursuit of keyboarding automaticity. Warm up as you review
some of the essential ingredients of AutoWords.

Create a **New** file and save it in the
Keyboarding folder. Name it **Lesson12.doc**.

Remember to:

• Clip your NoPeekee Keyboard to the top of
  the page.

• Place your book in the holder and set it to
  the right of your keyboard.

• Sit at your computer following the **Sitting
  Hints**.

• Set your timer to 5 minutes.

• Place your fingers lightly on the home row
  considering the **Home Row Hints**.

 Set your 5-minute timer. Go!

qqq ppp aaa ;;; www ooo sss lll eee iii kkk ddd ::: ccc uuu rrr jjj fff mmm vvv yyy ttt
nnn bbb sss lll ddd kkk ccc mmm vvv nnn bbb www qqq ppp aaa ;;; www ooo sss lll

is by be; and you see the for: your when with same used like more that know will;
letter moving finger should faster, respond correct letters: efficient automated.

Effective and efficient keying is developed by improving your keyboarding reflexes.
When you see a specific letter you should respond with moving the correct finger.

Expand this automated skill by developing the same responses for commonly used words. AutoWords should be automated like the alphabet letters. They should be keyed as a single unit. The more AutoWords you know, the faster your keyboarding will go.

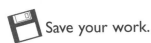 Save your work.

MORE AUTOWORDS

do, go, in, no, on, of, or, to, up, the, for, all, and, end

AutoWords will speed up your keying greatly. As explained in the past lesson, you need to develop the automaticity of keying AutoWords and AutoBlends. This lesson introduces an additional fourteen AutoWords. These AutoWords are all actual words. You will notice that all of them can also be found as parts of words in the English language. Whether you key them as AutoWords or AutoBlends, considering them as single units when you key them will increase your speed greatly.

Practice the words by keying them as a single unit. Say the word as a unit as you key the word. Two words introduced in this lesson may cause you a little trouble, namely, *no* and *on*. By themselves, they should be no problem. When keyed one after another, they can cause some finger fumbling.

Give it a go.

Key each of these AutoWords. Remember to pronounce each word as you key it. Begin slowly and increase your speed as you feel the process become automatic.

do do do do do do do do do do do do do do do do do do do do do do do do do do do

go go go go go go go go go go go go go go go go go go go go go go go go go go go go

in in in in in in in in in in in in in in in in in in in in in in in in in in in in

no no no no no no no no no no no no no no no no no no no no no no no no no no no

on on on on on on on on on on on on on on on on on on on on on on on on on on on

of of of of of of of of of of of of of of of of of of of of of of of of of of of of of

or or or or or or or or or or or or or or or or or or or or or or or or or or or or or or

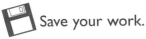 Save your work.

Let's create little digital disruption with these AutoWords. Here is your opportunity to practice them. Creating sentences with the two- and three-letter words introduced in this lesson is incredibly dull. You will notice that the selection of words in these exercises includes words composed of AutoWords and AutoBlends introduced in Lessons 6, 10, and 12.

by by by do do do go go go in in in no no no on on on of of of or or or by by do do go go in in no no on on of of or or by do go in no on of or by on by by by do do do

mat can wag dog one dodo door sits fast body beat when well tail goes gong gold golf quite whack clubs often Donna Gorky dozing stairs coffee shakes course player gonged Sunday playing kitchen Tuesday grabbed noticed country offered beginners snoozing

SELF-TEST

by by, do do, go go, in in, no no, on on, of of, or or, dog dog, out out, sits sits, door door, mat mat, wag wag, well well, tail tail, fast fast, body body, loud loud,

ball, ball, gold gold, golf golf, beat beat, birds birds, whole whole, whack whack, club club, quite quite, There There, shakes shakes, often often, mine mine,

course course, playing playing, offered offered, coffee coffee, Sunday Sunday, Monday Monday, dozing dozing, gonged gonged, napping napping, today,

Our dog goes in and out of the dog door or he sits by the door on the mat. He goes up the stairs. My dog can wag his tail fast. It is so fast that it shakes his whole body.

Donna can whack the ball with her gold golf clubs. There is no one on the course who can beat her. Donna is the best player of the beginners in the country club.

Gorky offered to go by my house to get some coffee. I asked Gorky to do it for me on Sunday or Monday. He agreed to wait until Monday to go in to my kitchen.

Noel noticed that all of the dodo birds were dozing. He gonged the gong. None of the birds were napping or snoozing after he did that. They flew off in the air.

 Save your work.

ADDITIONAL AUTOWORDS

to to to to to to to to to to to to to to to to to to to to to to to to to to to to to to to to to

up up up up up up up up up up up up up up up up up up up up up up up up up up

the the the the the the the the the the the the the the the the the the the the the the the the

for for for for for for for for for for for for for for for for for for for for for for for

all all all all all all all all all all all all all all all all all all all all all all all all all

and and and and and and and and and and and and and and and and and and and

end end end end end end end end end end end end end end end end end end end

 Save your work.

SELF-TEST

to to to up up up the the the for for for all all all and and and end end end to to to up to to to up up the the the for for all all and and end end to up the for all and end up up the

took took toys toys pups pups cups cups gall gall ball ball hall hall tons tons tote tote hand hand form form Ford Ford Today Today took took toys toys pups pups cups cups

Tokyo Tokyo toads toads tools tools forks forks forts forts balls balls walls walls bands wands wands bends bends force force torch torch night night football football

alloy alloy Sally Sally force force towers towers forged forged pandas pandas append stayed stayed stands stands fender fender toucans toucans keeping keeping grownup

Today Tom took toys to Tokyo. He had pups and cups and toads and tools and forks and balls and walls and bands and wands. He also sent a football to the grownup.

Sally had the gall to force the ball down the hall until it was up against the wall. She also had tons of tools to tote to the towers. There was a band on her hand.

Upendo forged alloy animals to put up on the housetop. He made pandas and alligators and toucans. They were difficult to append to the end of the roof.

Allen likes to work on cars. He stands by his workbench to form a fender for his Ford. All of his family drives Fords and they tend to drive at the speed limit.

 Save your work.

CORRECTIVE WORK

Proofread your work.

- Print the file **Lesson12.doc**.

- Identify the words that were keyed incorrectly.

- Create a new file and save it as **L12Practice.doc**.

- Key each of these words five times correctly and save your file.

IMPROVEMENT WORK

Return to the preceding sixteen lines. Open the file **Lesson12.doc**, and key these lines again. You should be able to complete the task more quickly and more accurately.

Do you want to build those AutoWord skills? The more you practice, the faster you will go. Remember your air keyboard. You can practice keyboarding whole AutoWords while you are sitting in your favorite chair . . . or anywhere.

The quick brown fox jumps over the lazy dog.

_ - DELETE AND AUTOBLENDS

OUTCOMES

- Keys: - _ and Delete
- AutoBlend Prefixes re, un, mid, mis, non, pre, sub
- Three-minute timing

Figure 13.1

Now it's time to learn about the *big stretch*. You have been learning how to strike keys that are one row above and one row below the home row (except for the space bar). On your keyboard you will see that there is another row above the QWERTY row. It is composed of numbers and symbols and the Backspace or, on some keyboards, Delete key.

Many people stop touch keyboarding when they want to use the numbers and symbols in this row. They stop, look at the top row, and then use their forefingers to hit the proper key. These people may be *good* keyboarders, but they will never be *great* keyboarders using this method. Yes, some characters or symbols (e.g., [{] } \ | ^ ` ~) are rarely used, and that is why they aren't being taught in this book. These keys will require you to stop, hunt, and peck to key them. However, the other characters and numbers and the Delete key (*especially*) are used often enough that it is useful to know where they are so that you can key them without stopping your flow.

WARM-UP (5 MINUTES)

Delete your digital doldrums with these challenging exercise experiences. Create a **New** file and save it in the **Keyboarding** folder. Name it **Lesson13.doc**.

Remember to:

- Clip your NoPeekee Keyboard to the top of the page.
- Place your book in the holder and set it to the right of your keyboard.
- Sit at your computer following the **Sitting Hints**.
- Set your timer to 5 minutes.
- Place your fingers lightly on the home row considering the **Home Row Hints**.

Set your 5-minute timer. Go!

Form DOES email GREAT Daily Build skills lesson involve online keying mental exercise memory complete writing discipline engaging chatting important NoPeekee

Daily practice of your keyboarding skills will provide the exercise and mental discipline necessary to become a GREAT keyboarder. This doesn't mean that you must complete a lesson every day. It DOES mean that you need to involve yourself in keyboarding through writing letters, answering email, engaging in online chatting, or just keying.

Speed isn't as important as form and discipline. You MUST use your NoPeekee Keyboard for reference when you don't know where to find keys. DON'T look at the keyboard. Build those memory traces to develop proper habits. Perfect practice makes perfect.

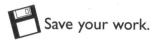 Save your work.

NEW CHARACTERS - AND _

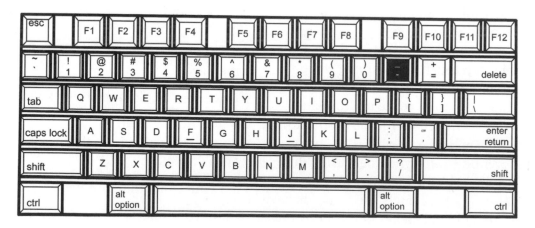

Figure 13.2

Look to the upper right region of your keyboard and find the (–) and (_) characters on the same key (see Figure 13.2). Considering the position of the key, you may think that it is another "pinky key." Some may recommend the pinky for this key but it requires you to swivel your whole right hand to reach it with your short pinky.

Therefore, it is recommended that you use your right ring finger to tap this key. You will produce a hyphen (–) with a single tap of your right ringer, but you will have to include a left Shift key with your left pinky to produce an underscore (_) (see Figure 13.3).

What is an *underscore?* you may ask. Some people call it a *line* and others may call it an *underbar* but this character is the one you use to make a continuous line across the page. On typewriters this character was used to underline/underscore/underbar words that were already typed. After typing the necessary words, the typist would return to the beginning

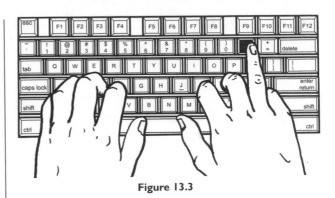

Figure 13.3

of the words to be emphasized and strike this underline key repeatedly to type a line below the letters. Today, you merely highlight the important words and click on the underline icon in the toolbar to underline them.

Place your hands in their favorite place on the home row. Move your right ring finger from the L key to the -_ (underscore) key. You will probably find yourself opening your hand quite a bit to extend to that key. Practice this a bit using the following exercise. Remember to name the keys as you tap them:

"L L L hyphen hyphen hyphen L L L hyphen hyphen hyphen L L L hyphen hyphen."

lll --- lll --- lll --- lll --- lll --- lll --- lll --- lll --- lll --- lll --- lll --- lll --- lll --- lll --- lll

Good job! Quite a stretch, wasn't it? Now you have the opportunity to make those same movements using your little left pinky as well. After hitting the L key a few times, you will hold down the left Shift key with your left pinky and then tap the underscore (_) key with your right ring finger. Use the following

practice line to give this a try. (You may not see three separate underscores when you key them, because your word processor is designed to merge them into a single line. That's OK.)

Remember to say the keys as you key them.

lll ___ lll ___ lll ___ lll ___ lll ___ lll ___ lll ___ lll ___ lll ___ lll ___ lll ___ lll ___ lll

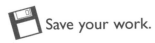 Save your work.

NEW CHARACTERS TRYOUT - AND _

Good job. Now, spend some time practicing your new characters.

lll --- lll ___ lll --- lll ___ lll --- lll ___ lll --- lll ___ lll --- lll ___ lll --- lll --- lll ___ lll --- lll ___

--- ___ ___ --- lll --- ___ lll lll ---LLL --- ___ lll --- ___ --- LLL ___ --- --- ___ ___ --- lll --- ___

Please fill in the following questions:

First Name: _____ Last Name: _____

Phone Number: ___ - ___ - _____ / Fax Number: ___ - ___ - _____

Gender: ___ Male ___ Female   Computer: ___ Macintosh ___ Windows

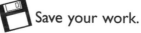 Save your work.

SELF-TEST

enjoyed enjoyed scared scared bail-out bail-out message message authority authority listening litigator litigator suggested suggested swimming swimming Constitution

uncomfortable uncomfortable Yesterday Yesterday pre-eminent pre-eminent little-used used-car used-car vice-president vice-president state-of-the-union state-of-the-union

seventy-year-old seventy-year-old recommended recommended under-secretary top-of-the-line top-of-the-line state-of-the-art state-of-the-art day-by-day day-by-day

The vice-president suggested that the under-secretary drive the little-used car. The under-secretary drove the little-used car and found it had uncomfortable seats.

Fill-in the blanks: Yesterday, I saw twelve _____ swimming in the _____. They looked _____. I _____ and scared them away. All of them _____ down the _____.

The seventy-year-old judge enjoyed listening to the state-of-the-union message. He was the top-of-the-line authority on the recommended bail-out program.

The Constitution of the _____ States of _____ was written by _____ _____ in _____. It has lasted for _____ years. It _____ _____ very well.

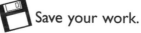 Save your work.

NEW KEY DELETE

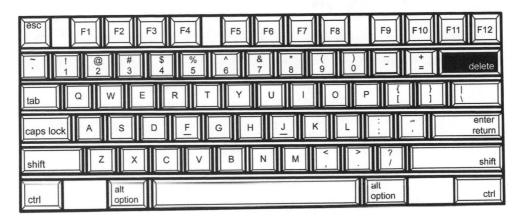

Figure 13.4

It is important to know about the Delete key in case you change your mind about what you are writing or make a mistake (see Figure 13.4).

Look at the upper right corner of your keyboard and find the Delete key. This is your ticket to freedom of expression (and the right to make mistakes). Because the Delete key is so far to the right, it needs to be tapped with your right pinky finger. Some people like to use their right ring finger because it is longer and makes it easier to reach the key, but you need to make your own decision.

It is difficult to list activities that will give you practice in using the Delete key. The following activities provide text to key and then instructions (in italics) to delete a specified number of characters.

Key this line all the way to the end of this sentence.

Now tap the Delete key 17 times. Key the following line to complete the sentence.

until three weeks from next Tuesday.

In the following exercise, key the alphabet two letters at a time. After keying two keys, tap the Delete key once. Then, key the next letters in the alphabet. Repeat this pattern until you reach Z.

abDelcdDelefDelghDelijDelklDelmnDelopDelqrDelstDeluvDelwxDelyzabDelcdDelef

Save your work.

MORE AUTOBLEND PREFIXES

re, un, mid, mis, non, pre, sub

Here are the rest of the AutoBlend prefixes. Have you noticed when these AutoBlends or AutoWords have appeared while you've been keying? Have they been increasing your feeling of competence when keyboarding? You may not have developed automaticity with these blends and words yet, but practicing these letter combinations will help develop it. Spend some extra time practicing the exercises in these lessons, or use the lists in the back of the book.

Try to key these prefixes as single units. Begin slowly and develop speed as you progress. Pronounce each AutoBlend as you work.

re re re re re re re re re re re re re re re re re re re re re re re re re re re re re re re re

un un un un un un un un un un un un un un un un un un un un un un un un un un un

mid mid mid mid mid mid mid mid mid mid mid mid mid mid mid mid mid mid

mis mis mis mis mis mis mis mis mis mis mis mis mis mis mis mis mis mis mis mis

non non non non non non non non non non non non non non non non non non

pre pre pre pre pre pre pre pre pre pre pre pre pre pre pre pre pre pre pre pre

sub sub sub sub sub sub sub sub sub sub sub sub sub sub sub sub sub sub sub sub

 Save your work.

NEW AUTOBLEND PREFIXES TRYOUT

re re re un un un mid mid mid mis mis mis non non non pre pre pre sub sub sub re mid mis mis non non pre pre sub sub re un mid dis non pre sub re re re un un un

Miss iss ippi Miss-iss-ippi Mississippi remake Rerun prequel preview retained mistakes returning miserable submarine mid-spring registering University responded reparations

Miss Rebun retained her dream to cruise in a submarine up the Mississippi River in mid-spring. Her preparations remain intact during non-spring days. It will happen.

Reginald stood in the line for pre-/re-/un-registering for classes at the Southern University of Mississippi. It was a long long long long line. He was in the middle of the non-traditional students. Yaumi saw the movie, "Mission: Suburban Midnight Fever." It was a remake of the prequel to "Mission: Seven-Year Rerun."

Joe responded, "No kidding -- Lorenzo called off his visit to Mexico City just because Aunt Myrtle told him the conquistadores were extinct." Lorenzo felt miserable.

 Save your work.

SELF-TEST

Field Field rebuffs rebuffs event event nonstop nonstop bagged bagged mistakes
Dreams Dreams Midwest Midwest mid-day mid-day remedy remedy tranquil tranquil

unsettled unsettled nonsense nonsense aardvarks aardvarks nonsense nonsense
Midor's Midor's Ebenezer Ebenezer Remembering Remembering remarkable remarkable

subconscious subconscious realized realized middle middle mishappenings
prefix prefix unexpectedly unexpectedly mid-summer mid-summer reaction reaction

Remembering Uncle Midor's mistakes and nonsense unsettled Presta's subconscious.
It was a difficult time of nonstop mishappenings and rebuffs.

Ebenezer unexpectedly bagged two tranquil aardvarks with his Jiffy vacuum cleaner.
It was a remarkable event at mid-day during mid-summer weather in the Midwest.

Now is the time for all good men to come to the aid of their party.
Now tap the Delete key 38 times. Key the following line to complete the sentence.
men and women to come to the aid of their party.

Six javelins thrown by the very quick athletes whizzed forty paces beyond the mark.
Now tap the Delete key 28 times. Key the following line to complete the sentence.
fifty meters beyond the mark.

 Save your work.

Take a break. Stand, stretch, and relax your body.
Now, return to do the final corrective work and three-minute timing.

CORRECTIVE WORK

Proofread your work.

- Print the file **Lesson13.doc**.

- Identify the words that were keyed incorrectly.

- Create a new file and save it as **L13Practice.doc**.

- Key each of these words five times correctly and save your file.

IMPROVEMENT WORK

Return to the Self-Test. Open the file **Lesson13.doc**, and key these lines again. You should be able complete the task more quickly and more accurately.

THREE-MINUTE TIMING

You are becoming more proficient with every key you tap. Here is your opportunity to measure how quickly you are keying for 3 minutes.

Remember these rules:

- Don't look at the keyboard!

- Use the NoPeekee Keyboard for reference.

- Use the **Sitting Hints** to address your keyboard.

- Use the **Home Row Hints** to position your fingers.

- Tap the Enter key at the end of each line.

and

- This is a **three-minute timing**. Pace yourself. Don't wear yourself down in the first minute.

The text for this timing has been formatted to make computing your WPM simple. There are 12 words (60 characters) per line. This means that if you key all of them in 1 minute, you will have completed 12 WPM. If you complete them all in 3 minutes, you will have keyed at 4 WPM. Notice that there are pairs of numbers throughout the text (e.g., 12/4). The first number (i.e., 12) indicates the number of words to that point. The second number (i.e., 4) indicates your WPM if you reach this point in 3 minutes.

 Now it's time for your three-minute test. Set your timer for 3 minutes. Go!

```
          3/1              6/2              9/3            12/4
Taking a three-minute test can be a different trial than when
         15/5             18/6             21/7            24/8
you are taking one-minute tests. It involves using your skill
         27/9             30/10            33/11           36/12
for a longer period of time. It means that you must learn to
         39/13            42/14            45/15           48/16
exercise discipline in how fast you key at the start. You may
```

```
        51/17            54/18            57/19          60/20
be tempted to begin at a quick pace. This is a good idea, but
        63/21            66/22            69/23          72/24
you don't want to wear down your strength at the beginning.
        75/25            78/26            81/27          84/28
Keep your keying at a relatively steady and constant pace.
        87/29            90/30            93/31          96/32
Try finding a rhythm in your keyboarding as you do your work.
```

Well done! Let's see how many correct WPM you keyed.

CALCULATING WPM

You did it again—you completed a 3-minute test. Do you feel more comfortable doing this? Did you find that you began developing a rhythm as you keyed your words for an extended amount of time?

Consider your performance on this test and enter the statistics in the "3-Minute Test #1" row of the following table. Complete the rest of the statistics by computing them as necessary.

	Total Words Keyed	Total Words Keyed in 1 Minute (Total Words/3)	Total Number of Errors	Total Errors in 1 Minute (Total Errors/3)	Correct WPM (Total Words Keyed in 1 Minute Minus Number of Errors in 1 Minute)
3-Minute Test #1					
3-Minute Test #2					
3-Minute Test #3					

Return to the three-minute timing and take it two more times. Enter each of the results and compute as necessary.

Enter your best time in Appendix K.

ALIGNMENT, TAB KEY, AND AUTOBLENDS

OUTCOMES

- Alignment Process
  Left, Center,
  Right, Justify

- Key: Tab
  Auto tabs
  Setting tab stops

- AutoBlend Suffixes
  al, ed, er, es, ic, ly

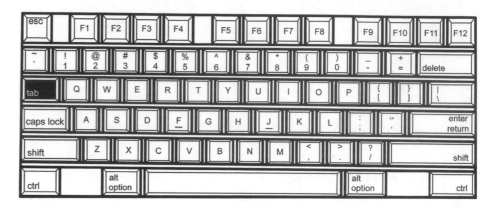

Figure 14.1

You know how to key most of the keys on the keyboard, and now it's time to deal with text placement. Placing your words at the appropriate location on the page is an important skill. You will first learn to maneuver location using your word processor's alignment capabilities. After you have become familiar with this capability, you will learn about using the Tab key and how to set the tabs (see Figure 14.1).

WARM-UP (5 MINUTES)

Placement is critical. Practice tapping the proper keys with these warm-ups.

Create a **New** file and save it in the **Keyboarding** folder. Name it **Lesson14.doc**.

Remember to:

- Clip your NoPeekee Keyboard to the top of the page.

- Place your book in the holder and set it to the right of your keyboard.

- Sit at your computer following the **Sitting Hints**.

- Set your timer to 5 minutes.

- Place your fingers lightly on the home row considering the **Home Row Hints**.

 Set your 5-minute timer. Go!

by, do, go, in, no, on, of, or, to, up, the, the, for, for, all, all, and, and, end by, do, go, in, no, or, to, up, the, the, for, for, all, all, and, and, end de, en, em, il, im, ir, dis, re, un, mid, mis, mis, non, non, pre, pre, sub, sub de, en, em, il, im, ir, dis, re, un, mid, mis mis, non, non,

tabs text left using words right belongs useful select lesson center trying cursor option center number defined covered identify aligning word processor document alignment settings aligning necessary location various middle full-align left-align right-align setting/using professional

Aligning text in a document can be done through a number of ways. The two that will be covered in this lesson include your word processor's alignment tool and setting/using tabs. Your word processor enables you to left-align, right-align, or center your text. You can also select the full-align option that aligns the words on both the left and right sides while adding spaces as necessary in the middle. The Tab key is used to move the cursor to various tab stops. You can define these stops to identify the exact location of text. Tabs are useful when you are trying to give a document a professional look. They move text where it belongs.

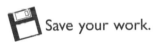Save your work.

TEXT ALIGNMENT

Keying text quickly is important, but it is more important to be able to make it look professional. Presenting text is more than just placing one letter after another. Making the text readable involves positioning, style, and size. Notice the heading for this section. It is boldface and placed next to the left margin. This placement is called *left alignment*. The text in this paragraph is also left aligned. Each line of text begins at the left margin and extends to the right until it runs out of space and continues the next line.

Your word processor probably uses left align as the default. This means that unless you change the alignment, the text that you key into a document will be left aligned. Left-aligned text is easier to read because of the consistent location for the beginning of each line. Reading a large quantity of text that is centered or right aligned is more difficult because there is no consistent location for the beginning of a text line.

Text can be aligned either before or after you key the text into your document. You will begin by keying text lines and then using the alignment tools to format the text. Follow the directions as they are explained.

Key the following line:
This text is being used to demonstrate alignment tools.

Highlight the line of text you just keyed. To *highlight* means to mark a menu option or a block of text with the highlight bar. At the top of the screen click on **Format** in the menu bar. A drop-down menu will reveal additional commands.

Select the **Paragraph** command.

Selecting the **Paragraph** command opens the Paragraph dialog box. You will find a drop-down menu named **Alignment**. "Left" is the type of alignment selected.

Select **Centered** from the drop-down menu. Click the **OK** button and you will see that the text is now centered on the page.

Highlight the text again. Select the **Paragraph** command and right-align your text using the same directions, but selecting **Right** in the **Alignment** menu.

Click the **OK** button and you will see that your text is aligned with the right margin. This alignment isn't used often, but it is useful when you do need it.

Alignment Using the Formatting Toolbar

You just used drop-down menus to align text, but you can also use tools on the formatting toolbar or palette. Look below the menu bar at the top of the screen and locate the toolbars containing icons. You should see some alignment icons that show lines of text that are aligned to the left, center, and right.

If you don't see the alignment icons at the top of your screen, you will have to make the formatting toolbar visible.

Select the **View** command from the menu bar at the top of the screen. A drop-down menu will appear.

Select **Toolbars** from the drop-down menu. Select **Formatting** from the toolbar options listed. You should now see the alignment icons at the top of your screen.

Alignment Using the Formatting Palette

The later versions of Microsoft Word/Office also feature a formatting palette. This is a box of formatting options that can be moved to any place on the screen and contains all the formatting options available in the **Formatting** menu option.

Select the **View** command from the menu bar at the top of the screen.

Select **Formatting Palette** from the drop-down menu. The **Formatting Palette** will appear on the screen.

Clicking on the triangle to the left of each title in the **Formatting Palette** will reveal or hide these options. Try it.

Click on the triangle to the left of the **Alignment and Spacing** option to reveal the formatting options. You should see the alignment icons, which are sets of horizontal lines showing the different alignment options.

Practicing Alignment

Key the following lines of text and then align them using the directions that follow them.

This line is aligned to the left margin.
This line is aligned to the right margin.
This line is centered.
This final line includes multiple lines of text because it is going to be used to demonstrate the full justify command. You will notice that all the lines are justified to both the right and left. Additional spaces are placed between words to create justification.

Highlight the first line. Click on the **Align Left** icon. (Not much happens because it is already left aligned.)

Highlight the second line. Click on the **Align Right** icon.

Highlight the third line. Click on the **Align Center** icon.

Highlight the fourth set of lines of text. Click on the **Justify** icon. You will see spaces inserted throughout the text, and lines will become flush with both the right and left margins.

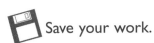 Save your work.

POSITIONING TEXT USING TABS

Right, left, or center aligning text is useful, but sometimes it is necessary to have greater control in positioning text on the screen or paper. Using the Tab key provides horizontal control of the location of text in a document. Tapping the Tab key moves the insertion point (cursor) across the screen to preset *tab stops*, which are locations on the ruler indicating where text will align when the Tab key is tapped. Most word processors have their tab stops automatically set to every 1/2". As you tap the Tab key, it inserts invisible *tab characters* to move the insertion point across the screen. This is similar to using the space bar to move the insertion point with an invisible space. The only difference is that the positioning of the tabs can be customized.

You will use your left pinky finger to tap the Tab key. This means that you move your pinky from the A key to the Tab. Give it a try. It's a bit if a stretch, but it can be done. Key the following line to practice this. First tap the A key and then the Tab key and then the A key and then the Tab key for the whole line. Use *only* your left hand and *only* your left pinky to do this!

a   a   a   a   a   a   a   a   a   a   a   a   a

Practice using the preset 0.5" tabs by completing the following exercise. Use the Tab key to move to the appropriate horizontal position before keying the text. Tap the Enter key to move to the next line before you tap the Tab key again.

Tab 1
    Tab 2
        Tab 3
            Tab 4
                Tab 5
                    Tab 6
                        Tab 7
                            Tab 8
                                Tab 9
                                    Tab 10
                                        Tab 11

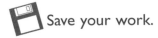 Save your work.

The 0.5" tabs are most often used for indenting the first line of a paragraph. Although this paragraph indentation is not used in all formats of writing, it is used in informal writing and in various formats for writing research reports (e.g., American Psychology Association (APA) and Modern Language Association (MLA)).

You can also use tabs to place text at specific horizontal tab stops. If you want to place a word 3" from the left margin, you can tap the Tab key six times to insert six invisible tab stops and then key the word.

You can simplify the process by creating a single tab stop at the 3" position. Look at the ruler at the top of the document. If you don't see a ruler at the top of the document, you can make one appear using the menu at the top of the screen.

Select the **View** command from the menu bar at the top of the screen. A drop-down menu will appear. There should be a check to the left of the **Ruler** option. If there is no check, place a check beside the **Ruler** option by dragging your cursor to the box next to the word Ruler and clicking on it. You should now see a ruler at the top of the document.

It is quite simple to place a tab at the 3" position in the document ruler. Move your cursor to the 3" marker in the ruler. Click on the 3 and a tab stop will appear (it is a small arrow or L-shaped mark). If the tab stop is in the wrong position, you can drag it to the proper position. Drag the tab stop down off the ruler to delete it.

When you insert a tab at the 3" position, it removes all the automatic 0.5" tabs to the left of it. This allows you to tap the Tab key only once to move to the 3" tab stop. The automatic tabs will return after you remove the inserted tab stops. This means that you will have 0.5" tab stops again.

Remove the tab stop at 3" (drag the stop off the ruler and onto the document. It will vanish).

Create tab stops at 1", 2", and 4.5".

Create the following Duty Roster. Center the title and then use the tabs to format the roster accordingly.

DUTY ROSTER

BREAKFAST

	Set up	Chris
	Cook	Jeff
	Clean up	Wes

LUNCH

	Set up	Jeff
	Cook	Wes
	Clean up	Chris

DINNER

	Set up	Wes
	Cook	Chris
	Clean up	Jeff

 Save your work.

AUTOBLEND SUFFIXES

al, ed, er, es, ic, ly

Here are the rest of the AutoBlend suffixes. Have they been increasing your feeling of competence when keyboarding? Have you noticed when these AutoBlends or AutoWords have appeared when you have been keying?

You may not have developed automaticity with these blends and words yet, but practicing these letter combinations will help it develop. Spend some extra time practicing the exercises in these lessons, or use the appendices in the back of the book.

Try to key these suffixes as single units. Begin slowly and develop speed as you progress. Pronounce each AutoBlend as you work.

al, al, al, al, al, al, al, al, al, al, al, al, al, al, al, al, al, al, al, al, al, al, al, al, al, al, al, al
ed, ed, ed, ed, ed, ed, ed, ed, ed, ed, ed, ed, ed, ed, ed, ed, ed, ed, ed, ed, ed, ed, ed

er, er, er, er, er, er, er, er, er, er, er, er, er, er, er, er, er, er, er, er, er, er, er, er, er, er, er
es, es, es, es, es, es, es, es, es, es, es, es, es, es, es, es, es, es, es, es, es, es, es, es, es

ic, ic, ic, ic, ic, ic, ic, ic, ic, ic, ic, ic, ic, ic, ic, ic, ic, ic, ic, ic, ic, ic, ic, ic, ic,ic, ic, ic
ly, ly, ly, ly, ly, ly, ly, ly, ly, ly, ly, ly, ly, ly, ly, ly, ly, ly, ly, ly, ly, ly, ly, ly, ly, ly, ly, ly,

Save your work.

NEW AUTOBLEND SUFFIXES TRYOUT

al, al, al, ed, ed, ed, er, er, er, es, es, es, ic, ic, ic, ly, ly, ly, al, al, ed, ed, er, er, es, es, ic, ic, ly, ly, al, ed, er, es, ic, ly, al, ed, er, es, ic, ly, al, ed, er, es, ic, ly, al, al, al, ed, ed, ed Vic sing epic ably trip aged They which folly dares bored elves likes waves lyric magic found These relics actual postal global picnic calmly cloves garlic listed sailed celery casual steered slowly carrier mutual clothes musical navigational wild-colored frequently

Hal, the postal carrier, dares to picnic calmly. He carries cloves of garlic and stalks of celery. Hal likes to wear wild-colored clothes frequently. He does fantastic magic.

Ted's barber bored Roger as he slowly listed names of lyric song titles. These musical titles included odes about doves, foxes and magic elves. They were lots of fun to hear.

Vidal sailed to Italy using a global positioning system navigational unit. He steered ably through the many waves and currents in the Mediterranean. It was an epic trip.

Vic invested in global mutual funds to prepare for his aged years. He is not casual about his epic investments. He recently made positive logical financial choices.

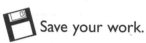 Save your work.

SELF-TEST

The foxes	slyly		stalked	the chickens.
The prey	did not	panic	when they	saw them.

Titles can be

Centered

Left Aligned

or

Right Aligned

Sometimes, when sentences are long enough to reach from margin to margin, writers can use justify to ensure that the text stretches from margin to margin. The only problem is that sometimes there are large spaces between words.

CORRECTIVE WORK

Proofread your work.

- Print the file **Lesson14.doc**.

- Identify the words that were keyed incorrectly.

- Create a new file and save it as **L14Practice.doc**.

- Key each of these words five times correctly and save your file.

IMPROVEMENT WORK

Return to the lines in the new AutoBlend Suffixes Tryout. Open the file **Lesson14.doc**, and key these lines again. You should be able to complete the task more quickly and more accurately.

6 7 &

OUTCOMES

- Keys: 6 7 and &
- Three-minute timing

Figure 15.1

You learned about the *big stretch* in Lesson 13. You stretched your pinky and ring fingers. Now you will move to the middle of the keyboard to key the 6 and 7 keys (see Figure 15.1). These keys will be your introduction to adding numerals to your repertoire.

WARM-UP (5 MINUTES)

Engage in these warm-up winners to prepare for numeral negotiation.

 Set your 5-minute timer. Go!

Create a **New** file and save it in the **Keyboarding** folder. Name it **Lesson15.doc**.

Remember to:

- Clip your NoPeekee Keyboard to the top of the page.
- Place your book in the holder and set it to the right of your keyboard.
- Sit at your computer following the **Sitting Hints**.
- Set your timer to 5 minutes.
- Place your fingers lightly on the home row considering the **Home Row Hints**.

aaa BBB ccc DDD eee FFF ggg HHH iii JJJ kkk LLL mmm NNN ooo PPP qqq RRR sss TTT uuu VVV www XXX yyy ZZZ ;;; ??? ''' --- """AAA bbb EEE fff III nnnOOO rrr UUU

body feet emails align touch floor rules center proper remain writing involved assume reading original material sitting written fingers automate thinking chatting prepare keyboard Sometimes automate especially composing positioning developing incredible

When developing your keyboarding skills, you must learn to automate the keyboarding process. You need to sit down at the keyboard and automatically assume the proper sitting position. Your feet must be flat on the floor with one ahead of the other. You must align the center of your body with a line between the G and H keys. Your fingers must touch the home row without thinking and your head must turn to the side to prepare for reading material that you will key.

Sometimes, you will not be keying material that is already written. You will be composing original material at the keyboard. You will key it as you think it. This is especially true when you are involved in writing emails and chatting. The rules for body positioning remain true but you don't have to worry about reading material at the side of your keyboard.

 Save your work.

NEW KEYS 6 AND 7

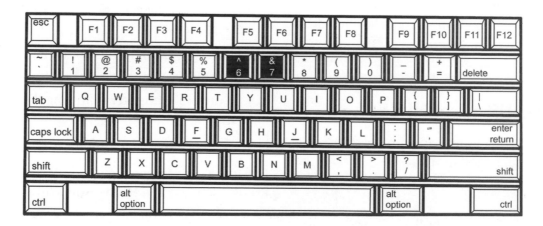

Figure 15.2

In the middle of the top row, above the T, Y, and U keys, are the 6 and 7 keys (see Figure 15.2). These keys are accessed using your forefingers.

Place your fingers on the home row and feel the J and F keys. Now, get ready for the *big stretch*. Move your right forefinger forward to tap the 7 key. Move your forefinger back home to the J key. Always return to the home row. Give it a try. Repeat tapping 7 and returning to the J key a few times.

jjj 777 jjj 777 jjj 777 jjj 777 jjj 777 jjj 777 jjj 777 jjj 777 jjj 777 jjj 777 jjj 777 jjj 777 jjj

Good job. Now it's time for the left hand. Reach your left forefinger into the top row to tap the 6 key. Move it back home to the F key. Do that again a few times until it feels natural.

fff 666 fff 666 fff 666 fff 666 ff 666 fff 666 fff 666 fff 666 fff 666 fff 666 fff 666 fff 666

 Save your work.

NEW KEYS TRYOUT 6 AND 7

Good job. Now, spend some time practicing the new characters.

jjj 777 fff 666 lll --- ___ kkk ddd lll sss ;;; aaa qqq uuu www iii eee ooo rrr ppp ttt yyy mmm ccc nnn vvv bbb xxx ,,, zzz ... aaa /// ??? ;;; ::: jjj 777 fff 666 lll --- ___ kkk ddd

76 76 7/6/67 7/6/67 6/7/67 6/7/67 76ers 76ers 67's 67's 766-6767 76 76 7/6/67 7/6/67 766-6767 '76 -- '77 '76 -- '77 trombones trombones Meredith Meredith Museum Museum

76 trombones led the big parade. You can find them at the Meredith Willson Museum Man Square in Mason City, Iowa 766-6767 They are presented throughout the museum.

7 sisters and 6 brothers went to Expo 67 that was Montreal's World's Fair. They left on 6/7/67 and returned on 7/6/67. Everyone had a wonderful time. 6 of the siblings laughed.

The Ottawa 67s is known as Canada's favorite junior hockey team. Their name recognizes '67 as their year of entry into the league. They often have over 676 supporters at their games.

The Philadelphia 76ers are an exciting team. In '67, they won the NBA title. In the '76 -- '77 season, they finished first in the Atlantic Division. They use 6 -- 7 buses.

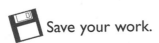 Save your work.

SELF-TEST

Route 66 Route 66; Boeing 767 Boeing 767; Boeing 777 Boeing 777; Route 66 Route 66; 67 AM 67 AM; 7/7/76 7/7/76; 76 76; 77 77; '76 '76; Crazy Crazy; 67 AM 67 AM;

jetliner jetliner; celebrated celebrated; fiftieth fiftieth; birthday birthday; Chicago; filled filled; feature feature; antique antique; transport transport; artery artery; range;

Los Angeles Los Angeles; following following; promptly promptly; intercontinental buckles buckles; Fredrick Fredrick; exquisite exquisite; medium-to-long medium-to-long

In '76, Route 66 celebrated its fiftieth birthday. This Chicago-to-Los Angeles route is a transport artery filled with folk lore. There is an annual Route 66 Fun Run in Arizona.

The Boeing 767 is a medium-to-long range jetliner. The Boeing 777 is a long-range jetliner designed for intercontinental transcontinental routes. These jets are huge.

The talk radio station for our area is 67 AM. They feature a call-in show 7 days a week. Babbling Bob has been hosting since 7/7/76. He has 6 guests per week.

We promptly judged 76 antique ivory buckles for the next 6 wonderful prizes. When we thought we were done, Crazy Fredrick brought over another 77 exquisite opal jewels.

NEW KEY &

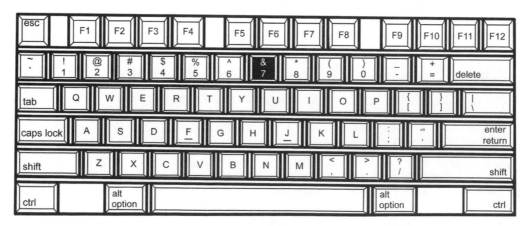

Figure 15.3

Did you hear about the law firm, Smith & Smith & Smith? Yes, a set of identical triplet sisters decided to become lawyers and team up together. The only problem is that the clients don't know which one is serving them when they meet. The & symbol is used a great deal in the English language (see Figure 15.3). Sometimes it is used because it is the proper symbol to use, and sometimes we do it just because we are too lazy to use "and."

This symbol is called an ampersand. It is located on the 7 key. Just hold down the Shift key and tap that 7 and you will see & on your screen (see Figure 15.4). We would typically learn the ^ (caret) as well, since it is above the 6 key, but it is used so seldom in everyday keyboarding, we won't bore you with learning that symbol.

You already found the 7 key in the last section. Just do what you did before. Place your fingers

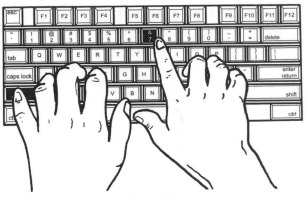

Figure 15.4

on the home row and feel the J and F keys. Move your left pinky to the left Shift key. Hold down the Shift key while you *stretch* your right forefinger forward to tap the 7 key. Move your forefinger back home to the J key. Always return to the home row. Give it a try. Repeat tapping 7 and returning to the J key a few times.

Use the following exercise to practice keying the ampersand.

jjj JJJ &&& jjj JJJ &&& jjj JJJ &&& jjj JJJ &&& jjj JJJ &&& JJJ &&& JJJ JJJ &&& jjj JJJ

 Save your work.

NEW KEY TRYOUT &

jjj JJJ &&& JJJ jjj 777 jjj fff 666 676 767 76&&67 & 6 7 j7&6f f6&7j & jjj JJJ &&& JJJ jjj k & l & L & d 6 7 & d & sss ddd aaa fff ggg hhh xxx xzx bzv /b? ghjfkd k & l & L & d 6

Smith & Smith; Attorneys-at-Law; 77677; 77th; research & development; courts; exciting insight & vision & a bit; specialize; contractual; business; Downtown; judicial;

Smith & Smith & Smith, Attorneys-at-Law specialize in business & contractual & tort law. They have an office at 77677 77th Street in Downtown. They are 6 blocks south.

Research & development in the manufacturing & production of technological innovations requires insight & vision & funding & a bit of luck. It is an exciting part of manufacturing.

THREE-MINUTE TIMING

You are becoming more proficient with every key you tap. Here is your opportunity to measure how quickly you are keying for 3 minutes. Look back at Lesson 11, page 81 to review the instructions.

Remember these rules:

• Don't look at the keyboard!

• Use the NoPeekee Keyboard for reference.

• Use the **Sitting Hints** to address your keyboard.

• Use the **Home Row Hints** to position your fingers.

• Tap the Enter key at the end of each line.

• This is a 3-minute test. Pace yourself. Don't wear yourself down in the first minute.

| 3/1   6/2   9/3   12/4 |

An effective way to grab your readers' attention in a

| 15/5   18/6   21/7   24/8 |

sea of words is to set some of your text in bold type. You

| 27/9   30/10   33/11   36/12 |

want to use this form of emphasis to highlight the important

| 39/13   42/14   45/15   48/16 |

parts of your message. Too many bolded words in a passage

| 51/17   54/18   57/19   60/20 |

will muddy the effect you are trying to achieve. Bolding

| 63/21   66/22   69/23   72/24 |

should be limited to titles; proper names; and key terms.

| 75/25   78/26   81/27   84/28 |

Italic type is thinner and slanted to the right. Italics are

| 87/29   90/30   93/31   96/32 |

used to set text apart to create an understated emphasis. The

| 99/33   102/34   105/35   108/36 |

use of italics should be limited to books, movies, magazines,

| 111/37   114/38   117/39   120/40 |

newspapers, trains, works of art, & foreign words or phrases.

How many correct WPM did you key this time?

CALCULATING WPM

You are getting pretty good at these 3-minute timings. Now, it's time to compute your speed, subtract the errors, and then post your mark of success.

Print your timing session. Circle each of the errors. Remember that you have to count only one error per word.

Also remember that you will have the opportunity to take this 3-minute timing three times and post your best score.

	Total Words Keyed	Total Words Keyed in 1 Minute (Total Words/3)	Total Number of Errors	Total Errors in 1 Minute (Total Errors/3)	Correct WPM (Total Words Keyed in 1 Minute Minus Number of Errors in 1 Minute)
3-Minute Test #1					
3-Minute Test #2					
3-Minute Test #3					

Return to the 3-minute timing and take it two more times. Enter each of the results and calculate your WPM.

Enter the best time in Appendix K.

EVEN MORE AUTOWORDS

OUTCOMES

- AutoWords
  we, you, his, her, him, are,
  but, not, has, had, have, they

- Using text styles
  bold, italics, underlined

Remember that the more AutoWords you know, the faster you will go.

You have keyed AutoWords and more AutoWords. Now you can practice even more AutoWords. The goal is automaticity.

WARM-UP (5 MINUTES)

Keep up the good work! Warm-up your finger, hands, and mind as you prepare for the ever-challenging four-letter AutoWord.

Create a **New** file and save it in the **Keyboarding** folder. Name it **Lesson16.doc**.

Remember to:

- Clip your NoPeekee Keyboard to the top of the page.

- Place your book in the holder and set it to the right of your keyboard.

- Sit up to your computer following the **Sitting Hints**.

- Set your timer to 5 minutes.

- Place your fingers lightly on the home row considering the **Home Row Hints**.

 Set your 5-minute timer. Go!

666 777 &&& """ ''' ggg hhh kkk ddd iii eee ooo www ppp qqq zzz bbb sss nnn xxx ,,, vvv ... /// ??? aaa ;;; ::: UUU ttt YYY666 777 &&& """ ''' ggg hhh kkk ddd666 777

about point daily chunk tricks skills single effort improve routing letters turning concept benefit between interesting keyboarders develop automaticity necessary AutoWords AutoBlends understand strings advance potential possible practicing

It is interesting to see that about 6 out of 7 keyboarders develop the automaticity necessary to benefit from AutoWords & AutoBlends. A few keyboarders seem to not understand or develop the concept of turning strings of letters into a single "chunk of effort." These keyboarders will never advance their keyboarding to the potential that is possible. Using these "tricks of the trade" makes the difference between a good keyboarder and a GREAT keyboarder. Practicing these skills in a daily routine will improve a keyboarder to the point of professionalism. It is fun too.

Save your work.

MORE AUTOWORDS

we, you, his, her, him, are, but, not, has, had, have, they

Expand your keyboarding vocabulary with this installment of AutoWords.

We introduce a couple of four-letter AutoWords in this lesson. As you remember, up till now we have limited the AutoWords and AutoBlends to three letters. In this lesson we introduce *they* which is the AutoWord *the* plus the letter *y*. If you have automatized *the* as a single set of strokes instead of three single strokes, adding the *y* shouldn't take too much effort. We are

introducing *have* as well because it fits nicely with *has* and *had*, and we know you can do it!

You may notice that the first two and last two words in the list are one-handed words. This means that you can key them using only a single hand. You will also notice that the two two-handed AutoWords, *his* and *her*, are composed of the AutoBlends *is* and *er* with an *h* added to the front. This is getting easier by the moment, isn't it?

Key each of these AutoWords. Remember to pronounce each word as you key it. Begin slowly and increase in speed as you feel it become an automatic process.

we we we we we we we we we we we we we we we we we we we we we we we we we we

you you you you you you you you you you you you you you you you you you you you you

his his his his his his his his his his his his his his his his his his his his his his

her her her her her her her her her her her her her her her her her her her her her her

him him him him him him him him him him him him him him him him him him him

are are are are are are are are are are are are are are are are are are are are are are

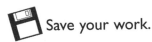Save your work.

SELF-TEST

Here is an opportunity to practice these new AutoWords.

we we we you you you his his his her her her him him him are are are we we you you her him him are are we you his her him are we you his her him are we you his her him

aid paid cash busy when zeal apron pluck young among keeps world change things listen office finish friends exciting provide looked learner gassing filled cashier requires students officer recognize financial application volunteer scholarship productive

We saw that you and Sam were gassing up his car. He paid the cashier when he filled his tank. He gave her a twenty-dollar bill. She gave him change from her cash apron.

You are among the top students for a scholarship. You need to go to the financial aid office by the end of the week. Your financial aid officer will provide help for you.

Mary and Jim recognize that his and her lives are filled with volunteer work. They are doing good things for the world. It is exciting to be friends with people like them.

His job requires extra pluck and zeal from every young wage earner. You know that if you listen closely, you will learn a great deal from him. He has lived a long life.

ADDITIONAL AUTOWORDS

but but but but but but but but but but but but but but but but but but but but but not not not not not not not not not not not not not not not not not not not not not

has has has has has has has has has has has has has has has has has has has has has has had had had had had had had had had had had had had had had had had had had had

have have have have have have have have have have have have have have have have have have they they they they they they they they they they they they they they they they they they

Save your work.

SELF-TEST

but but but not not not has has has had had had have have have they they they but has had had have have they they but not has had have they but but but not not not

life stars level theory effect opened quarry proven Street College entrees sizzled experience believes cultural restaurant visited excellent selection authentic new

Jesse has had a theory that stars have had an effect on his life but experience has not proven that they have had the effect he believes. He still depends on his star reports.

Paisley has had the level of cultural experience that her teachers had hoped in her study abroad. They appreciate her hard work and dedicated service to school.

A new Mexican restaurant has opened on College Street. We visited it last night and they had an excellent selection of authentic entrees. They had a great burrito.

Six big juicy steaks sizzled in a pan as five workmen left the quarry. They said that they had large appetites but they were not as big as they thought. They had leftovers.

USING TEXT STYLES

As descriptive and creative as your writing may be, sometimes you need to add format to the **actual** *text* that you <u>use</u>. Too often writers believe that they can EMPHASIZE WORDS BY PUTTING THEM IN ALL CAPITAL LETTERS. THE ONLY PROBLEM IS THAT WHEN ALL CAPITAL LETTERS ARE USED, THE ABILITY TO READ THE WORDS IS REDUCED DRAMATICALLY BECAUSE ALL THE LETTERS ARE RECTANGLES. A more effective way to emphasize words is sparingly to use **bold**, *italics*, <u>underline</u>, and combinations of these styles.

You have already learned about using the formatting toolbar or formatting palette to align text in Lesson 14. You can use these formatting tools to add styles to text. The styles icons are in the formatting toolbar/palette.

Styles can be assigned to text either before or after text is created, but styles are usually assigned after the text has been keyed.

Bolding Text

1. Key the following line:

This is a line of text that will be bolded.

2. Now, highlight the complete line of text.

- As you already know, you can highlight a single line of text by moving your cursor to the beginning of the intended text, and then holding down the left mouse button to drag the cursor to the end of the desired text passage, then releasing the mouse button.

- You can also highlight a complete line of text by clicking in the margin to the left of the desired line. Try moving your cursor to the left of the text you keyed above. It should cause your whole line to be highlighted. If it doesn't work, try moving the tip of the cursor arrow further to the left and clicking again. Sometimes it is a little tricky to make this technique work.

- You can also highlight words/paragraphs by clicking the left mouse button multiple times. Point to a word in a sentence/ paragraph. Double-click on the word to highlight it. Triple-click on the word, and the whole paragraph will be highlighted. If this whole paragraph happens to be a single sentence, as with the sentence you just keyed, the sentence will be highlighted.

3. No matter which method you used, now that you have highlighted the line you keyed you can bold the highlighted text by clicking on the **B** (Bold) icon in the formatting toolbar/palette. Depending on the font type and size you are using, you may not see much change in the darkness of the letters.

4. Click on the **B** (Bold) again and watch the text. You will see it unbold or at least become smaller.

Italicizing Text

1. Key the following line:
   This is a line of text that will be italicized.

2. Highlight the text using any of the three methods described above.

3. Click on the *I* (Italics) icon in the formatting toolbar/palette.

4. Click on the *I* (Italics) icon and watch the text. You will see it unitalicize.

Save your work.

Underlining Text

Follow the preceding steps but use the U̲ icon to underline some of the text.

Mixing Text Styles

You can also use mixed text styles. After keying some text and highlighting it just click the appropriate icons for the styles you wish to use. Key the following text and apply the mixtures of styles identified in the text itself.

This line of text is both bolded and italicized.

You might find the underlining and italicizing in this sentence to be redundant.

Include all three styles in these lines of text: bold, italics, and underline.

Stylizing Specific Words or Phrases

You can also stylize specific words or phrases in your writing. Just highlight the desired text in your writing and then stylize it accordingly.

Create these following lines of text complete with the styles shown in the example.

Bolding and *Italicizing* text can add character to your writing. Get it?

Depending on what report-writing format you are using, *italicizing* and <u>underlining</u> are often used to specify publication titles.

Save your work.

CORRECTIVE WORK

Proofread your work.

- Print the file **Lesson16.doc**.

- Identify the words that were keyed incorrectly.

- Create a new file and save it as **L16Practice.doc**.

- Key each of these words five times correctly and save your file.

5 % 8 * AND AUTOBLENDS

OUTCOMES

- Keys: 5 % 8 and *
- AutoBlend Suffixes ial, est, ful, ity, ion, ive, ous
- Five-minute timing

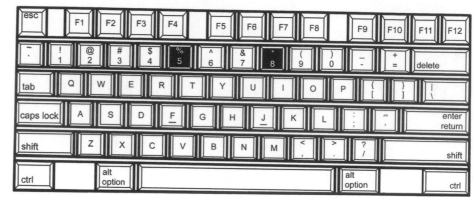

Figure 17.1

Expanding your numeric facility is important. This lesson will introduce you to two more numbers and a couple of symbols that you will use in your writing. These are in the top row, so you will be able to continue practicing your *big stretch* (see Figure 17.1).

WARM-UP (5 MINUTES)

Rehearse your responses with these warm-up workouts.

Set your 5-minute timer. Go!

Create a **New** file and save it in the **Keyboarding** folder. Name it **Lesson17.doc**.

Remember to:

- Clip your NoPeekee Keyboard to the top of the page.
- Place your book in the holder and set it to the right of your keyboard.
- Sit at your computer following the **Sitting Hints**.
- Set your timer to 5 minutes.
- Place your fingers lightly on the home row considering the **Home Row Hints**.

666 777 &&& fff kkk FFF KKK ppp qqq www OOO ccc nnn VVV mmm xxx bbb GGG aaa LLL sss xxx zzz EEE rrr ttt yyy uuu iii 666 777 &&& fff kkk FFF KKK ppp qqq www

half email level doing desire letters master driven keying quicker without looking Learning symbols difficult rewarding increase success keyboarding personal communication chatting probably academic professional keyboard remember perfect

Learning to key the symbols in the top row without looking is difficult but rewarding as you increase your level of success in keyboarding. Your desire to master these symbols will be driven by the type of keyboarding you will be doing. If you are going to be writing only personal communications like letters, email and chatting, then you will probably use only about half of the symbols. If your keying will be more on the academic or professional level, you will probably use most of the symbols. Either way, the more you learn, the quicker you will key your communication. Remember that perfect practice makes perfect so keep your air keyboard handy.

 Save your work.

NEW CHARACTERS 5 AND %

Figure 17.2

Once again, you will be working with a two-character key. Tap the 5 key in the top row with your left forefinger and you will key a 5. Add the Shift key when you tap the 5 key and you will produce a % sign (see Figure 17.2).

Place your fingers on the home row. Move your left forefinger from the F key to the 5 key and return to the F key in the home row. Do this again. It's a big *stretch*, but you can do it. Practice using the following exercise.

fff 555 fff 555 fff 555 fff 555 fff 555 fff 555 fff 555 fff 555 fff 555 fff 555 fff fff 555 fff

Good job. Now it's time to involve the character key %. Move your right pinky to hold down the Shift key and then tap the 5 key with your forefinger. Do it again. Give it a little practice with the following exercises.

fff FFF %%% fff FFF %%% fff FFF %%% fff FFF %%% fff FFF %%% fff fff FFF %%% fff

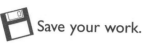 Save your work.

NEW CHARACTERS TRYOUT 5 AND %

Practice your new skills on these exercises.

fff 555 fff FFF %%% FFF fff 555 %%% 555 FFF fff FFF %%% 555 FFF fff 555 fff FFF
FFF 555 %%% fff FFF %%% 555 %%% fff FFF %%% 555 %%% fff FFF fff 555 fff FFF

55% 555 55555 555-5657 65 75% 5% 567 cancel senior Young discount showers
area code America assistance restaurants interesting Minnesota significant Roman

Did you know that you can get a senior discount at restaurants if you are over 55?
I would guess that over 55% of seniors use the discount. That is a significant %.

5 is an interesting number. 5 is written as V in Roman numerals. The zip code for Young
America, Minnesota is 55555. The 555 area code is reserved for directory assistance.

 Save your work.

SELF-TEST

555-5657 65 75% 56 5 67 55% 56% 5% 567 77 NASA NASA deal deal great great
report report probe probe cancel cancel support support computer computer dollars

showers showers operators operators whether whether probably probably planned
activities SPACEWARN SPACEWARN Bulletin Bulletin Number Number satellites

If you need support for your computer, call 555-5657. 65 operators will be there to assist
75% of the time. Full support costs 56 dollars each year. This can be a great deal.

The weather report on 67 AM says a 55% chance of showers over 56% of the valley. This will probably cause 5% of planned high school athletic activities to be canceled. SPACEWARN Bulletin Number 567 was published by NASA to report on satellites and space probe activity. It contains a great deal of useful information and is on the Web.

The July sun caused a fragment of black pine wax to ooze on the velvet quilt in 77 degree weather. 56% of the wax dripped to the ground throughout 65% of the day.

 Save your work.

NEW CHARACTERS 8 AND *

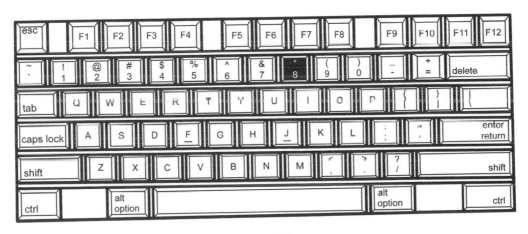

Figure 17.3

Adding 8 to your repertoire will now give you four numerals to use for your mathematical calculations (see Figure 17.3). The * character is also used to signify multiplication in spreadsheets, so you can now write a mathematical formula as well.

Place your fingers on the home row. Tap the K key a few times. Now make the big stretch to the 8 key. Tap the 8 key and return to the K key. Do this a few times and then practice the process using the following exercises.

kkk 888 kkk 888 kkk 888 kkk 888 kkk 888 kkk 888 kkk 888 kkk 888 kkk 888 kkk 888 kkk

Now it's time to kick your left pinky into action. Hold down the Shift key with your left pinky and then stretch your right forefinger to the 8 key. Do you see stars (technically asterisks)? Return to your K key and then key a * again. Practice these exercises.

kkk KKK *** kkk KKK *** kkk KKK *** kkk KKK *** kkk KKK *** kkk KKK *** kkk

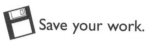 Save your work.

NEW CHARACTERS TRYOUT 8 AND *

kkk 888 kkk KKK *** KKK kkk 888 kkk KKK *** KKK *** kkk *** kkk 888 kkk KKK
jj aa kk ss ll ww ii ee oo dd 55 66 77 %% && 888 *** tt yy ee ww zz oo jj aa kk ss ll

* 7 * 8 56 58% ** 86 56th 75% 86ed 76% 87 55 writing writing papers papers indicate formula formula format format asterisks asterisks indicate indicate included included footnotes footnotes emphasize emphasize effective effective multiplication multiplication

The * symbol is sometimes used to indicate multiplication. You use this in the formula equals 56. This format is used less than 58% of the time. It originated with computers.

One * is an asterisk. Multiple ** are asterisks. Asterisks are often used to indicate footnotes in research papers. I once read 58 footnotes in a graduate-level research paper.

Albry placed 86 *s at the top of the 56th page to emphasize the ideas included. It was so effective that 75% of the people read the material. This became standard.

The project was 86ed so about 76% of the 87 assigned engineers were reassigned. The other ten engineers were over 55 and decided to retire. Over 67% of them were rehired.

 Save your work.

SELF-TEST

87 7 8 6 75% 85 dance dance people people strokes strokes sunny sunny beach beach pieces pieces bronze bronze playing playing least least excited excited quaint quaint

paddled jewelry jewelry wonderful wonderful beautifully beautifully coordinated excavations excavations landmark landmark Ocracoke Ocracoke North Carolina

Ana and Al loved to dance with their canoes. They paddled to music: 7 strokes forward, 5 strokes back, 6 strokes right and 8 strokes left. It was beautifully coordinated.

Terri shot an 87 in her golf game last week. She felt that she was playing up to about 88% of her potential. She tries to play at least once every 7 or 8 days. She drives well.

Robin and Magda have been having a wonderful time on the sunny beach in Ocracoke, North Carolina, for the past 6 days. They were in water 75% of the time.

While making deep excavations we found some 85 quaint bronze jewelry pieces. It was a landmark find that excited the people who were working at new the dig.

Save your work.

AUTOBLEND SUFFIXES

ial, est, ful, ity, ion, ive, ous

You have already been introduced to suffixes. Those are the endings of words that change and clarify their meaning. These are all three-letter suffixes. Two of these suffixes are one-handed AutoBlends. Can you figure out which ones they are?

Begin keying these suffixes slowly. Feel the flow as you key them. You may make consistent mistakes as you begin on a new AutoBlend that might be a conflict with a previously learned AutoBlend. Don't get frustrated. Recognize this and work your way through it. Pronounce each AutoBlend as you work.

ial ial ial ial ial ial ial ial ial ial ial ial ial ial ial ial ial ial ial ial ial ial ial ial ial ial ial

est est est est est est est est est est est est est est est est est est est est est est est est est est

ful ful ful ful ful ful ful ful ful ful ful ful ful ful ful ful ful ful ful ful ful ful ful ful
ity ity ity ity ity ity ity ity ity ity ity ity ity ity ity ity ity ity ity ity ity ity ity ity

ion ion ion ion ion ion ion ion ion ion ion ion ion ion ion ion ion ion ion ion ion
ive ive ive ive ive ive ive ive ive ive ive ive ive ive ive ive ive ive ive ive ive ive ive
ous ous ous ous ous ous ous ous ous ous ous ous ous ous ous ous ous ous ous ous ous

 Save your work.

NEW AUTOBLEND SUFFIXES TRYOUT

ial ial ial est est est ful ful ful ity ity ity ion ion ion ive ive ive ous ous ous ial ial est est
ity ion ion ive ive ous ous ial est ful ity ion ive ous ial ial ial est est est ful ful ful ity ity

best best jest jest dives dives Orion Orion fitful fitful action action vanity vanity levity
famous famous glacial glacial Erosion Erosion clarity clarity reunion reunion closest

playful playful greatest greatest sessions sessions deepest deepest gorgeous gorgeous
hilarious hilarious abrasion abrasion beautiful beautiful luminous luminous Gravity

Louise made five of her deepest dives in the gorgeous Barrier Reef in Australia. The
beautiful azure water had amazingly luminous clarity. Mark watched Reef Sharks.

Orion, the greatest hunter of all time, stands in the heavens as a constellation eternally
looking toward dawn. He is forever running from Scorpio, the scorpion, who attacked him.

Erosion is the destructive wearing away of land or soil by the action of wind, water,
or ice. Glacial erosion involves abrasion by a grinding effect of rock fragments.

During our reunion of closest friends we shared fitful sessions of hilarious levity. Our
playful times included some of the best jests I can ever remember. It was most jovial.

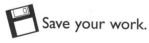 Save your work.

SELF-TEST

city city best best molar molar tooth tooth speed speed energy energy limits limits chance useful useful serious serious utility utility cavity cavity curious curious careful

youthful youthful direction direction vigorous vigorous reactions reactions conservation conservation hopeful hopeful dutiful dutiful zest zest thunderous thunderous publicity

Forrest had a serious cavity in his youthful molar. His dentist said there was an 87% chance that the tooth would have to be extracted in 6 or 7 days. Forrest was unhappy.

The Insurance Institute of Highway Safety states where speed limits were raised to 65 mph in '87, there was an increase of fifteen to twenty % more deaths annually.

The city utility company is careful to use resources in the best possible way. They provide useful direction for customers curious about energy conservation.

We quickly seized the black axle and just saved the wagon from going past him. He was most appreciative of our vigorous help and quick reactions.

CORRECTIVE WORK

Proofread your work:

- Print the file **Lesson17.doc**.
- Identify the words that were keyed incorrectly.
- Create a new file and save it as **L17Practice.doc**.
- Key each of these words five times correctly and save your file.

IMPROVEMENT WORK

Return to the preceding twelve lines. Open the file **Lesson17.doc**, and key these lines again. You should be able to complete the task more quickly and more accurately.

FIVE-MINUTE TIMING

You read that correctly: this is a 5-minute timing. You have been showing improvement with the three-minute timings. Now, it's time to raise the bar a little. You will compute your

WPM the same way you did the three-minute timing, except you will divide by 5 instead of 3. Take the timing twice and record your statistics in the chart at the end of the timing. Record your best time in Appendix K.

Here is your opportunity to show your improvement. Remember the rules!

• Don't look at the keyboard!

• Use the NoPeekee Keyboard for reference.

• Use the **Sitting Hints** to address your keyboard.

• Use the **Home Row Hints** to position your fingers.

• Tap the Enter key at the end of each line.

It's time to start your trial run. You will notice that the lines are only 10 words long. This will allow you to divide evenly by 5 minutes. If you get to the end of the text, start at the top again.

The text for this timing has been laid out to make computing your WPM simple. There are 10 words (50 characters) per line. This means that if you key them all in one minute, you will have completed 10 WPM. If you complete them all in 5 minutes, you will have keyed at 2 WPM. Notice that there are pairs of numbers throughout the text (e.g., 10/2). The first number (i.e., 10) indicates the number of words to that point. The second number (i.e., 2) indicates your WPM if you reach this point in 5 minutes.

 Set your timer for 5 minutes. Go!

```
                5/1                              10/2
    Keying numbers and symbols can be very difficult.
            15/3                            20/4
You may be tempted to look at the keyboard and to
            25/5                            30/6
hunt and peck when keying them. While you may be
            35/7                            40/8
more accurate while you are doing this method, it will
            45/9                            50/10
bring your keyboarding speed down to a slow crawl.
            55/11                           60/12
    Consider the process you must use when hunting
```

65/13   70/14

and pecking for keys. You recognize that you have

75/15   80/16

to use the top row. You then move your eyes from

85/17   90/18

the page to the keyboard. You find the key in the

95/19   100/20

top row and tap it. You look on the screen to see

105/21   110/22

if you got it correct. Finally, you return your

115/23   120/24

fingers to the home row and your eyes to the page.

125/25   130/26

    Spending extra time and extra effort learning

135/27   140/28

the positions of the keys on the keyboard will help

145/29   150/30

you greatly in the future as you learn to master

155/31   160/32

touch keyboarding. The most important benefit you

165/33   170/34

will experience is being able to key a stream of

175/35   180/36

thought without having to hunt and peck for keys

185/37   190/38

because you have well developed the memory traces

195/39   200/40

necessary to automate the keyboarding process.

CALCULATING WPM

Five minutes is a long time but you did it! You keyed a twenty-line document. That is almost a full page. Even if you didn't complete all of it, you are well on your way to keying full reports or long letters or composing manuscripts by yourself. Consider your performance on this test and enter the statistics in the "5-Minute test #1" row of the following table. Complete the rest of the statistics by computing them as necessary.

	Total Words Keyed	Total Words Keyed in 1 Minute (Total Words/5)	Total Number of Errors	Total Errors in 1 Minute (Total Errors/5)	Correct WPM (Total Words Keyed in 1 Minute Minus Number of Errors in 1 Minute)
5-Minute Test #1					
5-Minute Test #2					

Return to the 5-minute timing and take it one more time. Enter your statistics in the table and do the calculations.

Turn to Appendix K and enter the information about your best time in the Self-Progress Chart.

You're on your way to becoming a much better keyboarder.

3 # 4 $ AND AUTOBLENDS

OUTCOMES

- Keys: 3 # 4 and $
- AutoBlend Suffixes able, ible, tion, ation, ition, less

Figure 18.1

Now let's move down the line of numbers to the left. This lesson involves only your left hand, so give your right one a rest. You will stretch to the 3 and 4 keys (see Figure 18.1).

WARM-UP (5 MINUTES)

Rehearse your responses with these warm-up workouts.

Create a **New** file and save it in the **Keyboarding** folder. Name it **Lesson17.doc**.

 Set your 5-minute timer. Go!

Remember to:

- Clip your NoPeekee Keyboard to the top of the page.
- Place your book in the holder and set it to the right of your keyboard.
- Sit at your computer following the **Sitting Hints**.
- Set your timer to 5 minutes.
- Place your fingers lightly on the home row considering the **Home Row Hints**.

555 444 666 777 ### *** &&& ddd LLL SSS ttt DDD III ooo www ppp eee RRR QQQ zzz NNN bbb vvv CCC ggg HHH ;;; """ XXX uuu 555 444 666 777 ### *** &&& ddd

been said that born were when word hold does much Baby type write after older using fluid cover simple tools carbon errors Boomer Typing became advent grammar created Technology processing correction environment correction provides documents typewritten

It has been said that "Technology is anything that was invented after you were born." Therefore, if you were born after the mid-1980s when personal computers became popular, the advent of word processing does not hold much meaning for you. If you are a Baby Boomer or older, you remember the process of using a typewriter to type a paper. Typing errors involved using correction fluid to cover your errors or even completely retyping a page with too many errors. There was even a time when copies of typewritten documents could be created only using carbon paper to type two copies at the same time. Word processing allows writers to write in an electronic environment that makes correction simple and provides tools like spelling and grammar checkers.

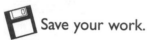Save your work.

NEW CHARACTERS 3 AND

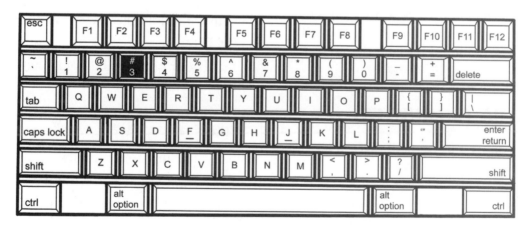

Figure 18.2

Once again, you will be working with a two-character key. Tap the 3 key in the top row with your left middle finger and you will key a 3. Add the Shift key when you tap the 3 key and you will produce a # sign (see Figure 18.2).

Place your fingers on the home row. Move your left middle finger from the D key to the 3 key and return to the D key in the home row. Do this again. It's a big *stretch*, but you can do it. Practice using the following exercise.

ddd 333 ddd 333 ddd 333 ddd 333 ddd 333 ddd 333 ddd 333 ddd 333 ddd 333 ddd

Good job. Now it's time to involve the character # key. This symbol may look like a tic-tac-toe board to the uninitiated, but # is a symbol used to indicate the word *number*, as in "Cubs are #1." The # is also used to represent pounds, as in "The hamburger weighed 1#." In editing, it is used to indicate the need to insert a space. Move your right pinky to hold down the Shift key and then tap the 3 key with your middle finger. Do it again. Give it a little practice with the following exercises.

ddd DDD ### ddd DDD ### ddd DDD ### ddd DDD ### ddd DDD ddd DDD ###

 Save your work.

NEW CHARACTERS TRYOUT 3 AND

Practice your new skills on these exercises.

ddd 333 ddd DDD ### DDD ddd 333 ### 333 DDD ddd DDD ### 333 333 ### 333 DDD 333 ### ddd DDD ### 333 ### ddd DDD ### 333 ### ddd DDD 333 ### 333

336 3:40 #3458 37 33 3333 76 .33% 3 '64 75% #376 leave active Chicago elation tranquil airport political science zestfully incredible studying semester learning meaningful education interest restoring pursue interest restoring painted mechanics completion

Jeff will zestfully enjoy his incredible 336 days of studying political science in France. He will leave from Chicago airport in August at 3:40 p.m. on flight #3458 at gate 37.

Chris was filled with elation during his first 33 days working at the Jamaican restaurant at 3333 Rainbow Drive. 33% of the customers eat there at least 3 times a week.

Wes wants to pursue his interest in auto mechanics. He has been restoring a red '64 Ford Mustang. He has painted #376 on its hood. He has completed about 75%.

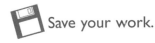 Save your work.

NEW CHARACTERS 4 AND $

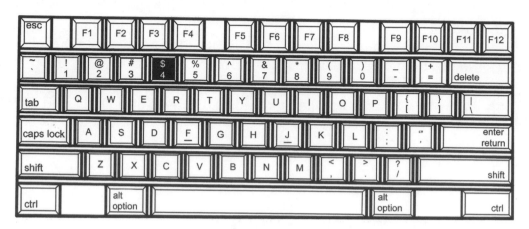

Figure 18.3

Do you have $4 in your pocket? Well, if you do, you will be able to key about it using the new skills you will learn in this section. The 4 and $ symbols are keyed using the middle finger (see Figure 18.3).

Place your fingers on the home row. Tap the D key a few times. Now, make the *big stretch* with your left middle finger to the 4 key. Tap the 4 key and return to the D key. Repeat this movement again and again. Now, practice the process using the following exercise.

ddd 444 ddd 444 ddd 444 ddd 444 ddd 444 ddd 444 ddd 444 ddd 444 ddd 444 ddd 444

Now, it's time to kick your right pinky into action. Hold down the Shift key with your right pinky and then stretch to the 4 key. Now you are "in the money ($)!" Return to

the D key. Tap the 4 key and then the $ key again and again. Expand your practice with the following exercise.

ddd DDD $$$ ddd DDD $$$ ddd DDD $$$ ddd DDD $$$ ddd DDD $$$ $$$ ddd

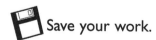Save your work.

NEW CHARACTERS TRYOUT 4 AND $

**ddd 444 ddd DDD $$$ DDD ddd 444 ddd DDD $$$ DDD $$$ ddd $$$ DDD $$$
kk dd ll ss ;; aa yy 66 uu 77 tt 55 dd 44 dd 33 ## 88 ** && %% $$ nn zz kk dd ll ss ;;**

**$44.44 444 44 $$$ 4 $44 44 fish rock Lane ledge doing happy teeth sports store
Court minutes extraordinary accountant employees guidance barracuda basketball.**

The basketball shoes cost $44.44. Eric had to go to the sports store at 444 East Court. It took 4 minutes to get there and 44 minutes to buy them. Eric ran 44 blocks here.

Beth saw $$$ in her eyes. This was good because she is an extraordinary accountant. Her 44 employees look to her for guidance. Lewis was happy to see Beth doing well.

It cost Dennis $44 to dive the reef in Cozumel, Mexico. He dove to 44 feet deep and saw a barracuda under a rock ledge. It is a fearsome fish with large sharp teeth.

 Save your work.

SELF-TEST

Kathy has developed a 4-level curriculum for her educational program. She has 43 students in 3 classrooms in her school. They have a busy year ahead of them in the teaching.

Ashworth was competing in the $60,000 Johnson & SonJohn Open Golf Tournament. He was hitting over two hundred yards on 73% of his tee shots. It was a combination of skill.

Aricia taught keyboarding to her 35 4th grade students. She integrated keyboarding with her writing program & 68% of her students increased their personal writing skills.

The job requires extra pluck and zeal from each of the 465 young wage earners. They can invest their $$ in a 6% interest Certificate of Deposit. Their money will double in twelve years.

 Save your work.

AUTOBLEND SUFFIXES

able, ible, tion, ation, ition, less

Now it's time to use four- and five-letter suffixes. Yes, earlier we noted that we would be limiting the AutoBlends to three-letter combinations, but suffixes can almost be thought of as "throwaway" word parts. If you automate commonly used suffixes like *tion*, *ation*, or *ition*, your keyboarding efficiency will skyrocket. You have had enough experience keyboarding to enable you to master these longer AutoBlends.

As before, begin keying these suffixes slowly. Build the rhythm for each AutoBlend. Pronounce each suffix as you key the letters.

Work faster as you master each one. Key like a pro! You can do it!

able able able able able able able able able able able able able able able able able able able able able

ible ible ible ible ible ible ible ible ible ible ible ible ible ible ible ible ible ible ible ible ible

tion tion tion tion tion tion tion tion tion tion tion tion tion tion tion tion tion tion tion tion tion

ation ation ation ation ation ation ation ation ation ation ation ation ation ation ation ation ation

ition ition ition ition ition ition ition ition ition ition ition ition ition ition ition ition ition ition

less less less less less less less less less less less less less less less less less less less less less

 Save your work.

NEW AUTOBLEND SUFFIXES TRYOUT

able able able ible ible ible tion tion tion ation ation ation ition ition ition less less less able ible ible tion tion ation ation ition ition less less able ible tion ation ition less able able able

fable Sable stable tables elation lotions potions tireless reckless hopeless portions creation faultless locations positions conditions condition incredible speechless partitions contradictions

The creation of the fable stable is incredible. The positions of the partitions provide an interesting condition for its speechless inhabitants, the horses. They are faultless creatures.

Both Lo's Mercury Sable and his excitement for driving were tireless. Unfortunately, these two conditions provided a hopeless contradiction of desire and access. Cannot find those tires.

Merlin provides portions of potions to use as lotions on the beaches of the oceans. When people use these lotions at these locations they are able to avoid bad sunburn.

West quickly gave Bert handsome prizes for six juicy plums. Bert's elation over these was reckless. He toppled tables and tumbled tulips. It was a creation of commotion.

 Save your work.

SELF-TEST

#34 #43 $34.43 #64 cable nation visible audible durable tuition credible fearless vocation bendable flawless feasible helpless deposition duration education adulation desirable population graduation connection preparation impossible ventilation corporation

Lakyle found it impossible to believe that the #34 cable was more bendable and durable in ventilation systems than #43 cable that cost $34.43 more per foot. It defied imagination.

Sibley Ontible offered a credible deposition as evidence for a feasible motive that was visible to the fearless jury who had been there for the duration of the lengthy trial.

Francis began tax preparation as a vocation. His calculations were flawless and he earned the adulation of desirable corporations from across the nation. He is able to select his clients.

Most of the student population is helpless in affecting the rising tuition costs for their education. For some, such escalation has dimmed their aspirations for graduation.

Whenever the black fox jumped, the squirrel gazed suspiciously. This $64 photo-op lasted for only about 3 or 4 seconds. It was an unusual collection of animal motion.

CORRECTIVE WORK

Proofread your work.

• Print the file **Lesson18.doc**.

• Identify the words that were keyed incorrectly.

• Create a new file and save it as **L18Practice.doc**.

• Key each of these words five times correctly and save your file.

IMPROVEMENT WORK

Return to the preceding thirteen lines. Open the file, **Lesson18.doc**, and key these lines again. You should be able to complete the task more quickly and more accurately.

9 (0) AND AUTOBLENDS

OUTCOMES

- Keys: 9 (0 and)
- AutoBlend Suffixes ment, ness, ative, itive, eous, ious
- Five-minute timing

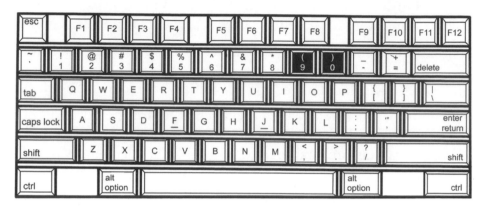

Figure 19.1

Now it's time to give your right hand that *big stretch*. You will be exercising your right middle and ring fingers by tapping the 9 and 0 keys (see Figure 19.1). You will be surprised about how often you use the related parenthesis symbols, (and), in your writing. This means that you can now expand the depth of your writing by including parenthetical phrases (phrases that further clarify something you just said).

WARM-UP (5 MINUTES)

Rehearse your responses with these warm-up workouts.

Create a **New** file and save it in the **Keyboarding** folder. Name it **Lesson19.doc**.

Remember to:

- Clip your NoPeekee Keyboard to the top of the page.
- Place your book in the holder and set it to the right of your keyboard.
- Sit at your computer following the **Sitting Hints**.
- Set your timer to 5 minutes.
- Place your fingers lightly on the home row considering the **Home Row Hints**.

 Set your 5-minute timer. Go!

333 444 ### $$$ sss ddd SSS DDD nnn vvv mmm ccc zzz /// NNN VVV WWW OOO
aaa ;;; AAA ::: 555 %%% 666 777 &&& 888 *** 333 444 ### $$$ sss ddd SSS DDD
World Wide Web water cycle phrase quotes simply really search engine Notice diagram

writing keying instead separate favorite actually planning sentence important searching describing information statement effective experience enjoyable words/phrases

Before you begin searching for information on the World Wide Web, you must first know what you really want to find. Instead of simply going to your favorite search engine and keying in a couple of words, you should begin by actually writing (or keying) a sentence describing what you want to find. It might read, "I want to find a diagram describing the water cycle." The important words/phrases in your statement are "diagram" and "water cycle." You will want to enter the first word, diagram, into your search engine. You will also want to enter the phrase "water cycle" into your search engine. Notice that water cycle is in quotes. That tells the search engine to look for the phrase instead of the separate words. This simple process of planning your search will make your searching experience more effective and more enjoyable.

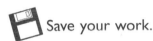 Save your work.

NEW CHARACTERS 9 AND (

Tapping the 9 key is not so difficult as it may appear. It's just a matter of flattening out your right hand to stretch your middle finger. Try it. Place your fingers on the home row and flatten out your right hand. Now move your hand a little to the right to touch the 9 key. Just a little to the right and stretch. To key the (symbol move your left pinky to hold the Shift key. Flatten out your right hand and stretch the middle finger to the 9(key. Tap it and you will see a (on your screen. Nice going. Do it again and again. Use the following exercise for your workout.

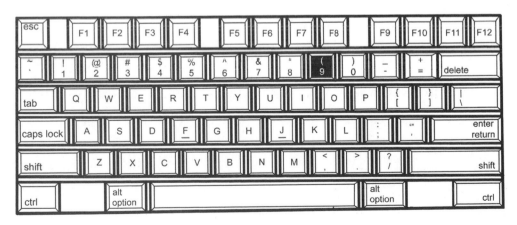

Figure 19.2

999 III (((KKK (((III 999 (((999 (((III KKK III (((III 999 III (((KKK III (((999 (((III

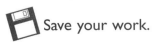 Save your work.

NEW CHARACTERS TRYOUT 9 AND (

Practice your newly developed skills here.

kkk iii 999 iii kkk (((III KKK iii 999 (((iii III kkk KKK 999 (((999 (((iii kkk iii 999 III KKK iii 999 (((KKK III (((III KKK 999 iii kkk III (((999 III iii KKK kkk (((999

999 (99 (9 (99-cent cost cents stores police twenty quickly England response sentence emergency customers purchased difficult incorporate Suburbia downtown different

England has a 999 emergency phone number contacting the police quickly. Only twenty calls made to 999 last year needed emergency response. That means a lot of false alarms.

99-cent stores are stores where all 99,999 of the items for sale cost 99 cents. Yesterday, 99 customers purchased 9 items or more at the 9 99-cent stores in downtown Suburbia.

Trying to write a sentence with a (is a difficult thing to do. I tried 9 different ways to incorporate (into a sentence but (doesn't fit except in sentences like this one.

Save your work.

SELF-TEST

39 9 34 5 99.9% 53% high high wire wire kept kept email email collect collect symbols enhance enhance phrases phrases closing closing amazing amazing creating creating

courage courage watching watching purchased purchased Glow-in-the-Dark Otherwise Otherwise expressive expressive emoticons emoticons parenthetical

Bazyli purchased 39 boxes of Oat-ios cereal. He wanted to collect all 9 of the Glow-in-the-Dark watches. Unfortunately, he ended up with 34 green watches.

(symbols can be used to enhance your email by creating expressive emoticons: smiling (-: frowning :-(crying :'-(winking (-; angelic (-: 0 and a moustache (*8

(99.9% of parenthetical phrases will end with a closing parentheses but not this one. Good writers need to spend 53% of their time writing, reading & thinking. Anyway, they should.

Jelly-like above the high wire, six quaking pachyderms kept the culmination of the extravaganza in a dazzling state of flux. Their concentration & courage was amazing.

 Save your work.

NEW CHARACTERS 0 AND)

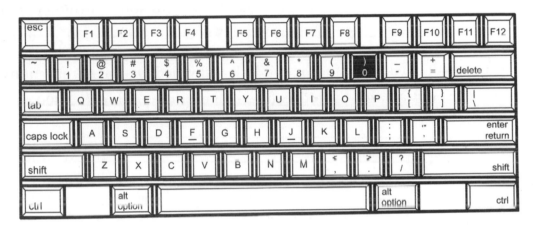

Figure 19.3

Stretching your right ring finger to the top row isn't too difficult. Just as you flattened your hand to reach the 9 key with your middle finger, you can flatten your right hand to place your right ring finger on the 0 key (see Figure 19.3). Try it. Your fingers automatically rest on the home row by now, don't they? Let them find their home and then flatten your hand. Use your right ring finger to tap the 0 key. It worked! Do it again. Practice with these exercises:

lll ooo 000 lll ooo 000 lll ooo 000 lll ooo 000 lll ooo 000 lll ooo 000 lll lll ooo 000 lll

Pinky time! Find the symbol that will complete your parenthetical phrases, the) [close parenthesis]. Hold down the left Shift key once again and then stretch your right ring finger to hit the) key. Do it again. Practice some more here.

LLL OOO))) OOO LLL OOO))) OOO LLL OOO))) OOO))) OOO OOO LLL OOO

 Save your work.

NEW CHARACTERS TRYOUT 0 AND)

lll ooo 000 LLL))) LLL lll 000 ooo lll LLL))) 000 lll OOO))) 000 LLL lll LLL))) 000 lll kk ss ll aa " aa 00)) 99 ((ii uu ee rr 33 44 ss ee ww dd tt)) 00 qq nn zz kk ss ll aa " aa

000s 99,000 99 85,000 50,000 35,000 10,000 25,000 brew toxic exotic wizards number Grumpy watching written questions difficult confusing thousands equations complicated

Large numbers in tables often drop the thousands (000s) so that 99,000 would be written as 99 (the 000 is just assumed as being part of the number.) It can be a confusing format.

Long equations like 85,000--50,000 equals 35,000 are easy to solve when they contain strings of 000. More complicated equations like (85,000--50,000)--10,000 are difficult.

Grumpy wizards make toxic brew for the evil Jack and veiled Queen. All questions asked by five watching experts amazed the judge. It was an exotic event for all 3,000 of them.

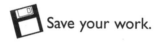 Save your work.

SELF-TEST

909 9th 836 3:30 10 #5 #9 90 900 oxen oxen scout scout acted acted jaded jaded troop leave leave river river people people fallen fallen village village spilled spilled Highway

liquids liquids aisles aisles bottles bottles camping camping cleaning cleaning chocolate attendants attendants zombies zombies necessary necessary quaintly quaintly

Dean is in scout troop 909 (the first scout troop in the Valley) that is going on its 9th camping trip of the year. They will leave on Highway 836 at 3:30 and travel 10 hours.

**ATTENTION: Please look out for spilled liquids on aisles #5 and #9. 90 bottles (and jars) of chocolate drinks have fallen (and broken) there. We have 3 attendants cleaning.

Learning the) symbol enables you to create more emoticons: Band-Aid (offering help) (::():::) Can't stop talking :-( ) yelling :-(O) hug ((((name)))) hugs & kisses (()):**

Jaded zombies acted quaintly but kept driving their oxen forward. These oxen were necessary for the 900 people in the village by the river. 900 zombies can be useful.

 Save your work.

AUTOBLEND SUFFIXES

ment, ness, ative, itive, eous, ious

Have you been able to key AutoBlends as a single action? This is a single action that involves multiple finger movements, much like tapping your fingers on the table in succession. If you don't feel comfortable with the four- and five-letter AutoBlends, think of how you are doing with the shorter two- and three-letter AutoBlends. The more you practice, the easier it will become.

Here is another half dozen AutoBlends. As always, begin keying them slowly. Look for a feeling of automaticity as you key each AutoBlend repeatedly. Say each AutoBlend as you key it.

ment ment ment ment ment ment ment ment ment ment ment ment ment ment ment

ness ness ness ness ness ness ness ness ness ness ness ness ness ness ness ness ness ness

ative ative ative ative ative ative ative ative ative ative ative ative ative ative ative ative

itive itive itive itive itive itive itive itive itive itive itive itive itive itive itive itive itive itive

eous eous eous eous eous eous eous eous eous eous eous eous eous eous eous eous eous

ious ious ious ious ious ious ious ious ious ious ious ious ious ious ious ious ious ious

 Save your work.

NEW AUTOBLEND SUFFIXES TRYOUT

ment ment ment ness ness ness ative ative ative itive itive itive eous eous eous ious ious ment ness ness ative ative itive itive eous eous ious ious ment ment ness ness ness ative

cement lioness basement fragment dampness kindness darkness fondness safeness snugness positive monument curiously formative sensitive competitive liveliness amazement environment pigment ornament creative enjoyment attachment preparedness

In the basement of the monument there is a fragment of cement. The dampness and darkness of the basement seems curiously prohibitive. The pigment of the ornament.

Our teacher's sensitive kindness creates a positive and noncompetitive environment in our classroom. This fills our learning experience with liveliness, amazement and enjoyment.

Jo had a fondness for the lioness at the zoo. She relished the formative positive safeness and snugness that the lioness provided for her mysterious cubs. They had a strong attachment. Big July earthquakes confound zany experimental vows of containment. It is difficult to contain something as quick yet ferocious as an unexpected earthquake.

 Save your work.

SELF-TEST

(980) 555-5555 45% 59% XYZ sales sales year year Idaho Idaho North North travel travel Oregon Oregon Alaska Alaska frozen frozen Caribou Caribou Digital Digital Carolina

talkative talkative fulfillment fulfillment competitive competitive consecutive consecutive improvement improvement attachment attachment telephone telephone adventure

Judy moved from Northern California to Oregon to Alaska to Southern California and then to Idaho. She has an attachment to travel. She receives fulfillment from traveling.

You can call Roberto in North Carolina at (980) 555-5555. He loves to talk about technology & learning & art. He can be talkative when you can call him by telephone.

The XYZ Digital Corporation has experienced a 45% improvement in sales for the past 3 consecutive years. Due to its competitive edge, this company has seen a 90% rise in profits.

The explorer was frozen in his big kayak just after making quizzical discoveries. Caribou are deer that live in North America & Greenland. They eat moss, green plants.

 Save your work.

CORRECTIVE WORK

Proofread your work.

- Print the file **Lesson19.doc**.

- Identify the words that were keyed incorrectly.

- Create a new file and save it as **L19Practice.doc**.

- Key each of these words five times correctly and save your file.

IMPROVEMENT WORK

Return to the preceding twelve lines. Open the file **Lesson19.doc**, and key these lines again. You should be able to complete the task more quickly and more accurately.

FIVE-MINUTE TIMING

Do you have another 5 minutes? Here is your opportunity to continue showing improvement with your keyboarding efforts. Remember that the only way you will increase your speed is to practice your keyboarding and receive feedback about your accuracy. Only perfect practice makes perfect.

Do the timing twice and record your statistics in the chart at the end of the timing. Record your best time in the back of the book. Look back at Lesson 17, page 126 to review the instructions for a five-minute timing.

Here is your opportunity to show your progress. Remember the rules!

- Don't look at the keyboard!

- Use the NoPeekee Keyboard for reference.

- Use the **Sitting Hints** to address your keyboard.

- Use the **Home Row Hints** to position your fingers.

- Tap the Enter key at the end of each line.

                    5/1   10/2
I like to collect a number of things. Of my many
                    15/3   20/4
collections, I think that I like my Pez collection
                    25/5   30/6
the best. I have over 95 Pez dispensers on a shelf.
                    35/7   40/8
    My Pez collection is separated into a number
                    45/9   50/10
of specific groups. I have an Animals section that
                    55/11   60/12
includes 9 cows, 10 cats, a crocodile, 4 dinosaurs, a
                    65/13   70/14
gorilla, and 3 elephants. I also have a blue tiger,
                    75/15   80/16
5 ponies and a panda bear. I have lots of Monsters.
                    85/17   90/18
I like monsters. I have vampires, a Scarewolf, 3
                    95/19   100/20
zombies and a 1-eyed monster. My favorite monsters
                    105/21   110/22
include the Creature, Wolfman and Frankenstein.
                    115/23   120/24
    The Pez Pals are real collectors' items. They
                    125/25   130/26
are based on Pezi Boy who changes his many looks by
                    135/27   140/28
dressing up in disguises to solve mysteries. This

145/29   150/30

means that there are a lot of accessories that are

155/31   160/32

interchangeable. I have all of the parts for the doctor,

165/33   170/34

engineer, fireman, policeman, pirate, teacher and nurse.

175/35   180/36

My Disney collection is not too big. I have Donald

185/37   190/38

Duck and 3 of his nephews. Dumbo and Goofy are at

195/39   200/40

the end of my shelf along with Jiminy Cricket.

CALCULATING WPM

You did it again. This time it was a twenty-line document. Did you complete the whole thing? That was a lot to key in one sitting.

Enter the statistics for this timing in the "5-Minute Test #1" row of the following table. Calculate the rest of the statistics.

	Total Words Keyed	Total Words Keyed in 1 Minute (Total Words/5)	Total Number of Errors	Total Errors in 1 Minute (Total Errors/5)	Correct WPM (Total Words Keyed in 1 Minute Minus Number of Errors in 1 Minute)
5-Minute Test #1					
5-Minute Test #2					

Take the 5-minute timing one more time. Enter your statistics in the table and calculate your WPM.

Turn to Appendix K and enter the information about your best time in the Self-Progress Chart.

You are continuing to become a faster and more efficient keyboarder. Good job!

1 ! 2 @ AND AUTOWORDS

OUTCOMES

- Keys: 1 ! 2 and @
- AutoWords
  are, was, with,
  from, this, that
- Five-minute timing

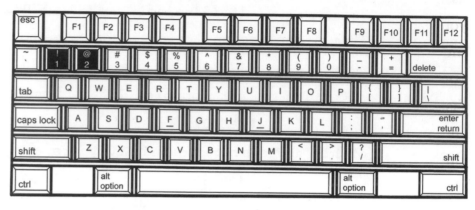

Figure 20.1

You have done it! You have reached the final lesson of learning new keys. At the end of this lesson you will have mastered all the keys (see Figure 20.1). You will be able to write about exciting exclamations! And you will be able to key e-mail addresses such as fastworker@keyboardingresearch.org.

WARM-UP (5 MINUTES)

Rehearse your responses with these warm-up workouts.

Create a **New** file and save it in the **Keyboarding** folder. Name it **Lesson20.doc**.

Remember to:

- Clip your NoPeekee Keyboard to the top of the page.
- Place your book in the holder and set it to the right of your keyboard.
- Sit at your computer following the **Sitting Hints**.
- Set your timer to 5 minutes.
- Place your fingers lightly on the home row considering the **Home Row Hints**.

 Set your 5-minute timer. Go!

999 000 ((( ))) kkk iii 999 lll ooo 000 KKK III (((LLL OOO))) jjj fff lll sss 333 444
$$$ 555 &&& 777 %%% yyy ttt eee ppp qqq zzz … ;;; 999 000 ((( ))) kkk iii 999

World Wide Web water cycle simply search engine Notice diagram information instead sentence important describing actually favorite planning statement effective experience

Learning to key rapidly benefits you more than just being able to complete assignments and correspondence in less time. Quick keyboarding is also healthier for you. Think about it. If you are able to key more rapidly, you don't have to spend as much time sitting at the keyboard trying to get things done. If a person (that means you) is able to key at 50 WPM instead of 25 WPM, then the work can get done 50% faster. This means that the would-be keyboarder can spend that extra time walking in the garden, exploring the outdoors, or "hanging out" with friends. The problem is when this extra time is spent at the keyboard playing games or "doing email" or watching TV. Be active and be healthy.

NEW CHARACTERS 1 AND !

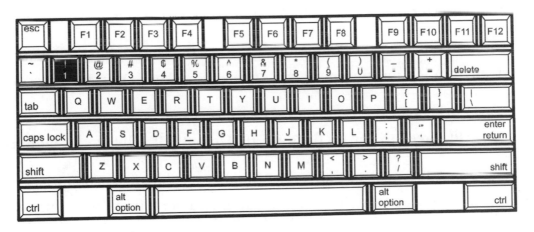

Figure 20.2

The 1! key is another *big stretch* but with the left hand. Just as you did on the right side, you need to flatten your left hand so that your ring finger can tap the 1 key (see Figure 20.2). You may think that you should use your pinky finger for the 1 key, but your pinky is not long enough. You can't reach the 1 key without moving your fingers from their home base at the home row. Try it. Move your fingers to the home row. Flatten out your left hand. Do you see that your left ring finger touches the 1 key? Practice this process with the following exercises.

sss www 111 sss www 111 sss www 111 sss www 111 sss www 111 www 111 sss www 111

That wasn't too difficult, was it? Flatten, stretch, and tap. You can do this with the ! (exclamation point) character as well. Hold down the right Shift key and stretch your left ring finger to the 1! key. Tap it and you will produce a ! on your screen. Do it again!

SSS QQQ !!! SSS QQQ !!! SSS QQQ !!! SSS QQQ !!! SSS QQQ !!! !!! SSS QQQ !!! SSS

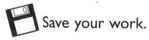 Save your work.

NEW CHARACTERS TRYOUT 1 AND !

Try it out:

sss www 111 sss www 111 SSS WWW !!! SSS WWW !!! 111 !!! 111 !!! sss www 111 sss www !!! sss SSS www WWW 111 !!! 111 !!! www WWW SSS sss WWW !!! !!! sss SSS www ssss

11 111 110 $111.11 F-111 111-111-1111 1111 1st 10011 #1 fox quail phone woods speeds month timber agreed capable freeway driving minutes tickets number John Deere house

address visited because Aardvark missions tactical upturned supersonic marvelous scampered surrounded multipurpose Los Angeles New York Over-Achievers fighter

Zack just got 11 tickets for driving his John Deere 111 Lawn Mower down the 110 Freeway Los Angeles!!! He agreed to pay his fines at $11.11/month. It will take 111 months to pay!

The F-111 was a multipurpose tactical fighter-bomber capable of supersonic speeds. It was nicknamed 'Aardvark' due to its long, slightly upturned nose. It can fly 11 missions.

Look at those Over-Achievers!! Their phone number is 111-111-1111 and their address is 11 1st Street, New York, NY 10011. They are #1 because they think like #1! It's good to be #1!

Jay visited back home and gazed upon 1 brown fox and 11 quail. It was marvelous!! They played for 10 minutes and then scampered off into the woods surrounding his house.

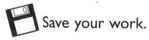 Save your work.

SELF-TEST

single single flight flight Creek Creek world world travel travel Willow Willow capital waxing waxing falling falling Footprints Footprints Airlines Airlines raindrop raindrop

linoleum creatures creatures discovered discovered Economical Economical acceptable frequently frequently Mississippi Mississippi assignment assignment Sasquatch Sasquatch

Willow Creek, CA, calls itself the Big Foot (Sasquatch) capital of the world. Footprints of these 7-8 foot tall (350-800 lb.) creatures were first discovered in 1958.

The Mississippi River begins 1,475 feet above sea level in Lake Itasca at Bemidji, MN. A raindrop falling in Lake Itasca takes about 90 days to travel the 3,705 km to Mexico.

Economical Airlines' flights #1389, #8903 & #5674 are on-time 73% of the time. This is acceptable on the single flight trips. Their rates are $110 cheaper than others.

The job of waxing 10 linoleum floors frequently peeves the 11 chintzy kids. "It's too much work for us to do!!!!" they often exclaim on the 3rd day of their 7-day work.

 Save your work.

NEW CHARACTERS 2 AND @

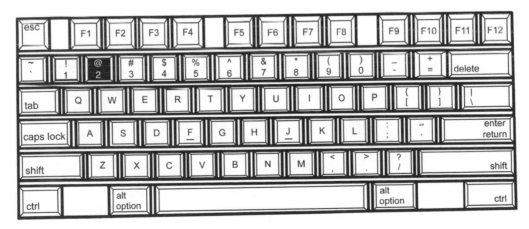

Figure 20.3

Here's the final key in the top row. Now you will be able to key e-mail addresses and write about shopping for pears @ $.79/pound. As with the 1! key, you will flatten your left hand and stretch your left ring finger to the 2 key (see Figure 20.3). Give it a try. Rest your fingers on the home row and flatten out your hand to stretch your left ring finger to the 2@ key. Do it a couple of times and then use the following exercises to perfect the process.

sss www 222 www sss www 222 www sss www 222 www 222 www 222 sss www 222

Let's add the @ character to your writing. Stretch out your right pinky. Wiggle it around a couple of times. Now, place it on the right Shift key. Flatten out your left hand and stretch your left ring finger to the 2 key. Tap that key and you will be @ the right place. Try it again and again. Continue with the following practice work.

SSS WWW @@@ SSS WWW @@@ SSS WWW @@@ WWW @@@ SSS WWW @@@

Save your work.

NEW CHARACTERS TRYOUT 2 AND @

sss www 111 sss ww 222 SSS QQQ !!! SSS WWW @@@ !!! 111 222 sss www 111 sss ww aa 22 ww dd 11 qq ss ww 22 11 !! @@ ww ss ee ll zz xx dd cc kk oo ii jj aa 22 ww dd

@ 12 21 22 112 111 12:00 5:20 2:45 5:20 1st per day zen tied spam prize vapor place monks course office joined vexed finish ground deletes through because quickly elevated

position jogging contact vertical Tuesdays WONDERFUL assistant interesting teammates themselves telepathic experience unfortunately Wednesdays irene@iamcheerful.com

Irene has an interesting email address. You can contact her at irene@iamcheerful.com. She gets over 112 emails per day. Unfortunately, about 102 of those are spam email.

Ashley is a WONDERFUL office assistant. She works on Tuesdays from 12:00 -- 5:20 and Wednesdays from 2:45--5:20. She is always @ the office on time! She does well.

Grace ran the course in 1 hour and 21 minutes. She was @ the finish line just as 12 of her teammates joined her. They were all excited because they tied for 1st place.

Harry, jogging quickly, vexed zen monks with beef vapor. All 22 of them fell to the ground but elevated themselves back to a vertical position through a shared experience.

Save your work.

SELF-TEST

12 -- 2 10 100 -- 22 78 $1 @wesellgoodfruit.com 25 16 212 WPM WPM ease ease diet price price relief relief jazzy jazzy flight flight exodus exodus people people numbers

discuss discuss complex complex improved improved borrowing borrowing difficult difficult process process thinking thinking healthy healthy expression expression

Subtraction is easy!! 12-2 equals 10. Larger numbers that require "borrowing" are more difficult. 100-22 equals 78. This involves a more complex process of thinking.

The pears @wesellgoodfruit.com are priced @ 2 fresh pears for $1! This is a wonderfully low price for a pair of pears. It is enough to make one want to begin eating healthfully.

27 of the boys and 18 of the girls in the 3rd grade were able to keyboard at least 25 WPM. This was great because they only handwrote about 16 WPM. This is better.

The exodus of jazzy pigeons is craved by squeamish walkers. While few people wish to actually discuss the problem, there is general relief when all 212 of the birds take flight.

 Save your work.

AUTOWORDS

are, was, with, from, this, that

The AutoWords in this section are commonly used with everyday language (notice that this sentence contains four of the six words.) These words should just become as automatic as the AutoBlends you have been learning in the last couple of lessons. There is an extended list of the most commonly used AutoWords in the appendix if you want to increase your speed by practicing them as well.

Give these six AutoWords a try. As always, begin keying them slowly. Look for a feeling of automaticity as you key each AutoWord. Pronounce each AutoWord as you key it.

are are are are are are are are are are are are are are are are are are are are are are was was was was was was was was was was was was was was was was was was was was

with with with with with with with with with with with with with with with with from from from from from from from from from from from from from from from from

this this this this this this this this this this this this this this this this this this that that that that that that that that that that that that that that that that that

 Save your work.

NEW AUTOWORDS TRYOUT

are are are was was was was with with with from from from this this this that that that are was was with with from from this this that that are are was with from this that this from

gown small World pieces desire poetry driven artistic quoted shivers invited running artistic survived etchings precious hometown Malaysia interested inspiration bridesmaids

Raina was beautiful in her wedding gown. She stood with her bridesmaids who are from her hometown. Most of the people from that small town were invited to this wedding.

Peter knew more about World War II than any man I have ever known. He was interested because he lived during that war as a boy in Malaysia. It was terrifying.

Edgar writes poetry that discusses this and that. He gets inspiration from the people and places that are part of his life. He was always driven with the desire and need to write.

Just keep examining every low bid quoted for zinc etchings. They are without a doubt the most precious artistic pieces that I have ever held. I got shivers from holding them.

Save your work.

SELF-TEST

8 11 18 23 50% 6,585.3 S&S S&S lunar lunar solar solar feats feats reach reach period urgent urgent jousts jousts budget budget pitiful pitiful eclipses eclipses savings savings

physical physical computers computers purchased purchased contestants contestants identified predicted predicted situation situation youthful youthful Babylonians

The recurrence & periodicity of lunar (and solar) eclipses can be predicted using the Saros cycle, a specific period of about 6,585.3 days (18 years 11 days 8 hours).

You can reach me at goodkeyboarder@ikeyquickly.com or you might get me at this address: goshiamgood@masterofthekeyboard.com. Either way, I check my email!!

We purchased 23 computers @ 50% savings. This was important because our S&S (supplies & services) budget had been drastically affected by the slow economy. Six crazy kings vowed to abolish my quite pitiful jousts. It was becoming only too evident that all 27 of the youthful contestants were better than me in this set of physical tests.

 Save your work.

CORRECTIVE WORK

Proofread your work.

- Print the file **Lesson20.doc**.
- Identify the words that were keyed incorrectly.
- Create a new file and save it as **L20Practice.doc**.
- Key each of these words five times correctly and save your file.

IMPROVEMENT WORK

Return to the preceding twelve lines. Open the file **Lesson20.doc**, and key these lines again. You should be able to complete the task more quickly and more accurately.

FIVE-MINUTE TIMING

It's time to test your skills again. You have improved a great deal over the course of this book, and this will be the last five-minute timing that is directly associated with a lesson in which you are learning new characters on the keyboard. There are plenty of other timings in the appendix, and you should do those about every other day so that you can monitor your improvement.

You know the drill. Do the timing twice, and record your statistics in the chart at the end of the timing. Record your best time in Appendix K.

If you need to review the instructions for a five minutes timing turn to page 126. Here is your opportunity to show your progress. Remember the rules!

- Don't look at the keyboard!
- Use the NoPeekee Keyboard for reference.
- Use the **Sitting Hints** to address your keyboard.
- Use the **Home Row Hints** to position your fingers.
- Tap the Enter key at the end of each line.

Remember to keep your eyes on the text and move as quickly as you are able. Start over if you finish keying this whole selection.

Set your timer for 5 minutes. Go!

```
                    5/1                          10/2
        It is very amazing how much I have improved while
                    15/3                         20/4
using this book. At first, I just looked for the various
                    25/5                         30/6
keys that I needed when I was at the keyboard.  It
                    35/7                         40/8
was totally a "hunt-and-peck" operation. But I have
                    45/9                         50/10
worked hard to keep my eyes on the book as I type.
                    55/11                        60/12
I also use the NoPeekee Keyboard when I don't know
                    65/13                        70/14
the location of a key. This has helped me build the
                    75/15                        80/16
memory traces that enable me to associate specific
                    85/17                        90/18
finger movements with certain letters. It has made
                    95/19                        100/20
an important difference in how I am keyboarding.
                    105/21                       110/22
        I have also learned a number of AutoBlends and
                    115/23                       120/24
AutoWords. I guess I would have learned about these
                    125/25                       130/26
on my own after I had been keyboarding for a few
                    135/27                       140/28
years but memorizing these combinations and trying
```

```
          145/29                        150/30
to key them as single movements is going to make my
          155/31                        160/32
keyboarding much more effective and efficient.
          165/33                        170/34
     The hardest part is going to be remembering to
          175/35                        180/36
use these good habits all of the time. I can do a lot
          185/37                        190/38
more composing at the keyboard now, and it is easy
          195/39                        200/40
for me not to look at the keyboard while I do my work.
          205/41                        210/42
It's just a matter of building self-discipline and
          215/43                        220/44
remembering that "Perfect Practice Makes Perfect."
```

CALCULATING WPM

Did you finish all twenty-two lines? You are getting better all the time, aren't you?

Enter the statistics for this timing in the "5 Minute Test #1" row of the following table. Calculate the rest of the statistics.

	Total Words Keyed	Total Words Keyed in 1 Minute (Total Words/5)	Total Number of Errors	Total Errors in 1 Minute (Total Errors/5)	Correct WPM (Total Words Keyed in 1 Minute Minus Number of Errors in 1 Minute)
5-Minute Test #1					
5-Minute Test #2					

Take the 5-Minute timing one more time. Enter your statistics in the table.

Enter the information about your best time in Appendix K.

Keep at it. Remember, "perfect practice makes perfect."

Keep practicing on your air keyboard!

USING THE NUMERIC KEYPAD

OUTCOMES

• Keys: 0 through 9 on the numeric keypad
  / * - + = .

Now that you have mastered all the keys on the regular keyboard, it's time to branch out to the numeric keypad (see Figure 21.1). Yes, you have just learned how to key all the numbers using the keys in the top row of your keyboard, but those are primarily for times when you have to key only a few numbers. You use the numeric keypad when you have to key many numbers for something like a spreadsheet.

Locate on the right of your keyboard the numeric keypad. This is found on all the "enhanced" keyboards. If your keyboard isn't enhanced, you can connect a numeric keypad as an add-on.

If you have a laptop computer, you may have a numeric keypad built into your keyboard. You just have to tap the Num Lock key to disable your keyboard except for fifteen keys that you can use as a numeric keypad. The keys may vary among keyboards, but the keys used for the numeric keypad often consist of the 67890UIOPJKL;M/ keys (see Figure 21.1). Examine your keyboard closely to see if you find any additional numbers and mathematical symbols on some of these keys.

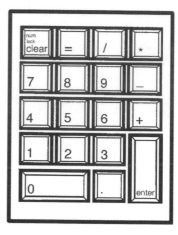

Figure 21.1

Figure 21.2

WARM-UP (5 MINUTES)

Warm up all your fingers and then begin learning about using the numeric keypad.

Create a **New** file and save it in the **Keyboarding** folder. Name it **Lesson21.doc**.

Remember to:

- Clip your NoPeekee Keyboard to the top of the page.
- Place your book in the holder and set it to the right of your keyboard.
- Sit at your computer following the **Sitting Hints**.
- Set your timer to 5 minutes.
- Place your fingers lightly on the home row considering the **Home Row Hints**.

 Set your 5-minute timer. Go!

333 888 222 000 111 --- sss ;;; eee ooo zzz ... ggg ''' aaa yyy www iii 333 888 222 000

::: AAA SSS YYY QQQ PPP BBB NNN XXX MMM ZZZ ??? $$$::: AAA SSS YYY QQQ

After mastering all the numbers on the top row of the keyboard, you will be able to key single and double digits with little difficulty. You should also be able to key characters like # & * & @ & ! & (&) & $ & % with little effort. When you have to key long strings of numbers like phone numbers or birth dates or all the digits on your paycheck, you will benefit from being able to use the keypad.

The keypad was used long before computers found their ways onto people's desks. Adding machines in the late part of the nineteenth century had keypads arranged in formats similar to what you find on your computer. They didn't work on electricity, though. After the adding machine user, often a bookkeeper, entered a number, he or she would pull down a lever on the right side of the adding machine. This would register the number and then calculate it using the previously entered numbers. It was a great way to exercise the right arm while balancing a bank account.

USING THE NUMERIC KEYPAD

Remember the home row on the keyboard that has become the "home away from home" for your fingers? Well, they are about to find a guesthouse on the numeric keypad. Find the four rows of keys on the numeric keypad. The row that contains the 4, 5, and 6 keys is your new home row. Place your fore, middle, and ring fingers over these keys, with the middle finger resting on the 5 key (see Figure 21.3). Unlike the QWERTY keyboard, which has no apparent form of organization, the layout of the numeric keyboard is quite logical. You can even figure out the location of keys here by using mathematical formulas.

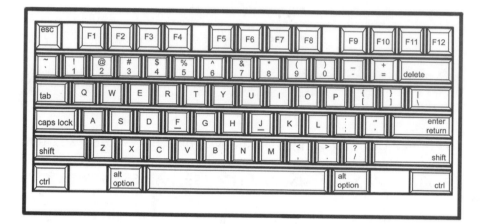

Fligure 21.3

Begin with the 5 key. The 4 key (–1) is just to the left of it. The 6 key (+1) is immediately to the right of it. The number directly below the 5 is the 2 key (–3). The number directly below the 4 key is the 1 key (–3). Yes, you guessed it—the number below the 6 key is the 3 key, which is 3 less than 6. The same is true for the top row. Each of the keys in the top row is just 3 more than the numbers on the home row. The 7 is above the 4, the 8 is above the 5, and the 9 is above the 6.

Move your hand to the home row of the numeric keypad. Place your middle finger on the 5 key. Now key the numbers below. Don't look at the keys. If you don't know which key to tap, you just need to do the math to figure out where it is located. This will help you build the memory traces that will enable you to key quickly and without looking.

55 66 44 88 99 77 22 33 11 55 66 44 88 99 77 22 33 11 55 66 44 88 99 77 22 33 11

What about adding a 0 to your number log? You have used up all your fingers, so use your thumb to hit the 0. Give it a try.

10 20 30 40 50 60 70 80 90 100 101 102 506 406 308 907 204 807 606

Now use your fingers and your thumb to put it all together in the following exercises.

NEW KEYS 0 THROUGH 9

555 444 666 777 888 999 111 222 333 555 444 666 777 888 999 111 222 333 888 999 777
444 222 333 111 888 999 777 555 666 444 222 333 111 555 444 666 777 888 999 111 222

345 543 534 435 645 789 987 897 879 978 123 321 231 231 312 741 852 963 369 258 147
693 159 357 951 753 853 158 259 752 345 543 534 435 645 789 987 897 879 978 123

555 444 666 546 564 456 123 321 52 41 63 363 252 141 74 85 96 897 345 543 534 435
987 897 879 978 123159 753 942 348 765 917 182 369 472 387 462 2916 9217 12 34 56

NEW KEYS TRYOUT 0 THROUGH 9

2 403 13 27 19 245 1,378 001-33-06-65-070-06-95 001-33-06-65-070-06-98
#39 678 98456 98 $2,898 $127, 989.65 ISBN 0 941681 37 8 onyx Paris farms quartz
found geodes course number jewels opened country paycheck mistake account chapters
Computer treasure expensive university embarrassing grandfathers calculated Applications

Cheryl said that I could call her in Paris @ 001-33-06-65-070-06-95. I tried but found that
her number was 001-33-06-65-070-06-98. What a mistake. It was expensive & embarrassing.

Xia told me that she had opened account #39 678 98456 98 at her bank. She was
able to deposit all of her $2,898 paycheck. She has 27 bank accounts in 19 banks.

Tiffany found the book with ISBN 0 941681 37 8. It was a wonderful book of 403 pages.
She had all 134 of her students in her Computer Applications university course use it.

My 2 grandfathers pick up 245 quartz geodes and 1,378 valuable onyx jewels on their
2 farms. They had $127,989.65 in rocks. It was a huge treasure chest of gems.

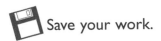Save your work.

NEW KEYS + - * / = .

Now that you know the numbers, it will be useful to use the mathematical operators that are on the keypad as well. As you can see, the symbols that are accessible on the numeric keyboard include + - * / =. As you probably know, the operations that these symbols represent are addition (+), subtraction (-), multiplication (*), and division (/). The location of the symbols on your numeric keyboard may not be *exactly* as shown in the illustration because there are some variations among models of computers. Learn the location of the function keys on your computer so that you can balance your checkbook and key long telephone numbers without looking at the numeric keypad.

Here is your opportunity to practice using these keys.

NEW KEYS TRYOUT + - * / = .

=== /// **** ---- +++ ... === /// **** ---- +++... === /// **** ---- +++... === /// **** ----

= / * - + . = / * - + . = / * - + . = / * - + . = / * - + . = / * - + . = / * - + . = / * - + . = / * - + .

7 + 9 − 2 = 14 ; 1/2 * 24 = 12 ; 45 + 23 − 50 * 4 = 72 ; 1/4 + 28.75 − 14 = 15 ; 2.3 − 1.7 = 4.0 ;140 * 12 + 78 = 1758 ; 8000 − 78 * .205 +403 = 8387.017 + 9 − 2 = 14 ; 1/2 * 24 = 12 ;

39-678-98456-98 ; 1-812-555-6554 ; 0-201-22678-2 ; 560-88-688844 ; 07-14-1953 ; 4/17 31-1981 ; 485/487/4958/454 ; +48148.97239-678-98456-98 ; 1-812-555-6554 ; 0-201-22678-

SELF-TEST

Dr. Smith asked us to solve these formulas; (100-23+13)/9*10=x; (22+11-33)*234987=y; and 23+87-41+44+275-92+16=z. They were challenging but not too difficult to solve.

Lewis has a birthday on 09/09/1922. His wife, Beth, has her birthday on 02/11/1924. They enjoyed celebrating their birthdays with their 3 children and 11 grandchildren.

The serial number on the computer was 0459812354. It was running software with SN 78-49-A5 1297-BN-981-AQ-845-F7W8-891-LZ-14. That last number was often transposed.

A boy, Max, felt his heart move 189 quick jumps during his zealous approach to the pole vault bar. He walked 2 steps and ran the remaining 18 steps to the 12' 3" bar.

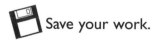 Save your work.

CORRECTIVE WORK

Proofread your work.

- Print the file **Lesson21.doc**.

- Identify the words that were keyed incorrectly.

- Create a new file and save it as **L21Practice.doc**.

- Key each of these words five times correctly and save your file.

IMPROVEMENT WORK

Return to the Self-Test. Open the file **Lesson21.doc** and key these lines again. You should be able to complete the task more quickly and more accurately.

WRITING A PERSONAL LETTER

OUTCOMES

• Writing a personal letter

Earlier in the book we said that mastering the keyboard would allow you to write letters. You have the skills, so now you can learn how to direct them toward writing a properly formatted letter. This lesson explains the format for writing a personal letter, and the next lesson describes the more formal format of a business letter.

Before you learn about writing a letter, you need to warm up a bit.

WARM-UP (5 MINUTES)

Exercise your digits with these activities.

Create a **New** file and save it in the **Keyboarding** folder. Name it **Lesson22.doc.**

Remember to:

• Clip your NoPeekee Keyboard to the top of the page.

• Place your book in the holder and set it to the right of your keyboard.

• Sit at your computer following the **Sitting Hints.**

• Set your timer to 5 minutes.

• Place your fingers lightly on the home row considering the **Home Row Hints.**

 Set your 5-minute timer. Go!

CCC sss kkk lll eee ''' aaa www ooo ppp qqq mmm ccc ,,, xxx … zzz bbb VVV ggg HH ttt iii WWW ddd FFF JJJ nnn /// ??? ;;; ::: " " CCC sss kkk lll eee ''' aaa www ooo ppp

Writing personal letters can be more than just writing your ideas and feelings. There are actually specific formats for writing such letters. A personal letter has five parts: the return address, the date, the salutation, the body of the letter, and the complimentary close.

The return address and date are indented to the middle of the screen. This means that you tap the Tab key five or six times until you reach the 3" tab. The return address is two lines long consisting of the street address, city, state, and zip code. This is immediately followed by the date on the next line.

The salutation is where you address the person to whom you are writing. This is flush to the left margin and ends with a comma. The body of the letter is where you write your message. You begin each paragraph with a tabbed indent. Unless you have set alternate tabs, your first line will begin at the 0.5" position.

The complimentary closing is always a few words on a single line. It ends with a comma. You will usually sign the printed letter below the closing, so there is no need to include your name at this point.

WRITING PERSONAL LETTERS

Writing a letter to a friend is very personal, and there are many types of letters. These may include thank you letters, letters of appreciation, apologies, complaints, condolences, congratulations, and invitations. Whatever the reason for writing to your friend, take the time to present it in the proper format.

The personal letter is written using a semi-block format. This means that the return address, date, and complimentary closing all begin at the middle of the page, and each paragraph is indented one tab. Personal letters are single spaced.

A personal letter contains five parts:

Sender's Address. The return address consists of the street address, city, state, and zip code and is two lines long. If your stationery contains your return address, you don't need to write it again.

Date. There is no specific format for the date, but it usually includes the full name of the month.

Salutation. This is your initial greeting. Since you are writing to a friend, you will begin your letter with "Dear LeRoy," or "Dear Jack,".

Body of the Letter. This is your message. It usually begins with an opening greeting that you might use in a typical conversation. You might ask about your friend's health or what he/she has been doing. The opening paragraph is also where you explain the reason for writing this letter. Having set the tone of the letter, you then go into the reason for the letter. This could be just telling your friend about things that have been happening in your life, or it could be for any of the reasons mentioned in the first paragraph. In the final paragraph, you should provide final encouragement or an explanation about your attitude toward the subject of the letter. It should be positive.

Complimentary Close. This appears double spaced below the body of the letter. It may include *Sincerely, Affectionately,* or a few encouraging words written on the same line and ending with a comma.

PERSONAL LETTER TRYOUT

Create a **New** file and save it in the **Keyboarding** folder. Name it **personalletter1.doc**.

Key the following letter into your new file. Save often as you work.

714 Digital Drive
National City, CA 91393
July 14, 20___

Dear Mom,

I just wanted to write you to tell you about the wonderful new skills I am learning. I recently bought a book, *Keyboarding Made Simple,* and it has taught me to keyboard without looking at the keys. I even got a rubber overlay that covers the keyboard so I can't see the letters on the keys. Sometimes I refer to my NoPeekee Keyboard when I don't know where to find a specific key or which finger to use, but I am doing pretty well.

I have learned a lot of things beyond keyboarding. Right now I am learning about writing personal letters. That is why I am writing this personal letter to you. It is an opportunity to display my newly developed keyboarding skills.

This book even taught me to use the numeric keyboard. I have played with it on my computer before, but now I know where to place my fingers on the numeric home row and how to enter numbers and operators without looking. It will be handy when I balance my checkbook.

Hope to see you soon,

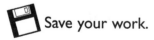 Save your work.

Review your letter for errors and print it.

Create a **New** file and save it in the **Keyboarding** folder. Name it **personalletter2.doc**.

Here's another personal letter. This one is a thank you note to your friend Pat.

714 Digital Drive
National City, CA 91393
November 20, 20___

Dear Pat,

I hope that you are doing well.

I just want to thank you for the wonderful folk-music CD that you gave me for my birthday last week. There are many artists with widely ranging abilities, and I have been playing the CD at least three times a day. My mom says that I will probably wear it out by my next birthday. That's funny, isn't it? CDs don't wear out, do they?

It was good to see you again. We haven't had a chance to sit and talk for a long time. Remember how we used to sit around the tree house and talk about everything in the world? Those were the days, weren't they?

Maybe we can get together again and share our worlds once more.

Your friend always,

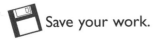 Save your work.

FORMATTING A PERSONAL LETTER

You've done a great job of copying these letters out of the book. Let's see what you have learned about formatting. Type the following using the same margins and format as your previous letters. Break the letter into paragraphs. Substitute your own return address and today's date. Sign the letter yourself.

Dear Rafiki,

I hope that you have recovered from all of the excitement of your graduation party. There were a lot of people there. It is nice to have a large group of friends who will support you as you move into the next chapter of your life. I just wanted to congratulate you on your recent graduation. You have worked very hard to succeed in school. Your many scholastic awards are indicators of your success, but I would guess that your greatest reward is the knowledge that you have achieved and been working toward these past 4 years. This will not be the last of your challenges in life, and I know that you will approach them all with the same courage that you approached your schooling. Congratulations on a job well done.

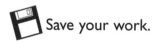Save your work.

Review your letter for errors and print it.

CHALLENGE WORK

Type a letter to a friend. This should be a letter concerning an actual situation in life. Use the semiblock format and today's date. Review your work before you print it. Make certain that you haven't made any errors.

Mail this letter to your friend. It will make both of you feel good.

WRITING A BUSINESS LETTER

OUTCOMES

- Writing a business letter
- Using your printer to address envelopes
- Folding and inserting letters into envelopes

You have learned how to properly format personal letters. You have copied letters that were already formatted and formatted prewritten letters. Unfortunately, you don't write letters only to close personal friends. Whether you do it at work or at home, you will have to write formal letters to businesses. This lesson will help you do that.

Before you learn about writing a letter, you need to warm up a bit.

WARM-UP (5 MINUTES)

Prepare to communicate with the business world by doing a little warm-up keyboarding.

Create a **New** file and save it in the **Keyboarding** folder. Name it **Lesson23.doc**.

Remember to:

- Clip your NoPeekee Keyboard to the top of the page.
- Place your book in the holder and set it to the right of your keyboard.
- Sit at your computer following the **Sitting Hints**.
- Set your timer to 5 minutes.
- Place your fingers lightly on the home row considering the **Home Row Hints**.

 Set your 5-minute timer. Go!

XXX 222 000 111 --- 333 999 444 888 555 777 666 @@@))) !!! (((### *** $$$ &&& %%% ___ ;;; ::: ''' """ /// ??? ttt III www OOO qqq PPP XXX 222 000 111 --- 333 999

Business letters are, by nature, more formal because you are trying to make an especially good impression. Although your close personal friends know you and will not judge you by the format of your letters, a business letter is usually your first contact with a person or organization. It is important to make a good first impression and to allow the reader to pay attention to your ideas instead of the format of the letter.

Business letters use a formal block style. This format includes seven parts: the return address, the date, the recipient's address, the salutation, the body of the letter, the complimentary close, and the signature information.

Notice that the recipient's address is included at the beginning of the letter. This is included to ensure that the letters make it into the properly addressed envelopes. In the days of the typewriter and typing pools, piles of letters and envelopes would be typed separately. Today, the computer allows the address to be used to print envelopes directly on a printer. This process is explained later in this lesson.

WRITING BUSINESS LETTERS

Business letters are less complicated to format than personal letters. Whereas personal letters require the writer to indent paragraphs and place certain sections in the middle of the page, business letters use the block format, which is flush to the left margin. Every section of the letter begins at the left margin; there are no indents. A blank line is placed between paragraphs to identify the differences.

A business letter contains seven parts:

Return Address. The return address consists of the street address, city, state, and zip code and is two lines long. If your letterhead stationery contains your return address, you don't need to include your return address.

Date. The date is written using the full name of the month (i.e., January 31, 200_) If your letter is written over a period of time, you should use the date it was finished.

Inside Address. This is the recipient's address. If you are writing to a company, it is best to write to a specific individual. You can identify this person through a phone call to the company or by searching the company's Web site.

Salutation. This is your introductory greeting. It is generally more formal than you would use in a social setting. Generally, you would use the recipient's last name. Although you can usually identify the gender of the recipient of your letter by the first name, sometimes it can be misleading. The author of this book, Leigh Zeitz, is a man. His first name has caused him to receive many letters to Ms. Zeitz. Go ahead and take a chance and use Mr. or Ms. based on your interpretation of the first name.

If you are addressing a letter to a woman, there is the issue of which salutation to use. It is safer to use Ms. instead of Mrs. or Miss unless you know the specific preferences of the woman you are addressing. If there is a possibility that the person to whom you are writing is a Dr. or some other professional, then you should use it. People usually don't mind being addressed by a title higher than they actually possess.

Body of the Letter. This is where the work is done. You are writing to a busy business-person, so be as concise as possible.

- Begin your first paragraph with a friendly opening and then make a statement concerning the main point of your letter.

- Justify the importance of your issue in the next paragraph.

- Explain the details of your arguments and provide background information as necessary in the following paragraphs.

- Restate the purpose of your letter and in some letters identify the type of action you would like seen taken in the closing paragraph.

Closing. This appears double spaced below the body of the letter. It may include "Sincerely," "Thank you," or another respectful phrase to end the letter. Capitalize the first letter only.

Sender's Name. Although your friends may be able to recognize your signature, it is essential for the recipients of your business letters to know your name. Sometimes your signature isn't completely legible, so you need to include your name below your signature. If appropriate to the intent of the letter, you may want to include your formal title as well. Sometimes the sender's phone number and/or email address are included under the sender's name if they are not part of the letterhead.

Enclosures. You may be including documents with your letter. If so, it is a good idea to indicate this by placing the word *Enclosures* one line below the closing. This ensures that your recipient will look for your résumé or sales materials, for example, that you included. If you have included multiple documents, you may want to follow *Enclosure* with a list of the documents, for the recipients benefit.

FORMATTING A BUSINESS LETTER

Create a **New** file and save it in the **Keyboarding** folder. Name it **businessletter1.doc**.

Key the following cover letter into your new file. Format it as a business letter. Save often as you work.

789 Fingers Road
Anytown, IA 50000

July 14, 20__

Uri R. Gude
Personnel Manager
My Book Company
150 Wall Street
Princeton, NJ 08555

Dear Mr. Gude:

I was excited to see your advertisement for a copy editor. I have been studying to become a member of the publishing field, and this would be a perfect opportunity to use my skills to benefit your company.

I have been studying for the past four years at Davis University. During this period, I majored in journalism and minored in French. I worked hard and graduated Magna Cum Laude with a 3.95 GPA.

Although studying was an important part of my life, it was not all of it. I was the editor of our university newspaper, *The UNInews Gazette*, for two years. During my tenure, we won awards for our news coverage and for the quality of our newspaper.

I am interested in becoming part of your team. My résumé is enclosed for your review. I am available to meet with you at your convenience. Please contact me at the address above or email me at kree@icanedit.com.

Thank you for your consideration.

Sincerely,

Kree A. Tive
555-555-1234
Enclosure

 Save your work.

Review your letter for errors and print it.

Create a **New** file and save it in the **Keyboarding** folder. Name it **businessletter2.doc**.

Here's another business letter. This one is a letter of complaint to a car dealer.

36963 Hubcap Road
Motor City, OH 39494

February 11, 20__

Your Choice Motors
838 Engine Blvd.
Motor City, OH 39494

Dear Ms. Garfield:

I have owned my Your Choice station wagon for 3 years. It has been a reliable vehicle, and we have used it on many enjoyable vacation trips throughout the country. We have always had your company do the periodic maintenance on our car as prescribed in the owner's manual.

Recently, we brought the car into your service department because of a rhythmic tick that we were hearing from the left rear wheel area. Your service person Charlie told us it was a suspension problem and that it would cost $600 to fix. We authorized the service to be completed.

The service was completed one week later. We paid the bill and drove the car home. On the way home, we still heard the tick. Upon stopping the vehicle and checking the left rear wheel well, we found a small branch stuck there. It was causing the tick by bouncing on the tire. We removed the branch and have not heard another tick since then.

I am writing to tell you that I feel that there was a problem with your service representative's diagnosis of the problem and that something should be done to correct the situation. Obviously your mechanic did not drive the car to hear the tick nor did he drive it afterward to see if the work corrected the problem. I just spent $600 on work that was not necessary and believe that the $600 should be refunded to me.

Thank you for considering this request, and I hope to hear from you within one week.

Sincerely,

Dr. Ican Drive
556-556-5556

 Save your work.

Review your second letter for errors and print it.

BUSINESS LETTER TRYOUT

This is your opportunity to write a letter of recommendation for a previous employee who is looking for another, more profitable position. Type this letter using a block format with the same margins as your previous letters. Break the letter into paragraphs. Create your own company and use your own return address and today's date. Sign the letter.

To Whom it May Concern: I have been Heather Flower's manager for three years. Although I wish her the best in her career and understand that she is moving to a better position than is available in our company, I am truly sorry to see her leave. Heather is a technical trainer of the highest caliber. She meticulously researches her subjects and prepares for her classes with the utmost care. While in the classroom her preparation pays off, as she creates a learning environment that is effective and individualized for her students. She always receives high evaluations from her students. Heather is an innovative self-starter who rarely requires supervision. She is on time and typically exceeds expectations. Heather is able to handle the pressure of deadlines as "just part of the job." She will stay late or take work home to ensure that the work is completed on time. Heather is a valuable part of our program, and I strongly recommend her for your department. I would be happy to discuss her work and potential in more detail if you would like to contact me. Sincerely,

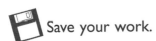Save your work.

Review your letter for errors and print it.

SENDING YOUR LETTERS

It's nice to write these letters but rather useless if you don't place them in envelopes and mail them to the recipients. Addressing envelopes used to be a somewhat difficult task of placing the addresses in "just the right places," but that process has been made simpler through technology. Your word processor probably has a capacity to print your envelopes from the information found in your letter. Follow these steps to do this using Microsoft Word.

Addressing Envelopes Using the Computer

Open the file for the letter you want to mail. Select the **Envelopes** command from the **Tools** menu at the top of the screen.

The **Envelope** dialog box will appear. Notice that the mailing address is already in the **Delivery address:** box. The program found the address on your letter.

You may also see your return address in the **Return address:** box. If you don't see your return address or if you want to use another address, you can do any of the following:

1. Try clicking on the check box next to **Use my address.**

- If this is your personal copy of Microsoft Word, your personal address should appear.

- If it doesn't appear, it may mean that you haven't personalized Microsoft Word with your own information.

- You can personalize Microsoft Word using the following directions:

  - On the **Word** menu, click **Preferences**, then **User Information**.

  - Under **Address**, type a return address.

  - This address will appear on all your future envelopes as a return address.

2. Enter your own address manually. This means that you leave **Use my address** unchecked.

3. If you are addressing an envelope that has a return address printed on it, you will

want to omit the return address. Click on the check box next to **Omit**.

Once you have the correct delivery address and return address settings, you can print your envelope. Click the **Print** button at the bottom of the **Envelope** dialog box. This will print the envelope to its own Microsoft Word document. Once the new document appears, you can just print the envelope as you would any other document.

The envelope may not print out correctly the first time. You may need to rearrange the direction and placement of envelope in the printer. You can modify these settings through the **Custom** button on the **Envelope** dialog box.

Folding a Letter

It may seem like a simple process, but just as the format of the letter can convey your professionalism, the placement of the letter in the envelope can be just as important.

Most letters in the United States are printed on 8.5" × 11" paper. Letters are usually mailed in No. 10 envelopes that are 9.5" × 4.125". These letters are folded into thirds and inserted into an envelope (see Figure 23.1).

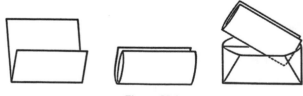

Figure 23.1

1. Fold the letter from the bottom to a little less than a third of the sheet.

2. Fold again to within about $1/_8$" of the top edge.

3. Insert the folded letter into the envelope.

   a. Hold the envelope with the reverse side facing you.

   b. Insert the letter with the open end at the top.

Sometimes personal letters are mailed in No. 6 envelopes that are 6.5" × 3.625". These are first folded in half and then folded in thirds as with No. 10 envelopes (see Figure 23.2)

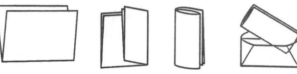

Figure 23.2

1. Fold from the bottom to $1/_8$" of the top edge.

2. Fold from the bottom to a little less than $1/_3$ of the sheet.

3. Fold again to within about $1/_8$" from the top edge.

4. Insert the folded letter into the envelope.

   a. Hold the envelope with the reverse side facing you.

   b. Insert the letter with the open end at the top.

CHALLENGE WORK

Type a complimentary letter to a company. Thank the company for producing a product that you use, a public radio station that you enjoy, or a company that provides a service that makes your life more enjoyable. This should be a letter concerning an actual situation in life. Use the block format and use today's date. Review your work before you print it. Make certain that you haven't made any errors.

Print the envelope for this letter as well.

Mail this letter to the company. It will make both of you feel good.

LESSON 24

ELECTRONIC COMMUNICATION

OUTCOMES

- Design and create a fax cover page
- Write a business e-mail
- Write a personal e-mail

Writing letters on paper is an important skill to master, but a great deal of your work (both professional and personal) is in an electronic format. This lesson explores a variety of electronic forms of communication. It begins with creating a fax cover page. Faxes are used for quickly transmitting copies of printed papers.

The majority of your communications are probably through e-mail. It may not seem that there is much to learn about sending an e-mail. You just need to create a new message, enter an address, add a subject, and then write your message, right? That's right for your friends, but there are a number of issues you need to consider when you are using e-mail for more formal correspondence, as we discuss in this lesson.

Let's begin with a warm-up!

WARM-UP (5 MINUTES)

Create a **New** file and save it in the **Keyboarding** folder. Name it **Lesson24.doc**.

Remember to:

- Clip your NoPeekee Keyboard to the top of the page.
- Place your book in the holder and set it to the right of your keyboard.
- Sit at your computer following the **Sitting Hints**.
- Set your timer to 5 minutes.
- Place your fingers lightly on the home row considering the **Home Row Hints**.

Remember to go back to the beginning if you complete this section.

 Set your 5-minute timer. Go!

Asdfghjkl;' poiuytrewq zxcvbnm,./ 1234567890- ARPAnet personal century electronic system telephone telegraph television broadcast invented development communication

Electronic communication has changed the world. Electronic communication is nothing new. It actually began in the 1830s with the telegraph. Alexander Graham Bell and Elisha Gray independently invented the telephone in the 1870s. The radio came around in the late 1800s and early 20th century. Believe it or not, television was first broadcast in the 1930s. The Internet was actually developed from the ARPAnet computer communication system that was developed in 1969. Email was first used over ARPAnet in 1971. It has gone through many developments since then. The World Wide Web was developed by Tim Berners-Lee and released to the world in 1993. The WWW has changed our way of life and communication. It has provided an easily accessible form of personal connection and communication.

FAX COVER SHEETS

Facsimiles, more commonly known as faxes, are used to transmit information from a printed page at one location to a printed page at another location. In the modern world of computers and e-mail, this may seem like an ancient way to communicate, but it can be fast and efficient if a person has only the printed copy to transmit. Think of it as a scanner at one end that is connected to a printer at the other.

It may not seem as though there is much to consider in the way of fax etiquette, but there are a few points to note.

Cover sheets are probably not needed if you are sending information to a friend or familiar business associate. You just call up your friend to tell her that the fax is on its way and she waits at the fax machine to receive it. In a more formal business setting, your company or the company to whom you are faxing may have established procedures for sending and receiving faxes. If they use cover sheets, you should do the same to display professionalism.

The typical cover sheet contains the following information:

- The name and fax number of the recipient
- The sender's name and fax number
- The number of pages being transmitted (including the cover sheet)
- Additional comments if necessary
- The phone number and person to be called if the fax is incomplete

Fax cover sheets have become very creative. You can find premade fax covers with formats that range from the formal business format to those decorated with various artistic expressions. Word-processing software like Microsoft Word provides templates for creating fax cover sheets.

FAX COVER SHEET TRYOUT

You have to decide what you want to convey in your fax cover sheet. Here is an opportunity to create a formal businesslike fax cover sheet.

Create a **New** file and save it in the **Keyboarding** folder. Name it **faxcover1.doc**.

Fax Cover Sheet
To: **Keyboards R Us**
Fax: **1-555-123-4567**

From: Ima Hunter
Fax: 1-555-765-4321

5 pages sent

Additional Comments: Please review these requests for new keyboards for our office. I look forward to your comments.

In case of fax error, contact:
Person: I. Fax Faster
Phone: 1-555-765-2222

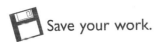 Save your work.

Review your fax cover sheet for errors and print it.

Adding Graphics to the Fax Cover Sheet

Return to the fax cover sheet you just created. Why don't you have some fun with your layout? At the very least, you can add some graphics to the page. Save it as **faxcover2.doc**.

- Move the cursor to the left of the *F* in *Fax* in the title.

- Click on **Insert** in the menu bar at the top of the page, then **Picture**, and select **Clip Art** from the drop-down menu.

- Select a picture to include on your cover page.

- Use the white handles around the graphic to resize it to fit your needs

- Make other creative changes to make your cover sheet more interesting

 Save your work.

Create Your Own Fax Cover Sheet

Create a **New** file and save it in the **Keyboarding** folder. Name it **faxcover3.doc**.

Now, create a fax cover sheet that you could use to fax a letter from you to a friend.

- Use your friend's name and fax number (you can make it up if you don't know the fax number).

- Use your own name and fax number (imaginary or real) as the sender.

- Indicate how many pages are being sent.

- Include some additional comments about the materials being sent.

- Identify the name and phone number of the person sending the fax. It can be you, or you can pretend to be a company executive who has hired a person to send faxes.

 Save your work.

Review your fax cover sheet for errors and print it.

MAKING E-MAIL WORK FOR YOU

Compared with the written letter, e-mail is almost conversational. Whereas it may take a week (if you are lucky) to receive a reply from a written correspondence, you may receive a reply to an e-mail within minutes. The telephone is useful if you want an immediate response, but e-mail allows you to "think about your answer" if you so desire. E-mail fills a necessary gap between the immediacy of using a telephone and the waiting involved with writing a letter.

The conversational nature of e-mail requires users to be careful about how they use it. E-mail has been accepted as an established channel of communication in both the more formal world of business and the less formal world of personal communication. The medium is the same, but the types of messages and expectations are different. Let's examine the different aspects of e-mail and how these should be considered based on how the e-mail is being used:

Be Brief. E-mail usually involves getting messages to other people quickly. For this reason, e-mails should be short and informative. E-mail messages should fill only one screen page. This is about 25 lines of text on a low-resolution monitor (640 × 800). The higher-resolution monitors (1024 × 768) can handle up to 40 lines of text, but it is better to keep messages short.

Make it Scannable. Surfing the Web has changed our reading habits. It is said that a Web page has about 5 seconds to capture a reader's attention before the reader clicks on a link and moves to another page. This means that the reader scans the page for important information. The same is true with other types of reading as well. If your reader doesn't see important information in the first 5 seconds, then your e-mail may be skipped.

Be Careful of What You Write. Unlike mailed letters, e-mail is not private. Don't write anything in an e-mail message you wouldn't want forwarded to other people.

Write Well. Proper spelling, grammar, and punctuation do count. The written e-mail is often the only representation of you to another person. Careless mistakes in spelling and grammar can make you appear uneducated.

Don't be Sarcastic. The conversational nature of e-mail makes it easy to be sarcastic in writing. Unfortunately, sarcasm can easily be misinterpreted because there is no body language or tone of voice to interpret. This problem has fostered the use of emoticons or smileys to indicate the emotion trying to be conveyed. These were introduced in earlier lessons, but here is a list of emoticons you might use:

:-)	smiley face	:-))	laugh
;-)	wink	:-D	shock
:-(	sad	:-C	really sad
;-(	crying	:-@	scream
:-0	yell	:-/	confused
:*)	clowning	0:-)	angelic

Use Salutations. Just as you would in a letter, begin each e-mail with "Dear David," or "Dear Mr. Mitchell." This is the proper way to address someone formally. You may drop the salutation for quick notes to friends, but it is best to err on the side of formality.

Limit Abbreviations. E-mail is a communication medium. Acronyms are the slang of electronic communication. Although acronyms save you time in writing, they are meaningless if your recipient doesn't know what they mean. Does your recipient use acronyms in his or her writing? You may be able to use common ones like BTW (by the way) or LOL (laughing out loud), but unfamiliar jargon like AFAIK (as far as I know) may confuse things.

Here are some useful abbreviations in writing e-mails:

AFAIK	as far as I know
AKA	also known as
ASAP	as soon as possible
B4	before

BTW	by the way
CU	see you
CUL8R	see you later
F2F	face to face
FYA	for your amusement
FYI	for your information
GMTA	great minds think alike
GR8	great
ICWUM	I see what you mean
IMO	in my opinion
IMHO	in my humble opinion
IOW	in other words
L8R	later
LOL	laughing out loud
MHOTY	my hat's off to you
NBIF	no basis in fact
OBTW	oh, by the way
OIC	oh, I see
OTOH	on the other hand
POV	point of view
T+	think positive
TIA	thanks in advance
TTFN	ta ta for now
TTYL	talk to you later
TTTT	to tell the truth
TX	thanks
TYVM	thank you very much
WTG	way to go!
WYSIWYG	what you see is what you get
2BCTND	to be continued
2	to

Use Meaningful Subject Lines. When your e-mail box is full, often you just scan the subjects to see what needs to be answered. Subject lines must be brief and descriptive. Message lines that say "Hi" or "For You" or "Website" mean nothing. More meaningful subjects might be "Meeting minutes – 11/5" or "Help with digital imaging" or "Latest version of the website."

Include http:// on URLs. Many e-mails involve referring the recipient to a Web site for more information. Most e-mail software will allow the reader to link directly to the site if the address (URL) includes the http:// prefix.

E-MAIL TRYOUT

Key the following e-mail into your new file. Save often as you work.

Create a New file and save it in the **Keyboarding** folder. Name it **businessemail.doc**

To: personnel@buyagoodcomputer

Subject: Thank you for the interview

Dear Mr. Hiring:

Thank you for allowing me to interview for the vacancy in your support services department. I enjoyed meeting you and hope I was able to demonstrate my interest in working for your company.

I want to direct you to another resource that demonstrates my background. Please visit my Web site at http://www.ifixcomputerswell.com. As you can see, I have an ongoing discussion about problems people are having with their computers. I offer advice on how they might fix them.

I hope that this Web site and the other materials I presented to you will provide some insight into how I can help people solve technical problems. I would be a great asset to your support services department and hope to hear from you soon.

Sincerely,

Uri Niceguy

 Save your work.

Review your letter for errors and print it.

That was a business letter that you might write as a follow-up for a job interview. Notice that it was brief and informative. It began with a proper salutation. No e-mail acronyms or emoticons were used. The Web address included the http:// prefix to make the link just a click of a mouse button away.

Try writing the following personal letter. You will see that it is also brief. It begins with just a name instead of a formal salutation. Acronyms and emoticons are used for fun. It is obvious that the two people are close friends and are using e-mail as a quick way to communicate.

To: Thelma@ilikeemail.com

Subject: It was good to see you again

Thelma,

I enjoyed talking with you last week. It was GR8 2 CU. It has been a long time since we last spoke. :-)

I can't believe that your sister has grown so much. I remember when she was just a youngster. Remember when we were kids? We used to hang around in our tree house for hours. I especially enjoyed the tire swing that swung out over the river.

It sounds like you have a lot of challenges in your life. You can make things work. T+

I hope that you can come over for dinner next week. Let me know ASAP.

TTFN,

Pat

OBTW there wasn't anything wrong with my car, it just needed gas. ;-)

 Save your work.

Review your letter for errors and print it.

CREATE YOUR OWN E-MAIL

Create a **New** file and save it in the **Keyboarding** folder. Name it **myemail.doc**

Now you have the opportunity to write your own e-mail to a friend. Using the heading format shown above, write an e-mail to a friend you haven't seen in a while. Use the abbreviations and emoticons sparingly unless you know your friend will understand them. Write a real message that you intend to send.

 Save your work.

Review your e-mail for errors and print it. Open a new e-mail message and send this e-mail to your friend. You may be able to get together again.

CREATING A NEWSLETTER

OUTCOMES

- Organize articles for a newsletter

- Write headlines and bylines

- Design a banner for the name of a newsletter

- Change margin settings to reformat a document to print in column format

You know all the keys and can write letters, so now it's time to do a little desktop publishing. Desktop publishing (sometimes known as DTP) is more than just keyboarding. It involves inserting graphics and formatting the text. An easy way to practice that is to create a newsletter. A newsletter has fonts of different sizes and multiple columns of text and graphics. It can be whatever you want it to be.

Begin by gathering some newspapers and newsletters that you have around the house/classroom. Review each of these documents and consider these questions:

- How many columns of text are on a page?

- How much larger is the headline than the text?

- Is the headline in the same font as the text?

- Are there bylines (author names) after the titles?

- Are the bylines smaller than the title and in bold?

- Are there graphics in the columns?

- Does the text wrap around the graphics?

- Are there headers and footers on the pages?

- Are the articles interesting?

These are all aspects you need to consider when designing your newsletter. A newsletter is a collection of information about a central topic. This topic is usually a city, school, business, or specific organization. It can also be about a common area of interest like rock climbing or fashion design. This information is usually presented in news article format, but this information can also be presented in the form of pictures, graphs, charts, personal letters, or even poetry. As long as it concerns the central topic, it can be included in the newsletter.

Once you have identified a topic for a newsletter, there is a series of steps you can follow to create your newsletter. You may find that you will develop a process of your own as you become more proficient at creating newsletters, but this lesson is organized using the following steps:

- Organize your articles

- Collect the articles you want to use

- Enter your articles into a single document

- Write a headline for each article

- Create your newsletter format

- Enter the title of your newsletter

- Insert a section break after the title

- Change format into two columns

- Right-align the columns

- Add a footer to the newsletter
- Insert graphics
- Insert graphics into the newsletter
- Set wraparound for the text

ORGANIZE YOUR ARTICLES

The first part of creating a newsletter is to identify a topic. You may select whatever topic you wish. We will be using keyboarding trivia as a demonstration for this newsletter, but you may identify your own topic and write your own articles if you desire. Here is your opportunity to create a newsletter for your organization or hobby interest.

In case you don't feel too creative today, you can use your wonderful keyboarding skills to enter the following articles into a word processing document.

Create a **New** file. Immediately save this new file as **newsletterarticles.doc**

Now, begin to enter the following articles. Save as indicated.

Dvorak Simplifies Keyboarding

In 1936, two efficiency experts, August Dvorak and William Dealey, reconsidered the QWERTY keyboard and decided it could be improved. They reassigned the keys so that the five vowels, AEIOU, are on the left side of the home row, and the most commonly used consonants, DHTNS, are on the right side.

With this layout, 70 percent of the keyboarding occurs in the home row and is evenly distributed between the right and left hands. Most computer keyboards can be configured to run as Dvorak keyboards, so it is only tradition and habit that keep QWERTY keyboards as the most popular keyboards on the planet.

 Save your work.

Keyboards Around the World Not Alike

Although the QWERTY keyboard is the most popular layout in the world, there are multiple variations.

The German keyboard has a QWERTZ layout, but the Y and Z keys are reversed. Three umlauted vowels and the "sharp-s" characters of the German alphabet have also been added at the right end of the keyboard.

The French keyboard has an AZERTY layout. The A and Q are exchanged, as are the Z and W. The M is placed to the right of the L, and the punctuation is moved to the bottom right row. Most of the accented vowels are accessed through the number keys.

These variations can make keyboarding awkward at first for visitors in a foreign country but can be learned without too much difficulty.

 Save your work.

Keyboarding Strikes a Chord

Imagine a keyboard with only eight keys. A chordic keyboard is designed that way.

Unlike the letters on a QWERTY keyboard, which have a separate key each, chordic keyboard letters and characters are represented by different combinations of multiple keys. Pressing these combinations of keys is similar to playing a chord on a piano, so the technique has been given the name of chording.

Chording has its advantages; the key combinations are easy to learn, and it is said that the novice keyboarder can work twice as fast using chording after a couple of days of training. The chording keyboard is also designed to be less stressful on the fingers and wrists of computer users. Finally, many disabled individuals who can't use a standard keyboard find they can achieve acceptable keyboarding speed with chording. With all these advantages, this new technology should strike a chord with the keyboarding community.

 Save your work.

Now that you have the text for your newsletter, let's format it to look like a newsletter.

CREATE A NEWSLETTER FORMAT

The primary difference between a newsletter and a standard word processing document is format. A newsletter has a title across the top and two or three columns of text. You have all your articles in your word processing document, so it is just a matter of formatting these articles into a newsletter.

Title

The first thing you need is a title for your newsletter. The title for the sample newsletter is "The Digital Doodler."

Move your cursor to the very beginning of your articles document. Place your cursor to the left of the D in Dvorak.

Enter the title, The Digital Doodler (or any title that seems appropriate.)

Tap the Enter key when you have finished so that the title is on a line by itself.

The title will be centered across the page, and the text will be in two columns. This means that there needs to be some sort of significant separation between the title section and the text section so they can have different formats. This type of significant separation is usually called a section break. When you insert the section break, notice that there are multiple kinds of section breaks. You need to select the "continuous" section break so you can have multiple sections on the same page.

Click on **Insert** in the menu bar at the top of the page and select **Break** from the drop-down menu. Select **Section breaks (continuous)** to place a continuous section break between the title and your first article.

The title needs to be larger, centered, and different. This will involve some formatting, so it will be easiest if you have the **Formatting** toolbar across the top of your screen.

Click on **View** in the menu bar at the top of your screen. Select **Toolbar** from the drop-down menu. Ensure that **Standard** and **Formatting** both have checks next to them. If they don't, then click on the desired selection. This will cause a check to appear beside the word and the toolbar to appear at the top of the screen.

Highlight the newsletter title. Increase the font size to 36 point by selecting the font size in the **Formatting** toolbar. The font probably says 12 now. Click on the down arrow next to the number and drag down to 36.

With the title still highlighted, center the title across the page by clicking on the **Align Center** button in the **Formatting** toolbar.

The title needs to be different from the rest of the text. Even though it's larger, it should also be a different font. You are probably using a Times or Times New Roman font right now. That is called a *serif* font. You will notice that it has light projections—"little feet" and "shoulders"—on letters like T and I and R. This is the easiest kind of font for reading large amounts of text. Fonts without these projections on their letters are called *sans serif*. Sans is Latin for "without." You can think of sans serif fonts as "without little feet or shoulders." A good selection for a sans serif font is Helvetica.

With the title still highlighted, select the Helvetica font in the font box next to the size box in the **Format** toolbar. Click on the down arrow and drag down to Helvetica. Release the mouse button and your title will suddenly appear as Helvetica.

Finally, bold your title. Highlight your title and then click on the dark B in the **Formatting** toolbar. This will give your title "body."

Do the same for each of the article titles. Change each of the titles to Helvetica 18, but don't bold them.

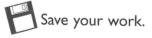
Save your work.

Columns

The titles are done, so now it is time to format the newsletter into two columns.

Highlight all the text in your articles. Click on the **Columns** button. A drop-down box with four columns will appear. Drag down your cursor so two columns are highlighted. Let go, and your text will appear in two columns. Now, we want to single space the article text. Highlight all the text then click **Format** from your toolbar and from the drop-down menu choose **Paragraph**. In the **Line Spacing** option choose **Single**.

You will probably find that a couple of lines of text extended onto the second page. You can try to find a couple of sentences to delete, or you can reduce the margins. Let's try reducing the margins a little to get these sentences all on one page.

Go to the **File** menu and select **Page Setup**. The **Page Setup** dialog box will appear. Notice that the left and right margins are 1.25". Let's reduce these margins to only 1" on each side to enable all the text to fit on one page.

Save your work.

Alignment

Most multicolumn newsletters and newspapers use a **Full Justify** alignment. This means that the borders are even on both the right and left sides. Such alignment does a good job of producing "ribbons of text" on the page. Unfortunately, this formatting can sometimes cause large gaps between words; this is a trade-off for the straight right margin.

Highlight the text in your first article but not the title. Click on the **Justify** button in the **Formatting** toolbar.

Your words will magically stretch to the right edge of the column.

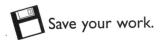 Save your work.

Add Footer

Every newsletter needs to have a dateline. It is often placed directly below the title but can also be placed at the bottom of the page in a footer. Placing the dateline in the footer will ensure that the information is included on every page of a multipage newsletter. The footer will also provide a place for the page number.

Select **Header and Footer** from the **View** menu.

Notice that the text turns gray and boxes made of dotted lines appear at the top and bottom of the page. The text for the headers and footers goes into these boxes.

Move the cursor to the footer box at the bottom of the page. Click inside the footer box, and the cursor will begin blinking at the left margin.

Tap the Tab key a couple of times and notice that there are three preset tabs in the footer: one at the left margin, one in the center, and one at the right margin.

Move the cursor to the left margin tab and enter the month and the year (e.g., July 2005).

Tap the Tab key twice to move to the right tab.

Enter "pg." here.

Your word processor can number each of the

pages automatically. You just need to select the **Insert Page Number** button (#) on the **Header/Footer** toolbar. Click on the # button on the toolbar.

Click on the **Close** button on the toolbar.

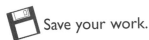 Save your work.

GRAPHICS

Your newsletter looks pretty good, doesn't it, with its two-column format with a fancy title at the top of the page? Your columns look rather professional with their right alignment. You even have a footer at the bottom of the page that identifies the date and page number.

The newsletter needs something, though—it needs some graphics. Although the world is full of photos and pictures and charts, we will just insert a clip art picture to see how it is done.

Move your cursor to the first letter of the second paragraph in the first article. You will insert a graphic here.

Select **Picture**, then **Clip Art** from the **Insert** command in the menu bar at the top of your screen.

The Clip Art Gallery will appear on your screen.

Enter *keyboard* (or a word that will provide appropriate graphics for your own newsletter) into the **Search:** box.

Click the **Search** button, and a number of pictures will appear.

Find the picture you want to use and double-click on it. (Don't click on the **Insert** button as well, or you will get two copies of the same picture in your newsletter.)

The graphic takes up the whole column. This is acceptable. You can have text above and below a graphic, but that causes the text to run onto the second page again, doesn't it? We need to reduce it to half the column width.

Click once on the graphic. Eight small white boxes will appear around it.

Point to the lower right box and drag it up and to the left. This will make the picture smaller. Continue doing this until the graphic is only half the width of the column.

Notice that the text isn't to the right of the picture. You need to tell it to "wrap" the text around the graphic.

Double-click on the graphic and a **Format Picture** box will appear.

Select the **Layout** button.

Select the Square "wrapping style." Click the **OK** button. This will move the text next to the picture.

 Save your work.

There you have it. You have just created your first newsletter. It's not fancy, but it provides a layout that you can use month after month.

Review your newsletter for errors. Save it again and print it. It should look like Figure 25.1.

The Digital Doodler

Dvorak Simplifies Keyboarding

In 1936, two efficiency experts, August Dvorak and William Dealey, reconsidered the QWERTY keyboard and decided it could be improved. They reassigned the keys so that the five vowels, AEIOU, are on the left side of the home row and the most commonly used consonants, DHTNS, are on the right side.

 With this layout, 70 percent of the keyboarding occurs in the home row and is evenly distributed between the right and left hands. Most computer keyboards can be configured to run as Dvorak keyboards so it is only tradition and habit that keep QWERTY keyboards as the most popular keyboards on the planet.

Keyboards Around the World Not Alike

Although the QWERTY keyboard is the most popular layout in the world, there are multiple variations.

The German keyboard has a QWERTZ layout, but the Y and Z keys are reversed. Three umlauted vowels and the "sharp-s" characters of the German alphabet have also been added at the right end of the keyboard.

The French keyboard has an AZERTY layout. The A and Q are exchanged, as are the Z and W. The M is placed to the right of the L, and the punctuation is moved to the bottom right row. Most of the accented vowels are accessed through the number keys.

There are multiple variations of the QWERTY board being used around the world. These variations can be difficult to visitors in a foreign country but can be learned without too much difficulty.

Keyboarding Strikes a Chord

Imagine a keyboard with only eight keys. A chordic keyboard is designed that way. Unlike the letters on a QWERTY keyboard, which have a separate key each, chordic keyboard letters and characters are represented by different combinations of multiple keys. Pressing these combinations of keys is similar to playing a chord on a piano, so the technique has been given the name of *chording*.

Chording has its advantages; the key combinations are easy to learn, and it is said that the novice keyboarder can work twice as fast using chording after a couple of days of training. The chording keyboard is also designed to be less stressful on fingers and wrists of computer users. Finally, many disabled individuals who can't use a standard keyboard find that they can achieve acceptable keyboarding speed with chording. With all of these advantages, this new technology should strike a chord with the keyboarding community.

July 2005   pg. 1

Figure 25.1

GLOSSARY

center
Alignment in which an item is centered between margins.

click
The process of selecting an item by pointing at it on the screen with the cursor and then pressing the mouse button.

clip art
Collection of graphic images available with a word processing program for insertion into documents.

cursor
An arrow that acts as the location indicator on the screen; the word *cursor*, Latin for "runner," is used because the cursor "runs" all over the screen.

dialog box
Box that appears on the screen where settings and selections are made.

drag
To move the cursor with the mouse button pressed down; often used to move items on the screen or to highlight a section of text.

drop-down menu
A group of selections in a box that appears ("drops down") when a selection on a menu is clicked.

ergonomics
The study of design factors in the workplace that maximize productivity.

file
An electronic collection of information that has a unique name; it may be stored on the hard drive of the computer or on a CD, DVD, or other external memory device.

footer
Information that is printed at the bottom of every page in a document or section of the document.

format palette
A movable collection of formatting commands.

header
Information that is printed at the top of every page in a document or section of the document.

highlight
To mark a menu option or a block of text with the highlight bar.

home row
Located in the middle of your keyboard and is where your fingers automatically go to rest.

icon
A small picture on the screen that is selected to execute a command.

insertion point
A blinking vertical line that indicates where text will be inserted in a document when a key is tapped.

justify
To adjust text format so that the text is flush with both the right and left margins.

left-align
To adjust text format so that all the text is flush with the left margin.

right align
To adjust the text format so that all the text is flush with the right margin.

sans serif font
A font (e.g., Geneva) in which the letters do not have serifs, or small projections at the top or bottom.

section
A selected part of a document that is separated from the rest of the document by section breaks; done to allow the section to be treated differently (e.g., formatted) from the rest of the document.

section break
> A formatting mark that is inserted into a document to indicate where a section begins and/or ends.

serif font
> A font (e.g., Times New Roman) in which the letters have small projections at the top or bottom.

style
> A collection of character formats including bold, italic, and regular.

tab stop
> A location on the on-screen ruler indicating where text will align when the Tab key is tapped.

toolbar
> A bar that contains a selection of buttons that can be clicked to perform specified commands.

underscore
> A line character.

undo command
> A selection from the Edit menu that reverses a change in the document (e.g, deleting, formatting, or inserting).

URL (uniform resource locator)
> A Web address.

word wrap
> A feature that causes text to move automatically to the next line after it has filled the current line.

HOME ROW HINTS

- Curve your fingers naturally. (Think of how you would bend your fingers if you were scratching someone's back.)

- Find the bumps on the F and J keys. Lay your forefingers on the bumps. These bumps are on these keys to allow you to return to them without looking.

- Having landed your forefingers on F and J, lightly lay the rest of your fingers on the home row keys.

- Keep your wrists low but *not* touching the keyboard or table.

- Keep your elbows close to your body.

- If you are right-handed, let your right thumb drop to the space bar below and let your left thumb curl under.

- If you are left-handed, use your left thumb for the space bar.

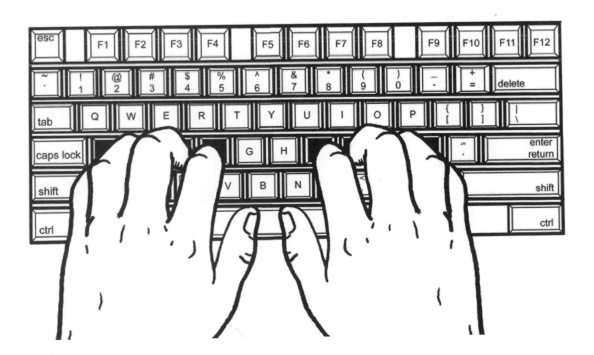

SITTING HINTS

- Sit at the center of the keyboard. Align the center of your body with the line that divides the G and H keys.

- Sit straight up in your chair in front of your keyboard.

- Make certain your lower spine is at the back of your chair.

- Keep about 9 inches between you and the keyboard.

- Position both feet flat on the floor with one foot slightly ahead of the other.

AUTOBLENDS

ag ag ag ag ag ag al al al al al al ag ag ag al al al ag ag al al ag al ag al ag al ag al ag

ap ap ap ap ap ap as as as as as as ap ap ap as as as ap ap as as ap as ap as ap as ap as ap

at at at at at at ay ay ay ay ay ay at at at ay ay ay at at ay ay at ay at ay at ay at ay at ay at

de de de de de de ed ed ed ed ed ed de de de ed ed ed de de ed ed de ed de ed de ed de ed

em em em em em em en en en en en en em em em en en en em em en en em en em en em

er er er er er er es es es es es es er er er es es es er er es es er es er es er es er es er es

ic ic ic ic ic ic im im im im im im ic ic ic im im im ic ic im im ic im ic im ic im ic im ic

ip ip ip ip ip ip ly ly ly ly ly ly ip ip ip ly ly ly ip ip ly ly ip ly ip ly ip ly ip ly ip ly ip

re re re re re re un un un un un un re re re un un un re re un un re un re un re un re un re

ack ack ack ack ack ack ail ail ail ail ail ail ack ack ack ack ail ail ail ack ack ail ail ack

ank ank ank ank ank ank dis dis dis dis dis dis ank ank ank dis dis dis ank ank dis dis

ell ell ell ell ell ell ell est est est est est est ell ell ell est est est ell ell est est ell est ell est

ful ful ful ful ful ful ial ial ial ial ial ial ful ful ful ial ial ial ful ful ial ial ful ial ful ial fun

ick ick ick ick ick ick ill ill ill ill ill ill ick ick ick ill ill ill ick ick ill ill ick ill ick ill ick ill

ing ing ing ing ing ing ion ion ion ion ion ion ing ing ing ion ion ion ing ing ion ion ing

ity ity ity ity ity ity ive ive ive ive ive ive ity ity ity ive ive ive ity ity ive ive ity ive ity ive

mid mid mid mid mid mid mis mis mis mis mis mis mid mid mid mis mis mis mid mis

non non non non non non ous ous ous ous ous ous non non non ous ous ous non non ous

pre pre pre pre pre pre sub sub sub sub sub sub pre pre pre sub sub sub pre pre sub sub

able able able able anti anti anti anti able able anti anti able anti able anti able anti able

eous eous eous eous fore fore fore fore eous eous fore fore eous fore eous fore eous fore

ible ible ible ible ious ious ious ious ible ible ious ious ible ious ible ious ible ious ible

less less less less ment ment ment ment less less ment ment less ment less ment less ment

ness ness ness ness tion tion tion tion ness ness tion tion ness tion ness tion ness tion ness

ation ation ation ation ative ative ative ative ation ation ative ative ation ative ation ative

ition ition ition ition itive itive itive itive ition ition itive itive ition itive ition itive ition

APPENDIX

D

AUTOWORDS

am am am am am am an an an an an an am am am an an an am am an an am an am an am an

be be be be be be by by by by by by be be be by by by be be by by be by be by be by be by

do do do do do do go go go go go go do do do go go go do do go go do go do go do go do go do

he he he he he he if if if if if if he he he if if if he he if if he if he if he if he if he if he if

in in in in in in is is is is is is in in in is is is in in is is in is in is in is in is in is in is in

it it it it it it me me me me me me it it it me me me it it me me it me it me it me it me it me

of of of of of of on on on on on on of of of on on on of of on on of on of on of on of on

or or or or or or my my my my my my or or or my my my or or my my or my or my or my or

no no no no no no to to to to to to no no no to to to no no to to no to no to no to no to no

up up up up up up we we we we we we up up up we we we up up we we up we up we up we up

all all all all all all and and and and and and all all all and and and all all and and all and all

are are are are are are but but but but but but are are are but but but are are but but are but

end end end end end end for for for for for for end end end for for for end end for for

had had had had had had has has has has has has had had had has has has had had has has

her her her her her her him him him him his his his his her her him him his his her him his him

not not not not not not the the the the the the not not not the the the not not the the not the

was was was was was was you you you you you you was was was you you you was you

from from from from have have have have from from have have from have from have from

that that that that they they they they that that that they they they that that they they that they

this this this this with with with with this this this with with with this this with with this with

THE 500 MOST COMMONLY USED WORDS

1	the	30	hot	59	many	88	over
2	of	31	but	60	then	89	know
3	to	32	some	61	them	90	water
4	and	33	what	62	would	91	than
5	a	34	there	63	write	92	call
6	in	35	we	64	like	93	first
7	is	36	can	65	so	94	people
8	it	37	out	66	these	95	may
9	you	38	other	67	her	96	down
10	that	39	were	68	long	97	side
11	he	40	all	69	make	98	been
12	was	41	your	70	thing	99	now
13	for	42	when	71	see	100	find
14	on	43	up	72	him	101	any
15	are	44	use	73	two	102	new
16	with	45	word	74	has	103	work
17	as	46	how	75	look	104	part
18	I	47	said	76	more	105	take
19	his	48	an	77	day	106	get
20	they	49	each	78	could	107	place
21	be	50	she	79	go	108	made
22	at	51	which	80	come	109	live
23	one	52	do	81	did	110	where
24	have	53	their	82	my	111	after
25	this	54	time	83	sound	112	back
26	from	55	if	84	no	113	little
27	or	56	will	85	most	114	only
28	had	57	way	86	number	115	round
29	by	58	about	87	who	116	man

117	year	151	sentence	185	off	219	thought
118	came	152	set	186	need	220	let
119	show	153	three	187	house	221	keep
120	every	154	want	188	picture	222	eye
121	good	155	air	189	try	223	never
122	me	156	well	190	us	224	last
123	give	157	also	191	again	225	door
124	our	158	play	192	animal	226	between
125	under	159	small	193	point	227	city
126	name	160	end	194	mother	228	tree
127	very	161	put	195	world	229	cross
128	through	162	home	196	near	230	since
129	just	163	read	197	build	231	hard
130	form	164	hand	198	self	232	start
131	much	165	port	199	earth	233	might
132	great	166	large	200	father	234	story
133	think	167	spell	201	head	235	saw
134	say	168	add	202	stand	236	far
135	help	169	even	203	own	237	sea
136	low	170	land	204	page	238	draw
137	line	171	here	205	should	239	left
138	before	172	must	206	country	240	late
139	turn	173	big	207	found	241	run
140	cause	174	high	208	answer	242	don't
141	same	175	such	209	school	243	while
142	mean	176	follow	210	grow	244	press
143	differ	177	act	211	study	245	close
144	move	178	why	212	still	246	night
145	right	179	ask	213	learn	247	real
146	boy	180	men	214	plant	248	life
147	old	181	change	215	cover	249	few
148	too	182	went	216	food	250	stop
149	does	183	light	217	sun	251	open
150	tell	184	kind	218	four	252	seem

253	together	287	fish	321	leave	355	true
254	next	288	mountain	322	song	356	during
255	white	289	north	323	measure	357	hundred
256	children	290	once	324	state	358	am
257	begin	291	base	325	product	359	remember
258	got	292	hear	326	black	360	step
259	walk	293	horse	327	short	361	early
260	example	294	cut	328	numeral	362	hold
261	ease	295	sure	329	class	363	west
262	paper	296	watch	330	wind	364	ground
263	often	297	color	331	question	365	interest
264	always	298	face	332	happen	366	reach
265	music	299	wood	333	complete	367	fast
266	those	300	main	334	ship	368	five
267	both	301	enough	335	area	369	sing
268	mark	302	plain	336	half	370	listen
269	book	303	girl	337	rock	371	six
270	letter	304	usual	338	order	372	table
271	until	305	young	339	fire	373	travel
272	mile	306	ready	340	south	374	less
273	river	307	above	341	problem	375	morning
274	car	308	ever	342	piece	376	ten
275	feet	309	red	343	told	377	simple
276	care	310	list	344	knew	378	several
277	second	311	though	345	pass	379	vowel
278	group	312	feel	346	farm	380	toward
279	carry	313	talk	347	top	381	war
280	took	314	bird	348	whole	382	lay
281	rain	315	soon	349	king	383	against
282	eat	316	body	350	size	384	pattern
283	room	317	dog	351	heard	385	slow
284	friend	318	family	352	best	386	center
285	began	319	direct	353	hour	387	love
286	idea	320	pose	354	better	388	person

389 money	423 pound	457 full	479 laugh
390 serve	424 done	458 force	480 thousand
391 appear	425 beauty	459 blue	481 ago
392 road	426 drive	460 object	482 ran
393 map	427 stood	461 decide	483 check
394 science	428 contain	462 surface	484 game
395 rule	429 front	463 deep	485 shape
396 govern	430 teach	464 moon	486 yes
397 pull	431 week	465 island	487 hot
398 cold	432 final	466 foot	488 miss
399 notice	433 gave	467 yet	489 brought
400 voice	434 green	468 busy	490 heat
401 fall	435 oh	469 test	491 snow
402 power	436 quick	470 record	492 bed
403 town	437 develop	471 boat	493 bring
404 fine	438 sleep	472 common	494 sit
405 certain	439 warm	473 gold	495 perhaps
406 fly	440 free	474 possible	496 fill
407 unit	441 minute	475 plane	497 east
408 lead	442 strong	476 age	498 weight
409 cry	443 special	477 dry	499 language
410 dark	444 mind	478 wonder	500 among
411 machine	445 behind		
412 note	446 clear		
413 wait	447 tail		
414 plan	448 produce		
415 figure	449 fact		
416 star	450 street		
417 box	451 inch		
418 noun	452 lot		
419 field	453 nothing		
420 rest	454 course		
421 correct	455 stay		
422 able	456 wheel		

This list is provided with permission from World-English at www.world-english.com

It is based on the combined results of British English, American English, and Australian English surveys of contemporary sources in English: newspapers, magazines, books, TV, radio, and real- life conversations—the language as it is written and spoken today.

as, at, ax, ed, we, ace, act, add, ads, age, arc, are, art, ate, awe, rex, sad, sag, sat, saw, sax, sea, sec, see, ser, set, sew, tab, tad, tag, tar, tax, tea, tee, vat, vet, vex, wad, wag, war, was, wax, web, wed, cart, casa, case, cast, cats, cave, caws, crag, craw, crew, czar, dabs, dace, dada, dads, dare, dart, data, date, deaf, dear, debs, debt, deed, gear, gets, grab, grad, safe, saga, sage, sags, save, saws, scab, scat, sear, seas, sets, stew, swab, swag, swat, tabs, tads, tags, tare, tars, tart, taws, tear, teas, teat, vase, vast, vats, verb, vest, vets, wars, wart, wear, webs, weds, weed, were, west, wets, zest, bards, bared, barer, barge, beads, beard, bears, beast, beats, crest, crews, czars, dares, darts, dated, dater, dates, draft, drags, draws, faxes, fazed, fears, frats, freed, freer, frees, frets, gages, scarf, scars, scats, sears, seats, seeds, sewed, sewer, stage, stags, stare, stars, start, trade, tread, treat, treed, trees, tress, tweed, tweet, vests, vexed, waves, waxed, waxes, wears, weave, zarfs, zebra, agreed, agrees, arcade, beaded, beards, bearer, braced, bracer, braces, braved, braver, braves, darers, darted, darter, feasts, grazed, grazer, grazes, grease, greats, redraw, redrew, reggae, seabed, seared, server, serves, straws, street, stress, traced, tracer, traces, tracts, traded, trader, trades, tweeds, tweets, zebras, adverbs, adverse, adverts, arcades, attract, avatars, average, barbers, bearded, bearers, created, creates, deafest, dearest, debased, debaser, debases, debated, debater, debates, decades, dredges, dressed, dresser, dresses, erasers, freebee, freezer, freezes, greases, greater, targets, tartars, tartest, tarweed, sweater, sweeter, swerved, asserter, assessed, assesses, carfares, defeated, defeater, dragster, drawbars, dredgers, refreeze, regarded, regattas, seawater, seaweeds, vertebra, vertexes, westward, actresses, addressed, addressee, addresser, addresses, cassettes, decreased, decreases, databases, deadbeats, degreases, desecrate, gazetteer, stargazed, stargazer, stargazes, vertebrae, vertebras, waterbeds, waterweed, westwards, abstracter, addressees, addressers, aftercares, aftertaste, afterwards, eggbeaters, stewardess, streetcars, wastewater, watercraft, aftereffect, aftertastes, extraverted, readdressed

These words are samples of a list provided with permission by Maltron at www.maltron.com

hi, ho, in, lo, mi, mm, my, no, oh, on, op, pi, uh, um, un, up, yo, him, hip, hmm, hop, huh, hum, hyp, ilk, ill, imp, ink, inn, ion, joy, kin, kip, koi, kop, lip, lop, mil, mom, moo, mop, mum, nil, nun, ohm, oil, ooh, phi, pin, pip, ply, pop, pun, pup, ump, yin, yip, yon, you, yuk, yum, yup, hill, holy, homo, honk, hook, hoop, hulk, hull, hump, hunk, hymn, hypo, inky, jinn, john, join, juju, jump, junk, kill, kiln, kink, kook, lily, limo, limp, link, lion, loin, look, loom, loon, loop, lull, lulu, lump, milk, mill, mini, mink, moil, mojo, monk, mono, moon, mull, nook, noon, noun, null, oily, oink, olio, only, pill, pink, plop, ploy, plum, poll, polo, poly, pomp, pony, pooh, pool, pull, pulp, pump, punk, puny, upon, yolk, hilly, hippo, hippy, holly, honky, hulky, humpy, hunky, imply, jimmy, jolly, jumpy, junky, knoll, kooky, lippy, loony, loopy, lumpy, lymph, milky, molly, mommy, moony, mummy, ninny, nylon, nymph, onion, oomph, opium, phony, pinky, pinup, plink, plump, plunk, polio, polyp, poppy, pulpy, pupil, puppy, pylon, union, unpin, yolky, yummy, homily, hominy, hookup, jokily, kimono, limply, limuli, linkup, lollop, lookup, minion, mukluk, muumuu, phylum, pinkly, pompom, pompon, poplin, unholy, unhook, unkink, unlink, uphill, uplink, homonym, jillion, jumpily, killjoy, kinkily, million, minimum, opinion, pumpkin, hokypoky, homonymy, lollipop, lollypop, monohull, monopoly, nonunion, polonium, homophony, monophony, monophyly, nonillion, pollinium, polyphony, hypolimnion

These words are samples of a list provided with permission by Maltron at www.maltron.com

PANGRAMS FOR PRACTICE

1. Brick quiz whangs jumpy veldt fox!

2. Quick wafting zephyrs vex bold Jim.

3. How quickly daft jumping zebras vex.

4. Quick zephyrs blow, vexing daft Jim.

5. Sphinx of black quartz, judge my vow.

6. Waltz, nymph, for quick jigs vex Bud.

7. The five boxing wizards jump quickly.

8. Jackdaws love my big sphinx of quartz.

9. Pack my box with five dozen liquor jugs.

10. Sympathizing would fix Quaker objectives.

11. The quick brown fox jumps over a lazy dog.

12. Five big quacking zephyrs jolt my wax bed.

13. Hick Jed wins quiz for extra blimp voyage.

14. Mix Zapf with Veljovic and get quirky Beziers.

15. Dumpy kibitzer jingles as exchequer overflows.

16. Turgid saxophones blew over Mick's jazzy quaff.

17. Brawny gods just flocked up to quiz and vex him.

18. Jim just quit and packed extra bags for Liz Owen.

19. A large fawn jumped quickly over white zinc boxes.

20. William Jex quickly caught five dozen Republicans.

21. Big July earthquakes confound zany experimental vow.

22. A boy, Max, felt quick during his hazy weaving jumps.

23. Six big devils from Japan quickly forgot how to waltz.

24. Harry, jogging quickly, axed zen monks with beef vapor.

25. Five or six big jet planes zoomed quickly by the tower.

26. Crazy Fredericka bought many very exquisite opal jewels.

27. Six crazy kings vowed to abolish my quite pitiful jousts.

28. The job of waxing linoleum frequently peeves chintzy kids.

29. Sixty zippers were quickly picked from the woven jute bag.

30. How razorback-jumping frogs can level six piqued gymnasts!

31. West quickly gave Bert handsome prizes for six juicy plums.

32. Just keep examining every low bid quoted for zinc etchings.

33. A quick movement of the enemy will jeopardize six gunboats.

34. The exodus of jazzy pigeons is craved by squeamish walkers.

35. We have just quoted on nine dozen boxes of gray lamp wicks.

36. Jay visited back home and gazed upon a brown fox and quail.

37. May Jo equal the fine record by solving six puzzles a week?

38. Fred specialized in the job of making very quaint wax toys.

39. Freight to me sixty dozen quart jars and twelve black pans.

40. Jeb quickly drove a few extra miles on the glazed pavement.

41. Grumpy wizards make toxic brew for the evil Queen and Jack.

42. We promptly judged antique ivory buckles for the next prize.

43. Whenever the black fox jumped the squirrel gazed suspiciously.

44. Jaded zombies acted quaintly but kept driving their oxen forward.

45. While making deep excavations we found some quaint bronze jewelry.

46. The job requires extra pluck and zeal from every young wage earner.

47. A quart jar of oil mixed with zinc oxide makes a very bright paint.

48. B, C, F, G, H, I, J, K, M, O, P, Q, U, V, W, X, Y, and Z are letters.

49. A mad boxer shot a quick, gloved jab to the jaw of his dizzy opponent.

50. Six big juicy steaks sizzled in a pan as five workmen left the quarry.

51. We quickly seized the black axle and just saved it from going past him.

52. The public was amazed to view the quickness and dexterity of the juggler.

53. The July sun caused a fragment of black pine wax to ooze on the velvet quilt.

54. Six javelins thrown by the quick savages whizzed forty paces beyond the mark.

55. Ebenezer unexpectedly bagged two tranquil aardvarks with his jiffy vacuum cleaner.

56. Jelly-like above the high wire, six quaking pachyderms kept the climax of the extravaganza in a dazzling state of flux.

57. No kidding—Lorenzo called off his trip to visit Mexico City just because they told him the conquistadores were extinct.

58. Forsaking monastic tradition, twelve jovial friars gave up their vocation for a questionable existence on the flying trapeze.

These pangrams were used with permission from Fun-With-Words (www.fun-with-words.com) and RinkWorks (rinkworks.com/words/pangrams.shtml)

THREE-MINUTE TIMINGS

Font: Courier **Point:** 12 **Left and right margins:** 1"

History of Chocolate

```
           3/1              6/2              9/3             12/4
     Although chocolate is now a prized food all the way around the
          15/5             18/6             21/7             24/8
world, it was unknown in Europe until explorer Christopher Columbus
          27/9             30/10            33/11            36/12
returned from his voyages in 1492. The people of the great ancient
          39/13            42/14            45/15            48/16
cultures of Mexico and Central America were the very first to mix
          51/17            54/18            57/19            60/20
ground cacao seeds with various seasonings to create a fabulously
          63/21            66/22            69/23            72/24
delicious drink. Chocolate even played an important role in the
          75/25            78/26            81/27            84/28
Maya and Aztec royal and religious events. When the many Spanish
          87/29            90/30            93/31            96/32
travelers brought the cacao seeds home, numerous new recipes were
          99/33            102/34           105/35           108/36
created and enjoyed. The once bitter drink was sweetened with
          111/37           114/38           117/39           120/40
sugar and milk for all to enjoy. But it was not until the mid
          123/41           126/42           129/43           132/44
1700s that an innovative confectioner created chocolate candy.
          135/45           138/46           142/47           145/48
The world's sweet tooth has never been the same again.
```

Biography of Houdini

<pre>
          3/1   6/2   9/3   12/4
Harry Houdini was perhaps the most greatest escape artist to
          15/5   18/6   21/7   24/8
ever live. Born in Budapest, Hungary, under the name of Erik
          27/9   30/10   33/11   36/12
Weisz, he arrived in Appleton, Wisconsin, at the age of 4 years
          39/13   42/14   45/15   48/16
old. The immigration officers changed his name to Eric Weiss upon
          51/17   54/18   57/19   60/20
his arrival. His name would soon change again.
          63/21   66/22   69/23   72/24
    Young Weiss was very athletic boy, which would be useful in
          75/25   78/26   81/27   84/28
his later career. Eric began performing magic tricks in his teen
          87/29   90/30   93/31   96/32
years. He called himself "Eric the Great." After he read a good
          99/33   102/34   105/35   108/36
autobiography by one of the greatest magicians of that day,
          111/37   114/38   117/39   120/40
Jean-Eugene Robert-Houdin, he was inspired. Eric then changed his
          123/41   126/42   129/43   132/44
name to Houdini in honor of his newly discovered mentor. He hoped
          135/45   138/46   142/47   145/48
that he might follow in the footsteps of this great man.
</pre>

Beauty of the Barrier

| 3/1 | 6/2 | 9/3 | 12/4 |

The Great Barrier Reef is the largest natural feature on

| 15/5 | 18/6 | 21/7 | 24/8 |

the earth. The reef stretches for more than 2,300 km along the

| 27/9 | 30/10 | 33/11 | 36/12 |

northeast coast of Australia. The reef is undisputedly one of the

| 39/13 | 42/14 | 45/15 | 48/16 |

world's most important natural resources. The Great Barrier

| 51/17 | 54/18 | 57/19 | 60/20 |

Reef is the world's largest marine protected area. The reef is

| 63/21 | 66/22 | 69/23 | 72/24 |

composed of over 2,900 coral reefs built from over 360 species

| 75/25 | 78/26 | 81/27 | 84/28 |

of hard coral. It is home to over 1,500 species of fish. It has

| 87/29 | 90/30 | 93/31 | 96/32 |

more than 1/3 of the world's soft coral species. Also, six of the

| 99/33 | 102/34 | 105/35 | 108/36 |

world's seven species of marine turtle live in the reef. The

| 111/37 | 114/38 | 117/39 | 120/40 |

Reef is a great destination for tourists as well. Every year

| 123/41 | 126/42 | 129/43 | 132/44 |

the Reef has almost 2 million visitors come to its shores.

Woodhull for President

3/1   6/2   9/3   12/4

Has the United States ever had a woman as a presidential

15/5   18/6   21/7   24/8

candidate? Why, yes. In 1872, Victoria Claflin Woodhull ran for

27/9   30/10   33/11   36/12

president as a nominee of the Equal Rights Party.

39/13   42/14   45/15   48/16

Victoria Woodhull was a social reformer. She believed in

51/17   54/18   57/19   60/20

women's rights, social welfare programs, 8-hour workdays, and

63/21   66/22   69/23   72/24

graduated income tax. She was a successful businesswoman who

75/25   78/26   81/27   84/28

owned her own newspaper and was the first female stockbroker on

87/29   90/30   93/31   96/32

Wall Street. Woodhull was able to finance much of her own campaign.

99/33   102/34   105/35   108/36

Her supporters believed that real reform was very necessary and

111/37   114/38   117/39   120/40

that Woodhull could lead it. They nominated the African American

123/41   126/42   129/43   132/44

abolitionist Frederick Douglass for her vice president. The duo

135/45   138/46   142/47   145/48

did not win, but they made great American history together.

More Than Just Old Faithful

          3/1   6/2   9/3   12/4

     Yellowstone National Park is known for its geyser, Old

          15/5   18/6   21/7   24/8

Faithful. But Yellowstone offers much more for the visitor to

          27/9   30/10   33/11   36/12

see. Did you know that this park's 300 active geysers make up

          39/13   42/14   45/15   48/16

more than two-thirds of all of the geysers on the planet? These

          51/17   54/18   57/19   60/20

geysers combine with over ten thousand thermal features to

          63/21   66/22   69/23   72/24

create a most unusual wonderland. They are evidence of one of

          75/25   78/26   81/27   84/28

the world's largest active volcanoes. This volcano erupted long

          87/29   90/30   93/31   96/32

before any recorded human history. The volcano is thought to have

          99/33   102/34   105/35   108/36

exploded enough ash into the air to cover most of the western

         111/37   114/38   117/39   120/40

and middle United States as well as northern Mexico. The wonder

         123/41   126/42   129/43   132/44

of this area led to the creation of the world's first national park.

FIVE-MINUTE TIMINGS

Font: Courier   Point: 12   Left and right margins: 1.75"

Duct Tape's History

                    5/1   10/2

Can you believe duct tape actually used to be duck tape?

                    15/3   20/4

During the World War II era, the Johnson and Johnson

                    25/5   30/6

Company developed a great waterproof tape to keep water

                    35/7   40/8

out of ammunition cases. Since it was waterproof so many

                    45/9   50/10

people referred to it as "duck tape" (like water sliding

                    55/11   60/12

off a duck's back). The name was also very appropriate

                    65/13   70/14

because it was made using cotton "duck," which is a

                    75/15   80/16

durable, closely woven, heavy cotton. Then the military

                    85/17   90/18

personnel found out that duck tape was good for a wide

95/19   100/20

variety of uses in their very busy lives that included

105/21   110/22

fixing their guns, packs, jeeps, shoes, jackets, and aircraft.

115/23   120/24

    Soon the tape became quite popular as it was

125/25   130/26

introduced into the civilian world. Interestingly

135/27   140/28

enough, duck tape was used in the housing industry to

145/29   150/30

connect heating and air conditioning ductwork. The

155/31   160/32

manufacturers changed the color to the sleek silver that

165/33   170/34

matched the duct work. It was now called "duct tape."

175/35   180/36

    Today, duck/duct tape has many diverse names,

185/37   190/38

colors, and sizes. The tape is used for everything from

195/39   200/40

fixing windows to putting broken bumpers back on NASCAR

205/41   210/42

cars. Duck tape is also used for decoration as much as

215/43   220/44

utility. Some enterprising students are even making lovely

225/45   230/46

duck tape tuxedos and formal gowns. Quite an invention.

Days of the Pony Express

5/1   10/2

The Pony Express provided a truly timely form of

15/3   20/4

direct communication between the city of St. Joseph, Missouri,

25/5   30/6

and California's capital, Sacramento. In 1860 the Express

35/7   40/8

was the fastest way to send news across the country.

45/9   50/10

It took about ten days for the riders on horses to pass

55/11   60/12

mail saddlebags from one to the other, then to travel the

65/13   70/14

almost two thousand miles across this large country.

75/15   80/16

Riders needed to be very courageous. An ad in a

85/17   90/18

California newspaper called for, "Young, skinny, and

95/19   100/20

wiry fellows. Not over 18. Must be expert daring riders.

105/21   110/22

Willing to risk death daily. Orphans preferred. Wages

115/23   120/24

$25 a week." Although most of the hired riders actually

125/25   130/26

were around twenty years old, the youngest rider of them

135/27   140/28

was eleven and the oldest was in his mid-forties.

145/29   150/30

    Although the great Pony Express has inspired many

155/31   160/32

legendary stories, it lasted only eighteen months.

165/33   170/34

It was the introduction of the telegraph and railroad

175/35   180/36

that brought an end to the need for the Pony Express in

185/37   190/38

1861. Even though the Pony Express was short-lived, the

195/39   200/40

communication provided by the Pony Express riders is

205/41   210/42

credited with keeping California state within the Union

215/43   220/44

during the pre-Civil War years.

Thom Cat

5/1   10/2

Cats were first domesticated by the great ancient

15/3   20/4

Egyptians over 4,000 years ago. They realized that cats were

25/5   30/6

effective vermin hunters so the Egyptians tamed the

35/7   40/8

cats to protect their precious corn supplies.

45/9   50/10

The Egyptians honored cats as hunters and they

55/11   60/12

worshipped them as gods and goddesses. The cats were

65/13   70/14

revered by all. Killing a cat was a crime ordered to be

75/15   80/16

punishable by death. Many cats were also mummified and

85/17   90/18

buried along with kings and queens in an effort to

95/19   100/20

preserve them in their eternal afterlives.

105/21   110/22

Today, cats can be helpful to human beings beyond

115/23   120/24

catching mice and rats. Many studies have shown that

125/25   130/26

sharing your home with a cat can decrease your high

135/27   140/28

blood pressure and other illnesses. You can relieve

145/29   150/30

stress by stroking a cat in your lap. It has to do

155/31   160/32

with a strong sense of serenity and comfort created

165/33   170/34

by the feel of a cat purring in your lap. While the

175/35   180/36

purring may be beneficial to your health, it is not

185/37   190/38

always a sign that your cat is a happy cat. Sometimes

195/39   200/40

cats purr when they feel distressed or are in pain.

205/41   210/42

Either way, it always feels very good to have my Thom

215/43   220/44

Cat sit on my lap purring on a cold winter evening.

Windmill Power

5/1   10/2

Humankind has used wind as a source of power

15/3   20/4

to help with accomplishing work since prehistoric times.

25/5   30/6

The idea of using wind to turn the blades of simple windmills

35/7   40/8

may have originated as early as the seventh century

45/9   50/10

AD in Persia (now known as Iran). These large windmills

55/11   60/12

were horizontal and turned a vertical shaft, used

65/13   70/14

for grinding grain and pumping irrigation water.

75/15   80/16

This technology then spread to Northern Europe in

85/17   90/18

the twelfth century as many warriors returned from the

95/19   100/20

Crusades. But instead, the Europeans positioned the windmill

105/21   110/22

vertically to create many post mills. The post mills stood

115/23   120/24

on a large rod that allowed the operator to direct the

125/25   130/26

face of the wind sails to face the wind direction.

135/27   140/28

Then the tower mill was developed in France in

145/29   150/30

the fourteenth century. This mill was a sturdy brick or

155/31   160/32

stone tower with a very large wooden cap that could be

165/33   170/34

rotated. The turning sails' axle used a set of complex

175/35   180/36

gears to transfer the power down to a turning mill

185/37   190/38

shaft to the milling machinery at the bottom of the

195/39   200/40

windmill structure. This power was useful for grinding

205/41   210/42

grain, running wood saws, pumping seawater, and pressing

215/43   220/44

oils. These very efficient forms of harnessing wind,

225/45   230/46

a renewable resource, were then adopted by the Dutch and

235/47   240/48

there were over 9,000 windmills in Holland by the 1800s.

Flamingo Fanatic

5/1   10/2

The American flamingo is a very long-legged and

15/3   20/4

long-necked pink bird that lives in Colombia, the

25/5   30/6

Galapagos Islands, Venezuela and several islands in

35/7   40/8

the Caribbean Sea. The diverse colors of the various

45/9   50/10

species may vary from bright red to pale pink hues.

55/11   60/12

The flamingo obtained its unique name from the Portuguese

65/13   70/14

word "flamenco," which means "flaming."

75/15   80/16

Flamingos are very tall birds. They may measure 5

85/17   90/18

feet in height but are skinny, weighing only 6 to 8 pounds.

95/19   100/20

Flamingos reside in shallow, salty lagoons and

105/21   110/22

lakes. They like to eat food like small animals, algae,

115/23   120/24

crabs and shrimp. Flamingos are also good waders and

125/25   130/26

swimmers. Their webbed feet are able to support them in

135/27   140/28

the mud. A bird will wade very deeply into the water

145/29   150/30

and hold its bill upside down in the water. Then the

155/31   160/32

flamingo sucks water through its big boomerang-shaped

165/33   170/34

beak and traps the food in a comb-like filter. It is

175/35   180/36

the chemicals in the foods that flamingos eat that give

185/37   190/38

them the pink color.

195/39   200/40

    Flamingos are very famous for standing on one leg

205/41   210/42

at a time. There is no special reason for this strange

215/43   220/44

behavior other than flamingos find it to be the most

225/45   230/46

comfortable position for resting, which also keeps

235/47   240/48

the lifted foot warm and conserves body heat.

SELF-PROGRESS CHART

Lesson	Date	Total Words Keyed	Total Words Keyed in 1 Minute	Total Number of Errors	Total Errors in 1 Minute (Total Errors/ Number of Minutes)	Correct WPM (Total Words Keyed in 1 Minute Minus Number of Errors in 1 Minute)
3						
5						
7						
9						
11						
13						
15						
17						
19						
20						

NOTES